Service Encou

D0332147

Service Encounters

CLASS, GENDER, AND THE MARKET
FOR SOCIAL DISTINCTION IN URBAN CHINA

Amy Hanser

STANFORD UNIVERSITY PRESS

STANFORD, CALIFORNIA

2008

Stanford University Press,
Stanford California
© 2008 by the Board of Trustees of the
Leland Stanford Junior University
All rights reserved

Library of Congress Cataloging-in-Publication Data

Hanser, Amy.
    Service encounters : class, gender, and the market for social
distinction in urban China / Amy Hanser.
        p. cm.
    Includes bibliographical references and index.
    ISBN 978-0-8047-5836-9 (cloth : alk. paper) —
    ISBN 978-0-8047-5837-6 (pbk. : alk. paper)
    1. Social classes—China. 2. Social stratification—China. 3. Sex
role—China. 4. Markets—China. 5. China—Social conditions—2000–.
6. China—Economic conditions—2000–. I. Title.

HN740.Z9S6154 2008
305.5'560951—dc22   2007035233

Printed in the United States of America on
acid-free, archival-quality paper

Typeset at Stanford University Press in 10/13 Palatino

To Mom and Dad

Acknowledgments

This research would not have been possible without the financial support of a number of organizations. These include the Fulbright IIE program, the Social Sciences Research Council's IDRF program, as well as support from the University of California's Institute for Labor and Employment and its Graduate Division, both of which funded the writing stages of the project. Preliminary research trips were supported by the Institute for East Asian Studies at UC Berkeley.

In Harbin, there are more people to thank than space allows, but I would like to recognize the indispensable aid and support from a few. At the Harbin Business University, Xu Xiaofei, Lu Guangyuan, and their staff; at the Heilongjiang Academy of Social Sciences, Zhao Ruizheng, Lu Rui, and their colleagues. Many supportive friends include Yi Yongwen, Shi Xiyan, Yang Yuanzhan, Li Jing and her family, Chi Yingge, Lin Lin, Teacher Zheng and his family, Lu Bo and her husband, and Wang Yanhong. In Beijing, thanks to Liu Fei for her friendly aid and Wu Xiaoying and her husband for their welcome and hospitality. I owe a tremendous debt to the managers and workers at both department stores I studied; Manager Liu and others from his cashmere sales office; and the people who welcomed me into The Underground. It is a gross understatement to suggest that this book could not have been written without their participation and help.

Teachers and mentors at UC Berkeley provided critical intellectual support. A Ph.D. student could not ask for a more patient, encouraging, and supportive mentor than Tom Gold, who read every chapter of the original dissertation with care, interest, and insight. Michael Burawoy challenged me to rethink my arguments in key ways, for which I am grateful. Raka Ray supplied critical insights as well as down-to-earth direction. Gil Eyal was somehow able to envision the core of the analysis long before I could. And Kevin O'Brien read and commented on the entire dissertation and provided kind and welcome encouragement. This work is greatly strengthened by each of your contributions.

Earlier versions of some of the chapters have been published elsewhere. Portions of Chapter 3 appear in "Serving the State, Serving the People: Work in a Post-socialist Department Store," pp. 91–109 in *How China Works: Perspectives on the Twentieth-Century Industrial Workplace*, ed. Jacob Eyferth (London; Routledge, 2006), reproduced by permission of Thomson Publishing Services. Parts of Chapters 1 and 4 appear in "The Gendered Rice Bowl: The Sexual Politics of Service Work in Urban China," *Gender & Society* 19(4): 581–600, reproduced with permission from Sage Publications, Inc. And portions of Chapter 6 appear in "Sales Floor Trajectories: Distinction and Service in Postsocialist China," *Ethnography* 7(4): 461–91, reproduced by permission of Sage Publications Ltd. I am grateful for permission to include these materials.

This book has benefited from the generosity of many people, though I have often been too stubborn or obtuse to follow their advice. Tom Gold's cross-disciplinary dissertation writing group at Berkeley provided me with outstanding advice, even while I was still in the field! Thanks in particular to Eileen Otis, Ken Foster, Bill Hurst, Seio Nakajima, Jaeyoun Won, Jianjun Zhang, Emily Yeh, Maranatha Ivanova, and Kun-Chin Lin. Other fellow students of China who have supported and shaped this project include Zwia Lipkin, Terry Woronov, Dan Buck, Eddy Yu, Jennifer Choo, Leslie Wang, Chris Sullivan, and Suowei Xiao. At the University of British Columbia, the China Studies Group has provided a crucial forum to develop some of the ideas included in this book, and my colleagues in the Sociology Department have provided an excellent intellectual home. My thanks also go to Ching Kwan Lee, Jacob Eyferth, Rachel Sherman, and Christine Williams. Comrades at Berkeley who provided a warm and engaging intellectual environment include Jennifer Utrata, Allison Pugh, Manuel Vallee, Cinzia Solari, Malcolm Fairbrother, Harold Toro, Bill Hayes, and many others.

Equal and likely greater debt is owed to the writing group who for many years read (and re-read) every chapter of this work. Teresa Sharpe, Isaac Martin, Lynn Rivas, Chris Neidt, and Jonathan VanAntwerpen were all central to this project at different and in some cases at every stage. You have nourished me in mind and . . . stomach! I am more grateful than I can express. And thanks, of course, to Elsa Tranter, without whose aid graduate school would have been unthinkable.

Finally, heartfelt thanks to my family: Mom, Dad, Bridget, Kate, and Dan; and to Nathan, for your exquisite sense of perspective.

Contents

Tables and Photographs

Service Encounters

CHAPTER ONE

Introduction

Under the bright fluorescent lights of the Harbin No. X Department Store, a large, state-owned retailer in the northern Chinese city of Harbin, a middle-aged woman sorted through the winter coat options spread about the sales counter. She pressed my fellow salesclerk, Big Sister Zhao, to lower the price. "Can't you make it a little cheaper?"

Big Sister Zhao responded with authority. "We're a state-run operation, we don't haggle over prices here, it's not like with those privately run places," she huffed, referring to the markets populated by *getihu*, small, independent hawkers and merchants. "Buy a down coat from those private merchants and the feathers will come out . . . this store, we have an excellent reputation. There are no fake goods here."

Just a few days earlier Zhao had complained to me about such people, customers who seemed determined to bring the free-for-all of the *getihu* marketplace into the department store. "Such people are of low quality [*suzhi bu gao*]," Zhao explained; "they should know they can't bargain here."

Several months later, a salesclerk from the state-owned store visited me at my new position as a salesclerk at the Sunshine Department Store, a glitzy, high-end department store filled with luxury goods. He complimented my glamorous new surroundings, adding: "The quality of the customers here at Sunshine is much higher than at Harbin No. X. You get all kinds of people at Harbin No. X. I once even had a customer who asked to see a razor, gave himself a shave, and left! I was so pissed off. . . ."

Management at Sunshine would have agreed with this assessment of No. X's customers and extended the judgment to its workers as well.

Upon our first meeting, a store manager explained that I would find the exclusive Sunshine a much better environment than Harbin No. X and its salesclerks far more disciplined. Another manager, in charge of hiring, explained that he would never hire a young woman who had spent any time working in the *geti* clothing bazaars to which Big Sister Zhao had referred, above. "Their whole manner is inappropriate for an expensive department store . . . and there's always the danger that they'll bring bad habits with them, like swearing and using uncivilized language."

Meanwhile, below the very streets where Sunshine's shining edifice sat, young women in gaudy attire hawked their wares from the clothing stalls of The Underground, a labyrinthine, subterranean *geti* market. One young woman in red-and-gold stiletto high heels, Xiao Li, thrust out her hip as she scolded a shopper. "We sell these trousers for 100 yuan retail here . . . they cost almost 400 yuan at Sunshine, they're exactly the same. Go take a look!" The customer seemed unconvinced.

"These are top quality, expensive trousers," Xiao Li added, implying that the customer couldn't tell.

In China, there is a market saying *huo bi san jia,* "compare the goods of three places before making a purchase." In the autumn of 2001, I took this advice to heart and embarked on a three-way comparison of market settings in the Chinese city of Harbin. My goal was to understand how the economic and social transformations of the past twenty or so years are reshaping social relations in urban China.

I began my study as a uniformed salesclerk at an aging state-owned department store, one of Harbin's premier retail establishments prior to the introduction of market reforms and still a major shopping destination for working-class shoppers. I then moved to a high-end private department store that offered luxury goods and solicitous service to the city's newly rich. Finally, I descended into a crowded, low-end clothing bazaar where independent merchants sold inexpensive goods to people from a range of social backgrounds. Each of these sites represented a different social position within Harbin society, and, as I will show, the social distinctions made in these settings are part of a larger story about inequality and social change in urban China today.

China is a society in the throes of rapid transformation. The country has experienced unprecedented rates of economic growth over the past

two-and-a-half decades, traveling rapidly from poverty to relative affluence. Alongside economic changes have come political and social ones:
China has shifted from a state socialist system to one that is market-oriented and, in many ways, fundamentally capitalist. These changes to
the economic, social, and ideological organization of the country have
been accompanied by new sets of social relations and a reconfigured social hierarchy. The rise of new elites has paralleled the fall of the urban
proletariat, and China's cities have witnessed the emergence of new social groupings, including a small but comfortable salaried middle class,
small-scale private entrepreneurs, and an influx of migrants and laborers from rural areas.

The core argument of this book is that relations among these dispa-
rate groups are understood and enacted through a framework of cultural distinctions that interpret—and legitimate—inequality as difference. I argue that a new "structure of entitlement" is being cultivated in
China through the marking of such social distinctions. The term "structure of entitlement" refers to the often-unconscious cultural and social
sensibilities that make certain groups of people feel entitled to greater
social goods. This sense of entitlement extends from seemingly mun-
dane aspects of daily social interactions all the way to more obviously
consequential and overt claims to formal power and material resources.
At the level of everyday life, this structure of entitlement finds expression in the realms of work, leisure, and daily social interaction. It is a
practical expression of one's place in society and a fundamental part of
the cultural scaffolding that supports larger systems of inequality.

This study explores China's emerging structure of entitlement and
the social distinctions upon which it is built by focusing on one setting
where people from different social groupings encounter one another:
the sales counter. It is across the sales counter, and in service work settings more generally, that entitlements are expressed and social distinctions are performed and legitimated. Key social divisions—along the
lines of class, gender, and even generation—solidify in the course of
service interactions. Because the resulting divisions make inequality
instead appear to be a question of difference, these social distinctions
play a central role in helping Chinese people make sense of—and accept—new forms of inequality.

But given the rapid, ongoing nature of change in contemporary
China, beliefs about inequality are not taken for granted. Rather, understandings of inequality and how acceptable it might or might not

be are the subject of struggles and negotiations in the course of daily life. China's "unsettled" context (Swidler 1986) provides a good opportunity to understand how systems of inequality are constructed and justified on a daily basis. In particular, performances of social difference in urban retail settings shed light on how inequality is experienced and legitimated during China's shift from a socialist system to a capitalist-oriented one.

At the same time that new socio-economic conditions reconfigure social relations in China, social inequalities are increasingly understood through a discourse that depicts the rise of the market and market values as both positive and inevitable while portraying socialism as a tarnished, not "radiant," piece of China's past (cf. Burawoy and Lukács 1992). The class, gender, and generational inequalities and distinctions that give form to the structure of entitlement in urban China are understood in reference to this transition from socialism to a market economy. In this context, people and organizations associated with state socialism and its planned economy are viewed as tainted by the past, and their perceived distance from the present signifies a lack of worth in the new market economy. This set of temporalized values is embedded in an emerging structure of entitlement in which some social groups and organizations invest and against which others struggle. This book is about the lives of ordinary people as they cope with—and strategize around—waves of social change and the new social values and entitlements that have arisen.

CLASS, CULTURE, AND THE ECONOMY

A study that deploys terms like "class" and "inequality" must, even if briefly, be situated within some of the larger scholarly debates that lie at the center of the social sciences. Traditionally, class analysis has tended to distinguish between class as a position in the economic order and class as a set of culturally shared meanings and experiences. One of the more contested of sociological concepts, definitions of class are often characterized as falling into various camps. For example, a Weberian-influenced tradition views economic class as just one of many forms of stratification and posits culturally defined status groups as potentially independent from classes. By contrast, Marxist approaches view class as "a set of fundamentally conflictual relations" (Ortner 1991) rooted in the economic sphere and determining relations in other (including the cultural) realms. Within each tradition, scholars also observe a division between more "objectivist" approaches that view class as a consequence of economic resources and more subjectivist perspectives that locate class in common lifestyle groups or shared identities (Ortner 1991).

Increasingly, this camp-like division has been critiqued as both unproductive and misleading. For example, Sylvia Yanagisako (2002), in her study of Italian family firms, argues that the economy and so-called "economic action" should not and cannot be separated from the cultural processes that produce them. In Mark Liechty's (2003) insightful analysis of the middle class in Nepal, he argues that neither Karl Marx nor Max Weber suggested that class, in practice, was divorced from cultural frameworks and motivations. Both Yanagisako and Liechty contend that treating culture (and the economy) as "process" or practice that is carried out in everyday life rather than static or stable structure provides an avenue for understanding class identities and practices as emerging out of *both* economic resources and cultural orientations (Yanagisako 2002: 6; Liechty 2003: 21–27).

This emerging tradition that treats social life as emerging out of social processes owes much to the work of French sociologist Pierre Bourdieu. For Bourdieu, linking objective structures to more subjective orientations (that is, wedding class and status) lay at the core of his intellectual project (e.g. Bourdieu 1990: 49–50). As Loïc Wacquant has noted, one of the hallmarks of Bourdieu's work is to affirm "the *primacy of relations*" over the "dualistic alternatives" that prioritize either structure *or* agency (Bourdieu and Wacquant 1992: 15–19). Class, according to this formulation, is not reducible to economic wealth, level of education, political position, or cultural knowledge but rather is realized through the interaction between objective and subjective factors and the complex mediation between economy and culture. Bourdieu portrays all of these different resources as setting limits upon one another, resulting in a set of dispositions that are best conceived not as fixed positions in the social structure but as potentials or likelihoods that must be enacted by social actors in real social situations.

THE STRUCTURE OF ENTITLEMENT AND THE PRACTICE OF INEQUALITY

Bourdieu's rejection of what Douglas Foley calls "a false dichotomy . . . between cultural status groups and economic classes" (Foley 1990 : 169–70) is echoed in a growing body of research that explores the cultural dimensions of the construction, maintenance, and reproduction of class boundaries.[1] Inspired by approaches like Bourdieu's, this research has explored how social distinctions contribute to the unequal distribution of both material wealth and non-material social goods like status and social esteem. Cultural sociologists in particular seek to understand how what Michele Lamont and Virág Molnár (2002: 168) call "symbolic boundaries"—the perception of groups of people as different or distinct—solidify into "social boundaries"—forms of social closure and exclusion that result in unequal access to and distribution of resources and opportunities.

One of the best-known works on social boundaries is Bourdieu's *Distinction* (1984), an analysis of the cultural production of taste in France. In a vast investigation of the class-coded nature of everything from dietary habits to hobbies and musical preferences, Bourdieu argues that "taste," in the form of preferences for certain lifestyle choices, represents a cultural counterpart to economic stratification. At the center of this argument is the concept of *habitus*, a term that refers to the largely unconscious dispositions that people internalize through the course of their lives by virtue of their social environment and their positioning in society (Bourdieu 1977, 1984: 169–72). For example, a working-class French habitus might produce a preference for "practical" clothing or "filling" food—what Bourdieu labels a "taste for necessity"—that simultaneously identifies this group outwardly as uncultured and even vulgar (1984: 379–80). Daily habits and practices that appear to reveal "natural" differences in fact reflect social inequalities that are viewed through a prism of both difference and hierarchy.

A host of other scholars have examined the role that symbolic bound-

---

[1] These range from Marxist-influenced studies of working-class cultures and life experiences (e.g. Thompson 1966; Sennett and Cobb 1972; Willis 1977) to more recent work that tends to focus on the role of cultural consumption in marking class distinctions (most famously Bourdieu 1984; more recently chapters in Lamont and Fournier 1992a, especially Collins 1992 and Hall 1992; Holt 1997; Katz-Gerro 2002; Zavisca 2004).

aries play in the cultural construction of social difference and class distinctions. Michele Lamont's research (1992, 2000) on the upper-middle and working classes in France and the United States demonstrates how class-specific cultural and moral categories create distinct understandings of personal worthiness. Such conceptual categories serve as the basis for strong symbolic boundaries that generate inequality through exclusion and hierarchy (Lamont and Molnár 2002; cf. Tilly 1998). Focusing on the level of daily practice, ethnographic research in schools has revealed how everyday understandings of social difference contribute to unequal outcomes—as demonstrated by Julie Bettie's (2003) study of cultural constructions of racial, class, and gender hierarchies in a California high school, or Paul Willis's influential book on working-class youth in England, *Learning to Labor* (1977). These studies all approach class as an activity or practice rather than as a category—they "processualize" class (Liechty 2003: 21). As such, this body of research not only points to the role of culture in structuring relations of inequality, it also suggests the practical, everyday ways this occurs.

One of the key sites where social distinctions are recognized and practiced is through daily social interactions (Lamont and Fournier 1992b), the realm that Erving Goffman (1983) dubbed the "interaction order." So, for example, anthropologist Douglas Foley (1990) relied upon an analysis of daily social interactions among students in his study of a rural Texas high school to demonstrate that "public face-to-face interactions become highly routinized aspects of a social order . . . reoccurring rituals in which people act out their proper [class] roles" (1990: 179). Similarly, Bettie's (2003) study of white and Mexican-American high school girls illustrates how gender, race, and especially class distinctions are "performed" and become meaningful in everyday life. Bettie, echoing Bourdieu, contends that "structures of inequality are not automatic but must be constantly reproduced in practice" (2003: 55). Recent ethnographic studies of service interactions in U.S. settings like luxury hotels (Sherman 2005, 2006) and toy stores (Williams 2006) vividly illustrate how concrete social interactions provide the stage on which performances of social class and recognition of class entitlements are enacted.

How do distinctions—class, gender, or otherwise—emerge in the course of social interactions like those conducted in a department store or marketplace? Following Bourdieu, I argue that social interactions involve an acting out—though not mechanistically—of our culturally coded habits and preferences. We rely on our *habitus* to tell us what feels right in a given situation and how we should behave. In a similar fashion, Raymond Williams has argued that lived reality is experienced through sets of feelings that guide social behavior, propelling or restraining action; Williams labeled this link between feeling and action "structures of feeling." Although Williams applied the notion of structures of feeling to literature, the class-differentiated "practical consciousness" (1977: 130) that he sought to describe applies well to daily social life. Much like *habitus*, structures of feeling provide an emotionally charged but often unspoken ordering to social life that emerges and hardens in the course of daily experience. Our habits and dispositions, our sense of what is right and what we are entitled to, not only reflect power relations in society but also create them.

Building on Bourdieu, Williams, Lamont, and others, I suggest that the cultural dispositions and the structures of feeling experienced by various social groups combine to form an overall *structure of entitlement*. Some social groups, by virtue of their elevated or powerful position in society, feel entitled to greater social goods—greater levels of respect and social recognition. The sense of entitlement people carry with them into social interactions with other people becomes a practical expression of social hierarchy and social location. This structure is neither automatic nor unchanging, but it nevertheless can guide and constrain individual action. In China today, a new structure of entitlement is under construction, and it is understood in terms of social distinctions that, while subject to disagreement and contestation, have important implications for the future shape of Chinese society.

THE WORK OF DISTINCTION

One set of key and very public sites where the structure of entitlement finds expression in urban China today is the range of retail settings that now vie for a piece of the consumer market. At the heart of this study lies the idea that the social relations performed in service settings like department stores and marketplaces—relations among managers, workers, and customers, and even relations *among* settings themselves—play a key role in the construction and reproduction of broader social hierarchies.

How does this happen? I suggest that social distinctions are produced in service settings in two ways. First, service organizations like department stores—especially those serving elite customers—engage in practices of *organizational distinction making*, relying upon hiring and labor control practices to distinguish themselves from institutions serving customers located further down the social hierarchy. Second, service workers produce social distinctions in the course of *service interactions* by recognizing customer claims to class position and social status. In either case, service settings are spaces where customers seek distinction and thus are important sites for the performance of social difference. Service institutions participate by organizing such performances and managing worker behavior in order to secure customers' loyalty. In this way, organizations like department stores actually become invested in recognizing and reinforcing a wider structure of entitlement.

The drive to produce social distinctions sets retail settings in conversation with one another, as hiring decisions, work activities, and service interactions are all organized in relation to—and in distinction from—other, similar service work settings. After all, something can only be distinguished as one thing if it is clearly *not* something else. An exclusive restaurant or retail establishment is only "exclusive" in relation to other restaurants or retail settings that are clearly *not* exclusive. When the tasks that make up interactive service work (Leidner 1993) are organized to produce social distinctions in such a relational way, the result is what I call *distinction work*. Distinction work is characterized by a *relational labor process*. A relational labor process organizes work activities in order to produce distinctions both among organizations and between individuals—the two levels I identified above. Here again I borrow from Pierre Bourdieu, especially the idea developed in *Distinction* (1984) that the production and consumption of cultural goods—in this case, the "good" of customer service—involve a struggle over symbolic categories that enables groups to define and assert themselves through simultaneously hierarchical and *relational* differences (Bourdieu 1984, 1998). Difference, in the form of the superior marks of "distinction," helps to reproduce cultural categories that create a structure of entitlement and that in turn help reproduce social inequality (Bourdieu and Wacquant 1992: 14–15).

The centrality of class distinctions in service settings has been revealed in a number of studies of service work in the U.S. context. Rachel Sherman's (2006) study of service work in American luxury hotels reveals how these settings serve as sites for the enactment and legitimization of inequality through the appropriation of workers' physical and emotional labor. Part of what workers do, Sherman demonstrates, is *recognize* hotel guests as entitled to luxury service, an entitlement which is in fact a marker of class privilege. Guests participate in the normalization of this inequality. Similarly, Christine Williams's (2006) study of U.S. toy stores demonstrates how class differences play out in retail settings. Williams found middle-class customers to be especially likely to enact a sense of class entitlement when dealing with service workers drawn from the working class and the working poor. In a China context, Eileen Otis's (2007) research on a Beijing luxury hotel details how new service work regimes are designed to extract worker deference for the benefit of moneyed and elite (and mostly male) hotel guests. All these studies demonstrate that because the *production* of service is simultaneously the *consumption* of service, service settings provide a key space for the reproduction of structures of inequality through the recognition of class entitlements.

INEQUALITY, ORGANIZATIONS, AND THE RETAIL "FIELD"

What these studies tend not to show, however, is the relational nature of distinction work and the ways in which this can create a dialogue among social settings. Relations *among organizations* are, in fact, what gives distinction work its most manifestly relational nature. Organizations like department stores become invested in the production of social distinctions in order to attract customers, but to produce distinction these stores must distinguish themselves, and their customers, from competitors serving customers located further down the social hierarchy. For this reason, the distinction work performed in Chinese department stores makes little sense without taking into account the larger organizational context or "organizational field" (DiMaggio and Powell 1991 [1983]).

A field can be thought of as an environment in which social actors (both organizations and individuals) interact and respond to one another (Bourdieu and Wacquant 1992: 97; DiMaggio and Powell 1991 [1983]; Martin 2003; Ray 1999). Relations among organizations in a field are both constrained and enabled by structures of domination and alliance, which shape their interactions. The boundaries of an organizational field are dependent on mutual recognition by organizations and are, as a result, always contested (DiMaggio and Powell 1991 [1983]: 65). The concept of field provides a way for thinking about the specific context in which distinction work is organized and performed and the concrete organizational forces that help create and maintain a structure of entitlement. Here, the field of interest is what I call the "retail field." Organizations (Chinese retailers) organize their workers' activities (the production of social distinctions) in relation to other organizations that they recognize as being engaged in the same "game" (retailing). This organizational context is a key environment in which the structure of entitlement is publicly constructed and defended.

The retail field is not, however, simply a sphere of economic competition. As I hope to demonstrate—and this is really the essence of the concept of distinction work—the "profits" to be earned and competed for in this field are not purely economic ones. The struggles among, and within, institutional actors in the retail field are as symbolic as they are economic. The symbolic side of business is important in part because it is so closely connected to the broader positioning of individuals and groups within China's changing social hierarchy. Indeed, the retail field in urban China is so interesting and important because it is *not* autonomous from larger social changes taking place in China. It is a field in which the "search for distinction" and the production of social differences tell us much about Chinese society writ large.

THE CONTEXT FOR DISTINCTION: CHINA'S ECONOMIC REFORMS AND RISING INEQUALITY

The economic reforms that China's Communist party-state implemented in 1979 have brought dramatic change to the country. Economic restructuring, and in particular the gradual dismantling of the socialist planned economy and its substitution by market mechanisms, has been a cornerstone of reform policies. The effects have penetrated every facet of contemporary Chinese society, reshaping everything from population movements and employment patterns to family structures and daily consumption activities, but several aspects hold particular relevance for this study. First, China's reform era has witnessed growing levels of social stratification and increasing gaps between rich and poor. Second, new class inequalities are popularly understood through what Lisa Rofel (1999) has called an "allegory of postsocialism," a highly gendered story that rejects the socialist "past" and embraces the marketized "present" in the name of progress, prosperity, and modernity. And third, economic reforms have given birth to a burgeoning consumer culture and a booming service economy where gendered class meanings are produced and performed.

Material and other inequalities did, of course, exist in pre-reform China (Bian 2002). The government's occupational ranking system produced a hierarchy of material wealth, status, and opportunity, and the party-state's class labeling system stratified those from "good" and "bad" class backgrounds (Zang 2000; Zhang 2004). China's *hukou*, or household residential permit system, further segregated the country along rural/urban lines, segmenting labor markets and offering urban dwellers a social safety net largely supported through the extraction of rural resources (Cheng and Selden 1994; Solinger 1999; Wang 2005). The vast majority of urban Chinese found themselves in the role of "supplicants to the socialist state" (Davis 1993), their lives organized by patterns of dependence upon their work units and workplace superiors for a vast range of goods and services (Walder 1986). Individuals' access to material goods and social services was largely determined by their status within their workplace (Walder 1986), the location of their workplace within the state bureaucratic hierarchy (Bian 1994), and their accumulation of *guanxi*, elaborate networks of personal connections (Yang 1994). In Mao's China, educational and especially political capital were the resources of the country's elite (Wu and Treiman 2004; Zang 2000; cf. Konrad and Szelenyi 1979).

In the course of the past two decades, however, economic disparities—and the importance of economic capital—have become increasingly apparent. Researchers have convincingly demonstrated that a growing gap between rich and poor has accompanied economic reforms, both nationally as well as between and within rural and urban areas (Fang et al. 2002; Khan and Riskin 2001; Li 2000; Riskin et al. 2001; Xue and Wei 2003; for an overview, see Nickum 2003). The average urban income is currently about six times the average rural income, while taxes in rural areas average three times higher than in cities (Yang 2005). One recent study found that the incomes of China's richest 10% rose from representing 24% of total wages earned in urban China in 1990 to over 38% in 1998 (Xu 2004: 91). As Riskin et al. have written: "One of the world's most egalitarian societies in the 1970s, China in the 1980s and 1990s became one of the more unequal countries in its region and among developing countries generally" (2001: 3). Khan and Riskin's (2005) most recent analysis of income inequality in China suggests that while national-level inequality remained roughly constant between 1995 and 2002, the rural-urban income gap grew during this time period. And when the wages of rural migrants working in cities are taken into account, the level of urban inequality grew as well.

Given these dramatic changes to the social structure, ongoing research probes the mechanics of stratification in contemporary China (Bian 2002). While theoretical claims are often inconclusive (Wu 2002), it is clear that both economic and political elites are reaping great profits from China's rapid economic expansion (e.g. Walder 2002; Goodman 1995), and the two groups are often closely allied (Wank 1999). Most of these stratification studies draw upon large data sets and largely focus on the gradational distribution of social actors in China, asking questions such as who gets ahead in reform-era China, what social groups are elites drawn from, and what resources do they rely on for their power, influence, and economic success.[2]

Ethnographic approaches like the one used in this book offer a different perspective. By focusing on the texture of relations of inequality—in Arthur Stinchcombe's words, "what powerful people can get others to do" (Stinchcombe 1965: 180)—an ethnographic approach allows us to frame inequality in terms of relationships among people and enables us to highlight the place of class and other inequalities in everyday social interactions. What does inequality *feel* like? How is it constructed and understood in the course of everyday life? Most importantly, along what lines are social divisions perceived and drawn, and how do these social distinctions serve to create new structures of entitlement in China?

THE POLITICS OF TIME AND IMAGERIES OF POSTSOCIALIST TRANSITION

"The play of difference is highly political," writes Pun Ngai (2005: 131) in her study of women factory workers in southern China. Indeed,

---

[2] This is an extensive literature, but key publications include: Nee 1989, 1996; Walder 1996; Zhou 2000; Cao and Nee 2000; and most recently Walder 2002 and Zang 2002. These scholars propose different stratification mechanisms and theoretical frameworks for understanding social change in China, often dividing into what have been termed "market transition" and "path dependent" approaches, but this research tends to ask similar sets of questions about the mechanisms of stratification (Zang 2002; Bian 2002).

the categories utilized to convey social distinctions are critical to understanding inequality in China today. In urban China, the "play of difference" is reflected in a cultural conversation about the relationship between the past and the future that rejects the socialist "past" and embraces the marketized "present." This temporal framework is the central context in which social distinctions based on class, gender, and generation get constructed, serving as an interpretive framework in which social distinctions take on significance and power.

In the mind's eye of the Chinese public, the pre-reform years are often characterized as a combination of planned economics and revolutionary politics that left China backward and impoverished. People do not commonly use the term "socialist" to refer to this time—they are more likely to say "when there was a planned economy" (*jihuajingji de shihou*)—in part because the Chinese state still lays claim to the socialist label (now accompanied by the modifier "market"). However, I will use "socialism" and "socialist" to refer to Maoist-era China, its planned economy, politics, and the daily patterns of behavior it fostered. Borrowing Ching Kwan Lee's (2002: 193) formulation, I understand contemporary China to be "postsocialist" in that the planned economy no longer plays a central role in production or consumption. China is also "postsocialist" in the sense that the present is very much understood in relation to, and as a rejection of, a socialist "past" that encompasses both institutional and interpersonal levels of social organization (Rofel 1999; Zhang 2001).

The irony, of course, is that there is no clear dividing line between "past" and "present" or between which social practices should be embraced in the name of progress and which must be rejected. Critical analyses of social change in formerly state socialist societies often involve a complex attempt to separate the legacies of socialism from newly imported influences of the market. What remains? What has changed? In China, given that the dismantling of the planned economy and depoliticization daily life have not been accompanied by the unseating of the Chinese Communist Party, this labeling of "old" and "new" is even more fraught with ambiguity.

Of special importance in this context are the patterns of behavior that are evocative of the socialist past and thus are *perceived* as remnants of China's planned economy. The past, and especially people associated with the past, are cast as "abject" figures against which the future is to be defined (Rofel 1999; Pun 2005). Like workers in other state socialist contexts (Burawoy and Lukács 1992; Dunn 1999, 2004; Kideckel 2002), China's state sector workers have been portrayed as inefficient, undisciplined, and lazy, people unsuited to the demands of a modern, market-driven economy (Rofel 1992, 1999; Won 2004; Lee 2007). In industrial settings, the taint of socialism can even extend to young rural migrants, who never benefited from the security and stability of socialist urban work units but are nevertheless viewed by managers as "socialist" bodies exhibiting the "red" and "lazy" characteristics of a workforce contaminated by the anti-competitive, collectivist, and undisciplined mentality of state socialism (Pun 2005). In a cultural drama reminiscent of other contexts of rapid and dramatic social change, the mapping of a new time schema onto social groups creates distinctions that justify exclusion and inequality. China's urban working class, much like the laid-off autoworkers in Kathryn Dudley's (1994) study of the de-industrializing American rustbelt, are characterized as possessing an "obsolete" set of cultural values; they are a "lost generation" (Hung and Chiu 2003; cf. Dudley 1994: 89), out-of-step with China's progressive forward movement.

Indeed, China's economic take-off has been accompanied by an almost evolutionary perspective on society and social groupings, and other groups in contemporary China are similarly viewed as backward (*luohou*) or even primitive (Yan 2003; Zhang 2001; Schein 2000; cf. Dudley 1994). In China's cities, this is especially true of rural migrant workers, whose poverty and resistance to market reforms get reinterpreted as a lack of *cultural* resources as much as a lack of material resources (Yan 2003: 499). At times, small-scale merchants and their workers are also viewed as operating at a "low level" of capitalism that will be naturally superseded by more advanced forms of business.

The portrayal of the urban working class as trapped in a socialist time warp, and of small-scale merchants and their often-rural employees as located on a lower rung of a ladder of economic and cultural development, represent two ways in which time—and the past in particular—shapes contemporary social distinctions in urban China. But if, as the following chapters will show, the rejection of China's state socialist past serves to produce social distinctions that bolster the sense of entitlement borne by new elites, those claims are nevertheless subject to contestation and struggle. Groups like the urban working class, increasingly marginalized both symbolically and economically, nevertheless evoke the past as a resource in the present (Lee 2000, 2002). For the workers who were part of this study, China's state socialist history operated as both a cultural legacy that structured a working-class sense of entitlement as well as an object of nostalgia to be redeployed as a source of value—and a mark of distinction—in the contemporary marketplace. Likewise, the *geti* merchants and their hired help reinterpreted their marketplace as a space of dignity and personal development and not as one of chaos and disorder.

SERVICE WORK, THE GENDERED RICE BOWL, AND THE PLAY OF DIFFERENCE

Ideas about gender combine with this powerful imagery of China's transition from a socialist planned economy to a market economy to operate as a key means for marking social distinctions (Hanser 2005). In particular, modern constructions of "proper" femininity map onto class and generational distinctions, associating young urban women with affluence and modernity while working-class, middle-aged women are cast as unproductive and unreformable remnants of the past. Ideas about femininity also lay down distinctions among young Chinese women, and relatively well-educated urban women are distinguished from their uncultured and morally suspect rural and less-educated urban counterparts. In China's burgeoning service sector, these gendered and generational differences often translate into class distinctions on the sales floor, as class meanings are produced for and consumed by status-conscious customers (Otis 2007).

Feminist scholars point to the interconnectedness of class and gender distinctions, reminding us that performances of femininity are always class-coded (Bettie 2003; Freeman 2000; Steedman 1987). Sherry Ortner, writing of the American context, notes that class "is rarely spoken in its own right. Rather, it is represented through other categories of social difference: gender, ethnicity, race" and sexuality (Ortner 1991: 164). In China today, there are a number of reasons why gender has become a powerful way of "speaking" class. First, while discourses about class have not historically been muted or absent in China, during the reform era a new ideology of individual enterprise and achievement has gradually displaced class-based analyses of Chinese society (Hoffman 2001; Hanser 2002; Won 2004; Croll 1991), such that class understandings of Chinese society have come to seem as anachronistic and dysfunctional as the socialist planned economy. One consequence is that class may increasingly be spoken, as Ortner puts it, "through other categories of social difference."

Second, the rise of a naturalized, biologized understanding of gender in the reform era facilitates the expression of new class differences through gendered meanings. Numerous scholars have identified a trend toward the sexualization and commodification of women's bodies in China (Brownell 2001; Schein 2000; Yang 1999), a trend viewed as a departure from both the rhetoric and social practices of the Maoist era (Chen 2003a; Rofel 1999; Croll 1995) and more traditional conceptions of gender difference rooted in earlier Chinese history (Barlow 1994; Furth 2002). Lisa Rofel (1999: 217) characterizes this rise of essentialized notions of gender as "an allegory of postsocialism" that portrays newly sexualized gender relations as a return to the natural and inevitable. With Mao-era gender neutrality now viewed as unnatural and even ludicrous, this naturalized understanding of gender and sexuality is powerfully associated with everything socialism was not—especially an affluent, market society and a new, modern future for China. In many Chinese work settings, essentialized gender categories become a means to justify and mask inequalities between women and men (Lee 1998; Ong 1997; Rofel 1999; Woo 1994).

In the service sector, this allegory of postsocialism takes shape as the "rice bowl of youth" (*qingchunfan*), a term that refers to a woman's ability to convert her youth and beauty into potentially lucrative employment opportunities (Zhang 2000; see also Hyde 2007, who translates the term as "eating spring rice"). The rice bowl of youth stands opposed to the traditional, socialist "iron rice bowl" (*tie fanwan*), once the symbol of the guaranteed employment, housing, and social services of state socialism but today more often associated with the drab poverty and immobility of China's old planned economy—and the middle-aged female bodies of workers in state enterprises. As cultural critic Zhang Zhen has written: "The robust image of vivacious, young female eaters of the rice bowl of youth symbolizes a fresh labor force, a model of social mobility, and the rise of a consumer culture endorsed by current official ideology" (2000: 94; see also Wang Zheng 2000). Young urban women, through their adoption of new, feminized identities and practices, are simultaneously identified with productivity and modernity, while older workers are "marginalized by new imaginaries of modernity" (Rofel 1999: 95; on femininity in the service sector, see Otis 2003

and 2007; for parallels in industry, see Lee 1998 and Pun 2000; on pros-
titution, Hyde 2007). At the same time, proper urban femininity is defined against lower-class urban and rural versions, portrayed as overly
promiscuous or ridiculously unsophisticated (e.g. Lei 2003; Pun 1999).

As a result, the "rice bowl of youth" imagery and its associations with
sexualized femininity and capitalist modernity have become a powerful formula for conveying social distinction in China's burgeoning retail sector. These elements of difference—gender and generation—are
set within a broader imagery of transition and become the raw material for the production of class and status distinctions in contemporary
Chinese department stores, marketplaces, and service interactions. In
the service sector labor market, these profoundly gendered symbolic
distinctions ultimately solidify into the exclusion of middle-aged and
rural women from the most lucrative, high-end jobs.

FIELD SITES AND METHODS

The research on which this book is based began as a straightforward comparison between two department stores—one state-owned,
one privately owned. The rationale behind a two-pronged comparison
was to explore how retail work and consumer practices were changing
in the course of China's economic reforms, and a contrast between an
entrenched, state-owned store and a new retailer using more modern
managerial practices seemed apt. Once I entered these two field sites,
however, it became apparent that not only would I have to expand my
comparison to include a third setting—the *geti*-dominated clothing bazaar—but also that these three settings were in no way discrete and
separate cases. The people in each department store setting were acutely aware of one another (and of other department stores in the city)
as well as of the activities going on in the *geti* marketplaces scattered
about Harbin.

Although Harbin possesses a distinctive history, the city's experiences during the reform era are generally representative of large urban settings in the way that reforms have reshaped the city's economic
and social structures. A fishing village transformed into an urban base
for the Russian development of the Trans-Siberian Railroad in the late
nineteenth century, Harbin once acted as a center for Russian and East
European émigrés in the early 1900s, fell under the control of Japanese
imperialist forces in the 1930s, and then was liberated by the Chinese

communists in the 1940s (Wolff 1999; Lahusen 2001). The city has since become an unequivocally "Chinese" city (Carter 2002), and it served as a center of heavy industrial production and state planning in the Mao era.

Today, this city of over 3 million people and the capital of Heilongjiang province in China's far northeast has witnessed innumerable changes, including the rapid rise of private business, the decline of state industry, and an increasingly visible gap between the material circumstances of the city's richest and poorest residents. In this context, Harbin's increasingly stratified retail sector serves as a barometer of broader changes. Although economic reforms came later to China's northeast than coastal areas, in this regard Harbin is similar to the bulk of China's non-coastal provinces and cities and is especially representative of the country's ailing industrial Northeast.

Indeed, Harbin lies in what is sometimes termed China's "rust belt," the northeastern provinces that once served as a center of state industrial production but where a troubled and declining state sector has created high regional levels of unemployment (Hurst 2004; Lee 2000, 2007). Much like the situation in Liaoning province detailed by Ching Kwan Lee (2007), actual unemployment rates in Harbin in the early 2000s were likely double, or more, the official registered unemployment rate of 3.7% in 2002 (*Statistical Yearbook of Harbin* 2006: 29). A city in which the state-employed working class once enjoyed high status and job security, Harbin's experiences of economic and social transformation puts the contemporary social struggles faced by much of China into somewhat starker relief.

My first field site was a state-owned department store that I call the Harbin No. X Department Store, one of Harbin's oldest and largest department stores, employing almost 3,000 people. Since it was nationalized in the late 1940s, the store has symbolized the bounty of state socialism. Physically, the store was a socialist behemoth, a massive structure engulfing a full square block of land in one of the city's central districts. Inside, working-class salesclerks dealt with mostly blue-collar shoppers. Here I worked as a uniformed salesclerk selling down coats in the women's department.

At the top of the retail hierarchy, my second field site was a high-end, privately owned department store that I call the "Sunshine" Department Store. A glistening structure located in Harbin's downtown, this luxury department store first opened in the early 1990s, employed over 1,000 staff, and offered six floors of expensive merchandise to

Harbin shoppers. Run by a private mainland-Chinese business group, Sunshine was generally acknowledged by shoppers and retail industry specialists alike as one of the city's most exclusive department stores. Here I worked as a salesclerk in a cashmere sweater boutique.

My third field site was known as "The Underground," a label mirroring its low status and socially dubious position in the city. The marketplace was literally located underground, sitting just below the Sunshine Department store in a series of converted and later extended air raid tunnels that stretched for several kilometers below the city streets. The Underground was a large wholesale/retail clothing market where small-scale private merchants—*getihu*—rented counter space and sold their inexpensive wares to both rural and urban people. Here I spent time observing and occasionally selling in two separate "rooms" of the market, each housing about ten clothing merchants.

In the chapters that follow, I primarily rely on ethnographic data gathered during thirteen months of field research in China, conducted between March 2001 and September 2002. In each site I spent about two-and-a-half months working seven-hour days, six days a week. I also spent lengths of time observing in a number of other stores, markets, and service work settings in the city. I supplemented ethnographic work with over 40 interviews with workers, store managers, merchandise suppliers, and other industry experts, and I conducted archival research on institutional changes to China's retail sector since the introduction of economic reforms in 1979.

Until the moment I actually found myself on the sales floor at Harbin No. X, suited up in a store uniform, I was uncertain if I would be able to work as a salesclerk in a Chinese store. I was turned away at the first store to which I tried to gain access—a new, private department store in Harbin run by a large, Beijing-based company—by managers who cited fears about revealing "business secrets." It was my good fortune that managers at state-owned stores are unaccustomed to thinking in terms of business secrecy, and so when I approached a manager (a friend's acquaintance) at Harbin No. X, I was received with little hesitation. The store's assistant-general manager agreed to allow me to do an unpaid "internship" (*shixi*), explaining that the store might use me as an opportunity to engage in "a little publicity."

On my first day of work, upper management outfitted me in the striped shirt, tie, and numbered badge of a regular store employee. They then took me down to the sales floor, where they held a "welcome ceremony" for me—and where I found not one, but two TV cameras awaiting me, plus a small knot of newspaper reporters. One of the newspaper reporters collared a passing girl, and he made me move the zipper up and down on her coat while he tried to get a "candid" of me at work selling down coats. I appeared in a number of local papers, often on the first page and under the headline "Western Ph.D. works Harbin No. X counter." As my countermates at the store would tell me, "Hey, you're famous now."

For a week or two, all this media attention was disruptive, and I found myself in the position of the observed more than of the observer. But people quickly grew accustomed to my presence in the store. Initially I thought the store might restrict me to simply observing the activities of salesclerks in the store, but I was wrong. My co-workers enthusiastically coached me in almost all aspects of the job—organizing stock, introducing merchandise to customers, and writing out sales receipts for shoppers to take to the cashier for payment. On one occasion, two of my co-workers left me to work the counter alone for an entire morning while they reorganized stock in our storage area.

Ultimately, the media attention I received at Harbin No. X eased my entry into other sites, especially the Sunshine Department Store. My sales position at Sunshine was arranged by a sales manager at a cashmere sweater company, one of Sunshine's suppliers. As the following chapters show, Sunshine was a dramatically different workplace—and field site—from Harbin No. X. At Sunshine, workers were far more anxious about making mistakes and workplace discipline more strictly enforced. It also took me a much longer time to learn the ropes. There were certain tasks—such as writing out receipts—that I never felt comfortable performing. As I note in Chapter 4, my co-workers worried that they would be held responsible for my mistakes, and yet to my surprise the clerks in my sales area, with the exception of one young woman, seemed loathe to instruct me. The first few weeks on the job were excruciatingly uncomfortable, though I eventually came to understand that this was a feature of the workplace and not simply of my personal reception by my co-workers. Unprompted, a number of salesclerks individually expressed to me that they had had similar experiences when they first arrived at Sunshine. By the time I left Sunshine, however, I had become familiar enough with the work that my co-workers had come to rely on my assistance on the sales floor.

Gaining access to the *geti* marketplace, The Underground, was the most straightforward in the sense that an acquaintance simply introduced me to people operating a sales counter. In this setting I was more observer than participant, largely because selling merchandise involved negotiation and haggling over prices. I was and still am a poor bargainer. Given that the merchants in the market often get by on very slim profit margins, I did not want to negatively impact anyone's business through my incompetence.

If getting myself into The Underground proved very easy, there were occasions when it looked like staying would be more difficult. I received no formal permission to spend time in the market, but as long as I was not selling merchandise the management company that oversaw the market did not seem to care much about my presence. The Underground was also regulated by a district office of the Bureau of Industry and Commerce (*gongshang ju*), whose mandates were theoretically carried out by a group of officers who in practice tended to bully Underground merchants and fine them for minor infractions. On one occasion, one of these men appeared at my sales counter, somewhat drunk, and suggested that I might have to "pay a little something" in order to stay in The Underground. I was extremely angry at the attempted bribe, but I acted as if I did not understand what the man was saying. For a number of weeks I waited anxiously for the man to reappear and either make the demand for money again or force me to leave. I also worried about the negative impact my presence might have on the merchants in the room, especially "Xiao Li," who was my host. But Xiao Li was on very good terms with the management company, and ultimately nothing came of my worries.

In the end, although I never "blended in" in any of my three sites, in each setting my presence achieved a kind of normalcy as I became another fixture of the environment. My foreignness also meant that my research was never covert, that I could take field notes openly, and that I could raise all sorts of issues and questions with my informants. However, as a "white" person in department store uniform, I was without question an oddity. At Harbin No. X, store publicity attracted many well-wishers from the city, and store Communist party officials bestowed a "friendship ambassador" award on me. At Sunshine, customers frequently mistook me for a young Russian woman driven by Russia's weak economy to find employment in Harbin, department store work being a respectable option. By contrast, in The Underground, I was read as a Russian trader—a fairly despised group in Harbin—and as a result I was frequently the subject of disparaging and even racist comments made by passersby who assumed that I could not understand them. These variable perceptions of me in each site also reflected the gendered and classed nature of the three retail settings and their relative positions in Harbin's urban hierarchy.

Finally, while I want to acknowledge that my authorship of this book has given me the power to reconstruct and frame the words and actions of other people, I want also to note that this rarely reflected the dynamic I experienced on the sales floors. As indicated above, frequently I was observed more than I was observing. Not only was I highly dependent on my informants for almost every piece of information in this study, but they also kept me under their thumb for much of the time I was their companion. In some cases, I felt as if I had become a kind of public property—down to having personal mail opened and read for me by my co-workers at Harbin No. X, being teased mercilessly by raucous merchants in The Underground, and receiving intimate advice on how to improve my figure by a fellow salesclerk at Sunshine. Perhaps this is just as it should be: Where there is deep curiosity on both sides, the researcher can expect to share herself with her subjects, just as they share with her.

THE CHAPTERS THAT FOLLOW

There are many more discrete positions within China's, and Harbin's, retail field than I could possibly attend to in a single book. The range and kinds of retailing businesses found in urban China have proliferated rapidly over the past fifteen or twenty years, with some businesses targeting very small and specific groups of consumers. The three market sites examined here, however, hold special symbolic weight in urban China as the shopping spaces identified with the new urban rich, the working "masses," and rural people and the less respectable segments of urban society. These three locales, and the organization of sales interactions within them, were also very much in dialogue with one another.

But while the clothing retailers I studied conceived of themselves as arrayed along a vertical hierarchy of marketplaces, the image of a ladder is a misleading one. Instead of viewing positions as locations in a market hierarchy, I suggest that these positions were in fact *stances* that retailers took vis-à-vis one another. These stances were translated into relational labor processes in which workers were expected to distinguish themselves and the service they produced from that found in other settings through gender- and especially class-coded distinctions. In this way, the stances or positions managers and merchants took within the retail field could be literally transposed onto the physical stances workers were directed to adopt on the sales floor.

I explore the broader, historical context in which this particular retail field is situated in Chapter 2, where I describe changes to retailing in China during the course of economic reforms and the accompanying transformations in the lives of workers and consumers. Chapter 3 then explores one site—Harbin No. X, the state-owned department store—in detail, arguing that because this store was originally organized under the conditions of a centralized, planned economy, service work there was *not* organized relationally and was *not* structured to produce class distinctions. By contrast, Chapter 4 demonstrates how work at the Sunshine Department Store, an expensive, luxury establishment, was carefully organized to produce and recognize markers of class distinction. In that chapter, I argue that class distinctions become coded in highly gendered ways, and in direct dialogue with both Harbin No. X and The Underground, as managers sought to mold a sufficiently high-class workforce to serve its elite customers. The store was, as a result, deeply invested in upholding a new structure of entitlement.

Subsequently, Chapter 5 turns to The Underground, the chaotic, subterranean clothing bazaar, economically vibrant but low-status. I characterize The Underground as a space of counter strategies, where merchants and saleswomen challenged the symbolic boundaries produced in settings like Sunshine by blurring the distinctions that separated the "high" from the "low." In Chapter 6, I return to the Harbin No. X Department Store and explore how the market environment—and competition from markets like The Underground in particular—reshaped worker practices in this working-class department store. I argue that Harbin No. X workers themselves began to innovate elements of distinction work as they attempted to convert their store's—and their own—socialist-era symbolic capital into reform-era resources. And finally, I conclude with Chapter 7, where I draw out more clearly the implications the links between production, consumption, and inequality explored in earlier chapters hold for an emerging structure of entitlement in urban China today.

CHAPTER TWO

Revolution and Reform:
The Business of Retail in Modern China

Orville Schell's book on the early years of China's economic reforms begins with a stark description of urban life during the Mao era:

> For anyone familiar with the great cities of Asia, which teem with activity, it was eerie to walk the streets of urban China while Mao still lived . . . all private enterprises, even individual street venders, had been branded "tails of capitalism." And so diligently had the government gone about chopping off these tails that the streets looked as if a neutron-bomb-like device had been detonated, destroying small businesses while leaving everything else intact. There were no curbside restaurants with their smells of food wafting in the air, no peddlers hawking their wares, no throngs of shoppers browsing and haggling with merchants on the sidewalks. The streets of Mao's China were crowded, but with silent, purposeful people, buying the bare necessities of life from dreary state-owned stores or going to and from work. (Schell 1984: 3–4)

By the mid-1980s, just a few years into the country's new program of economic liberalization and decentralization, urban marketplaces already had begun to multiply, transforming the urban landscape. Schell describes the new strata of the burgeoning retail sector: merchants occupying rented stalls and stands, small shops converted to private ownership, and sidewalk hawkers selling everything from designer jeans to home-made medicinal concoctions (1984: 50–52).

By the start of the twenty-first century, massive glass-and-chrome structures housing new shopping complexes and modern department stores had sprung from the soil of China's largest cities, replacing the dour shopping spaces and small shops that characterized pre- and early reform periods. In May 2005, the *New York Times* reported that China had become home to the world's largest shopping mall, and by

2010 the country is expected to have seven of the ten largest shopping complexes in the world (Barboza 2005). More goods and more stores generated more competition, and newly acquired mantras like "The customer is never wrong," unheard of in the days when store clerks could act as surly gatekeepers to scarce merchandise, began to reflect the dramatic rise in stature of that once-neglected entity in China, the consumer. Urban China had become a "buyer's market," where merchants scrambled to attract shoppers now confronted with a vast and growing array of goods and services to consume.

This chapter provides an overview of economic reforms in China's urban retail sector and of the impact these changes have had on store organization, retail workers, and urban consumers. The scope of these changes has been enormous and spans radically different forms of social and economic organization. In contrast to market economies, where the forces of supply and demand drive production, prior to 1978 China's economy was a "planned" or "command" economy in which both production and distribution were dictated by output quotas issued by government ministries and planning bureaus. But in the span of just over two decades, China has shifted from the shortage-plagued distribution system of its planned economy to a market system straining under an explosion of goods now sold in a diverse and expanding range of retail settings. New patterns of business have emerged that are tied to broader socio-economic changes, and retailers have come to trade not only in an array of newly plentiful goods but also in new sets of cultural meanings.

Below, I outline changes to the structure of both the retail sector and consumption patterns in urban China, starting from the founding of the People's Republic of China, to the early years of reform, and through to the present day some twenty-odd years later. This historical context frames the discussion of workplace organization in later chapters and underscores the massive scale of change in urban China. At the same time, I consider the links between the growing stratification among retailers and among urban consumers. I trace the contours of a new field of economic and symbolic competition that defines an emerging structure of entitlement and in which the ethnography of the subsequent chapters is situated. Perhaps most importantly, this chapter sheds light on the dramatic changes—and, in truth, decline in status—experienced by department store salesclerks over the course of the past twenty years.

The themes covered in this chapter—retailing and the structure of commerce, the practices and cultural meanings associated with consumption, and inequality—are of course not limited to China after 1949. Numerous historical studies convincingly demonstrate that consumerism was not only a part of life in China in the late 1800s and early 1900s (or even earlier, Clunas 1991) but also of considerable social and political significance. For example, Gary Hamilton and Chi-kong Lai (1989) have argued that in Late Imperial China (and in particular from the late 1800s onward), consumer goods became an increasingly important means for conveying social status, a situation they tie to the particularly fluid nature of China's social structure at the time (see also Bergère 1989). As historian Karl Gerth notes (2003: 49), the elimination of the imperial examination system in 1905 "ended the traditional and primary road to wealth, power, and status" at roughly the same time that China saw an influx of new consumer goods from abroad. It was in this context that consumerism and consumer goods became central to the development of nationalism and conceptions of the nation in Republican-era China (Gerth 2003).

Modes of retailing during the Late Imperial and early Republican years also underwent change. As business historian Sherman Cochran (2006) demonstrates, Chinese medicine retailers pioneered new retailing practices, including the development of extensive production and distribution networks, chain store retailing, and the marketing of both "Western" and "Traditional" medicines across China. Department stores, perhaps the retailing form at the time most closely associated with the West, first appeared in China in the early 1900s in port cities like Hong Kong, Guangzhou, and Shanghai and explicitly drew on foreign models (Yen 1998; Chan 1998). As in North America and Europe, the development of these stores was tied to industrialization and the rise of new urban middle and upper classes who sought new ways to convey their social status (Chan 1998; MacPherson 1998; Yen 1998; see also Bergère 1989).

The actual forms these stores took, however, were powerfully shaped by other trends and social movements in China. For example, the sentiments of nationalism and anti-imperialism, activated by political upheavals during the 1920s and '30s, gave rise to nationalistic buying movements (Gerth 2003), and there was even a department store set up in Shanghai specifically to sell only *guohuo*, or domestic goods (Department of Commerce 1989: 7–12). And as in Europe and North America (e.g. Leach 1984), China's department stores also reflected

changing understandings of women's role in society. Women, their mobility less limited by the demands of propriety and no longer so dependent on door-to-door peddlers for many goods, were an important part
of emerging department stores' clientele (Chan 1998: 67). Eventually,
department stores became key sites of employment for women, though
this did not happen until the 1930s.[1]

The rise of the Chinese Communist Party to power in 1949, however,
brought dramatic changes to retailing and consumption throughout
China. As the following sections detail, the dictates of central planning,
the politics of a proletarian ethos, and anti-bourgeois aesthetics, coupled
with the daily realities of scarcity and shortage, came to characterize retail and consumption in China for much of the next three decades.

SHOPPING WITH MAO: RETAIL AND CONSUMPTION PRIOR TO 1978

From the outset in 1949, China's new Communist leaders were faced
with tensions between their political goals and constraining economic
realities. As a result, the history of the commercial sector in the People's
Republic has been far from straightforward, characterized by policy in-
novations and retrenchments and punctuated by major political and
economic upheavals. Nevertheless, far-reaching state controls over the
distribution of material goods typified the planned economy during
the Mao era. For the average person, the inefficiencies of this system,
coupled with strong national investment in heavy industry and a general neglect of commerce, meant that shortage of consumer goods was
simply a fact of life.

Pre-Reform Retail: Everything According to Plan

During the early years of the People's Republic, the dispersed nature
of existing wholesale and retail businesses, especially those dealing in
consumer goods, made state reliance on the non-state sector important.
Over time, however, the Chinese party-state greatly expanded its con-

---

[1] An early effort to introduce "salesgirls" in Hong Kong's newly opened Sincere
department store in 1900 led to an uproar, for "fashionably dressed 'salesgirls' created a sensation that led to gawking crowds" (Chan 1998: 71). These saleswomen
were soon replaced with men.

trol over and ownership of the distribution channels of both industrial and consumer goods. In the realm of domestic commerce, government controls extended first into the wholesale sector, as private wholesale businesses were either forced to close or absorbed into state entities through the course of the 1950s (Department of Commerce 1989: 21; Solinger 1984: 307–12). These measures began on a large scale in 1953, and by 1955, private wholesalers had shrunk to a mere 4.4% of the total volume of wholesale business (Solinger 1984: 313, 315).

In the 1950s, the retail sector also underwent considerable change. Large and mid-sized retail operations were the first targets of reorganization; most of these enterprises were converted to state ownership by 1956 (Solinger 1984). In the early 1950s, efforts were made to tie stores and shops into the state distribution system by forcing retailers to source their merchandise from state wholesalers. In urban areas, mergers and the imposition of state ownership often followed (Solinger 1984: 307–12, 316–18). By 1956, state-owned and collective retail outlets were conducting over 70% of the total retail sales volume in China (see Table 1).[2]

Bringing small merchants and peddlers under the umbrella of the state was a slower and less complete process. These merchants usually operated from either small booths or mobile carts and employed no workers. They were also dispersed across both urban and rural areas and dealt in small, everyday-use items not included in the purview of state industrial planning. Campaigns for socializing private business peaked in 1956, as small merchant and peddler businesses in urban areas were organized into cooperatives (*hezuo she*) and cooperative groups (*hezuo xiaozu*), many of which were later converted into state-run stores or incorporated into urban communes. The remaining merchants were sent to work in industry, agriculture, or transportation, or were simply retired (Solinger 1984; Department of Commerce 1989).

The implementation of these changes was not without problems. While the insertion of small merchants into the state sector was considered a jump in status ("reaching heaven in a single bound," *yi bu*

[2] In northern China, the conversion of private wholesale commerce happened earlier and faster; as early as 1950 state businesses there represented 80% of the businesses engaged in wholesaling such products as grain, cotton, coal, salt, and kerosene (Department of Commerce 1989: 18). The conversion of retail to state control also occurred more quickly; in Harbin, over 40% of sales of daily-use items (*riyong gongye pin*) in the retail sector belonged to state-run businesses as early as 1952 (*Harbin City Almanac* 1996: 45).

TABLE 1

Percentage of Total Retail Sales Volume by Ownership, 1952–98

Year	State-owned	Collective	Joint	Individual	Peasant to non-peasant
1952	16.3%	18.2%	0.4%	60.9%	4.3%
1956	34.0%	37.5%	20.8%	5.1%	2.6%
1965	53.0%	43.2%		1.9%	1.9%
1975	55.7%	42.2%		0.1%	2.0%
1978	55.0%	43.3%		0.1%	2.0%
1980	51.4%	44.6%		0.7%	3.2%
1985	40.4%	37.2%	0.3%	15.4%	6.8%
1990	39.6%	31.7%	0.5%	18.9%	9.3%
1991	40.2%	30.0%	0.5%	19.6%	9.7%
1992	41.3%	27.9%	0.7%	20.3%	9.8%
1993	37.5%	22.0%	0.3%	24.2%	16.0%
1994	31.9%	20.8%	0.4%	28.4%	18.4%
1995	29.8%	19.3%	0.4%	30.3%	20.2%

Year	State-owned	Collective	Joint	Individual	Other
1996	27.2%	18.4%	0.5%	32.0%	21.8%
1997	23.3%	17.5%	0.5%	34.8%	23.9%
1998	20.7%	16.6%	0.6%	37.1%	25.2%

SOURCE: *China Statistical Yearbook*, 1991, 1995–97, 1999
    NOTE: "Collective" ownership includes both urban collectives and rural supply and marketing cooperatives. "Joint" ownership up to 1958 and from 1980 includes various forms of domestic joint ownership as well as Chinese and foreign joint ownership. "Individual" ownership refers to private ownership. "Other" was a residual category that replaced "peasant-to-non-peasant" in 1996. Numbers do not add up to 100% due to rounding.

deng tian), consolidation of state-run commerce also eliminated many of the subsidiary channels through which goods had been distributed, contributing to shortages and bottlenecking of consumer goods (Department of Commerce 1989: 23–24; *Harbin City Almanac* 1996: 22–23). Nevertheless, the reorganization of retail continued apace, and in cities like Harbin, by 1958, 83.3% of retail sales were conducted by state-run enterprises. In the '60s, this figure was close to 100% (*Harbin City Almanac* 1996: 45–46; for national figures, see Table 1).[3]

   Over the succeeding years, policies governing the distribution of

[3] Dorothy Solinger argues that the socialization of rural commerce was less complete and unwieldly, with less than a third of small-scale rural merchants converted by the end of the 1955–56 campaign (1984: 323–24). Greater reorganization may have come with the Great Leap Forward, when most of the existing cooperative stores and groups were turned into rural state-run stores and communal supply and marketing cooperatives (*gongshe gongxiao bu*), and remaining merchants were sent to take part in agricultural production (Department of Commerce 1989: 23).

material goods fluctuated with political debates over the legitimacy of market forces. Control over distribution vacillated between centralized and more local forms, frequently contributing to greater inefficiencies and fragmented distribution chains. The ideological aims of major political campaigns like the Great Leap Forward (1958–60) and the Cultural Revolution (1966–76) included efforts to reduce bureaucracy, eliminate markets, and enhance local economic self-reliance. Agricultural free markets were closed in 1958, reopened in the early 1960s, then closed again in 1967, not to reopen in urban areas until 1979 (Donnithorne 1967; Solinger 1984; Naughton 1995: 116). During the Great Leap, policies promoting self-sufficiency sought to localize the production and sourcing of commodities, which led to local protectionism, broken supply networks, and faltering production. As early as 1959, economic disruptions forced the central government to begin reinstituting centralized purchasing contracts (Donnithorne 1967: 282, 290, 295–98, 307; Solinger 1984: 234–37).[4]

The Cultural Revolution involved similar politically induced economic disruptions. State commercial units and ministries were merged and reduced in 1970. At the retail level, collective and cooperative groups and shops that had been re-established after the Great Leap were again folded into state retail units, in name if not always in practice (Department of Commerce 1989: 31–33). During the 1970s, commerce was once again seen as operating primarily in the service of industrial production, and wholesalers and retailers were forced to buy and then sell whatever industry produced. At the same time, private enterprise was virtually eliminated, representing only a miniscule 0.1% of retail sales conducted in the country in 1978 (Table 1). These arrangements were so disruptive that they did not last long, and the resulting "disregard for consumers" and "wasteful inventories" laid the ground

[4] One of the ironic consequences of attempts to eliminate any trace of markets was the rise of a "second" or "gray" economy that involved "out of plan" trade and barter. For example, Donnithorne describes how disruption of the industry-trade links that had supplied industry with the raw materials led to "tea-house exchanges" in Shanghai, "an acknowledged mart for metals and machinery . . . where goods unprocurable elsewhere could be obtained" during the early years of the Great Leap Forward (Donnithorne 1967: 290). Enterprise purchasing agents, who would often try to circumvent local commercial systems to secure supplies and equipment, were another manifestation of the pressure to work outside state distribution frameworks in the face of shortages or bureaucratic inefficiencies (Donnithorne 1967: 290–91; Schell 1984: 83–84).

for a quick return to more market-like purchase arrangements between commerce and industry (Solinger 1984: 241).

On the eve of the introduction of economic reforms, China's retail sector was beleaguered by shortages and limitations. As economist Barry Naughton (1995) has noted, this government monopoly over both production and distribution meant extreme shortages for ordinary Chinese citizens, and over half of all household purchases were subject to some kind of rationing. There was even a shortage of retail outlets: between 1957 and 1978, the number had shrunk from one per 331 residents to only one per 914 (Naughton 1995: 46). These figures help explain the quiet city streets devoid of peddlers and street-side venders that Orville Schell described in the quotation that begins this chapter.

Shopping in a Shortage Economy

The dynamics of planned economies have earned them the label of "shortage economies" (Kornai 1980), because such economies tend to produce hoarding behaviors, inefficiencies, and consequent shortages both of raw materials and finished goods. For ordinary urban Chinese, shortage manifested itself in daily life in the form of rationing, queues, and a general scarcity of consumer goods, phenomena which were exacerbated by the central government's emphasis on the development of heavy industry at the expense of consumer goods production (Naughton 1995). Many everyday goods could only be purchased with government-issued ration tickets, including staple grains, cooking oil, cotton cloth, and laundry detergent.

In cities, access to consumer goods was mediated almost exclusively by urban work units, or *danwei*, casting China's urban population as, in the words of Deborah Davis (1993), "supplicants to the socialist state." In his study of China's industrial workplaces, Andrew Walder (1986) described a condition of extreme "organized dependence," where the urban worker was forced to rely upon his or her work unit not only for wages but also for a range of goods and services not available through other channels—housing, ration coupons, and even hotel reservations. Often the only alternative to long queues—both physical and paper— was reliance upon elaborate networks of personal connections. The accumulation of such *guanxi* networks was far more useful than money for gaining access to scarce goods and services (see, e.g., Yang 1994; for a parallel situation in the Soviet Union, see Ledevena 1998).

Grain ration ticket from Heilongjiang province. In author's possession.

Conditions of shortage produced particular strategies of consumption and gave scarce goods great levels of social significance. For example, one Harbin man in his late 50s described for me the difficulties of acquiring peanuts in the city when he was a young man. Peanuts were not a local product and were difficult to find in state-run stores, and so often the only way to procure the nuts was to get relatives in a peanut-growing region to buy and mail some. Nevertheless, there were government restrictions on the amount of peanuts that could be privately mailed to prevent individual stockpiling (and black market selling) of scarce goods. As a result, he told me, "Peanuts were something we rarely got to eat. They were the kind of thing you would pull out when a special guest came for a visit." He recalled a visit to a friend in a hospital, where peanuts were a special gift. "Someone brought peanuts, and I remember a group of us sitting around sharing them, taking just three peanuts each. Those peanuts were so very *xiang* [flavorful]."

Consumption was also highly and overtly politicized, especially during the Cultural Revolution (1966–76) when merchandise available for purchase was further reduced by political campaigns aimed at cleansing society of all the hallmarks of a bourgeois lifestyle. High-heel shoes, along with such items as high-end cosmetics, gold and silver jewelry, Western-style suits, and even mechanized toys and playing cards were labeled "problem" merchandise and removed from store shelves (Department of Commerce 1989: 34). The color of clothing narrowed to proletarian grays, blues, and whites and to military greens, and clothing styles were laden with ideological meaning (Chen 2003b). Political pressures also meant that groups like middle-class professionals, who often rely upon the display of cultural refinement to signal group identity, avoided distinctive patterns of consumption (Davis 2000a). As one history of retailing in China has declared of the period, "The sales counter became another site of class struggle" (Department of Commerce 1989: 35).

In such conditions of shortage, store clerks often acted as gatekeepers to goods, and they might hoard desirable merchandise for distribution within their own personal networks. In China's production-oriented society, clerks were notorious for their abuse of customers, frequently chastising customers or ignoring them altogether. One young man told me, "It was like you were begging them for something, not like you were giving them money for something." He recalled that a sales assistant might respond to a question like "How much for a *jin* of rice?" by saying, "Isn't it written down [on the sign] [*bushi zai nar xie de ma*]??!" Asking to see an item before buying it might elicit a comment like "No purchase, no touching" (*bu mai bu mo*, or *bu mai bu peng*). One woman I met remarked of the early reform years, "Service was just dreadful! There was one time my mother and I purchased some preserved eggs in a government food market. We opened one egg at the counter to eat right away, but it had gone bad. So my mother put the egg on the counter and told the salesclerk. The salesclerk swept the rotten egg off the counter with her arm—whup!—and said, 'Even if it's bad, you bought it.' Nowadays, not only would the clerk switch the bad egg for a good one, but she would probably apologize as well!"

Perhaps that particular salesclerk was herself a "bad egg," because service was not, of course, always as terrible as in that particular story. As with industry, model service workers were identified and praised. For example, in the late 1960s, Beijing's Number One Department Store designated a candy counter clerk, Zhang Binggui, as "model sales assistant" (Guo and Fei 1998). Praised for his efficiency in dealing with shortage-induced queues, Zhang was a socialist "service hero" cast in the idiom of industrial production. Skills such as *yi zhua zhun* (measuring accuracy in "one grab"), *yi kou qing* (quick tallying of purchases), and the Taylor-esque analysis of service transactions attributed to Zhang all depicted the candy counter as an assembly line. At my state-run field site, Harbin No. X, managers and salesclerks still told stories of the remarkable salesclerk who could accurately gauge customers' shoe sizes from the size of their hands. And the *Harbin City Almanac* (1996) records municipal cloth-measuring contests in which salesclerks competed for accuracy and speed.

Yet bad experiences were common enough that this is very much how people remember service under a planned economy. Given the small number of retail outlets and the lack of competition among them, customers had to return there regardless of how they were treated by salesclerks. As one commentary noted of service in China's shortage economy, "The emperor's daughter doesn't fret about finding a husband [*huangdi nu'er bu chou jia*]" (Department of Commerce 1989: 131). Or, in the words of Orville Schell: "Chinese consumers were prisoners. They had to shop *somewhere*, and every store was run by the state" (1984: 194).

THE DOOR OPENS: RETAIL IN THE ERA OF REFORM

In 1978, China's commercial sector was basically a state-run monopoly characterized by shortages of basic consumer commodities, rationing of many key goods, and inconvenient access even to goods officially available. At the same time, the country's economy was plagued with problems and faced a crisis of stagnant agricultural, industrial, and energy outputs accompanied by growing urban unemployment (Naughton 1995). These economic quandaries precipitated the major policy changes laid out at the Third Plenum of the Eleventh Central Committee held in December 1978, a meeting which set into motion a gradual but nonetheless dramatic reorientation of China's economy and the transformation of its society. The resulting shift in resources away from investment in heavy industry and toward consumption, light industry, and agriculture would have a powerful effect on retailing in China.

Reconfiguration of the Retail Sector

Through the course of the 1980s, China's retail sector and the distribution of consumer goods in cities went from what essentially had been a state monopoly to a proliferation of retail venues and forms. Orville Schell (1984), for example, describes the early reappearance of capitalist "tails" on city streets in the forms of peddlers, street vendors, and small-scale private merchants selling in more organized urban markets. As domestic light industry expanded and goods began to fill Chinese marketplaces, state distribution channels increasingly fell into disuse, and rationing and many price controls were lifted. Most important for this study, China's urban retail sector developed into a highly competitive market made up of ever-more stratified shopping venues. The earliest steps to revitalize Chinese retail marketplaces involved both the internal reorganization of existing retail businesses and the expansion of the non-state portion of the retail sector.

Reforms affecting the internal organization of retail units increased enterprise autonomy and relaxed restrictions on the distribution of consumer goods. In late 1979, experimental "autonomy trial sites" (*zizhuquan shidian*) were identified and given greater control over their own operations.[5] At the time, many day-to-day business decisions were subject to approval by local administrative organs, and increased retail enterprise autonomy was meant to enhance productivity and flexibility. For example, prior to being identified as an autonomy trial site, the management in one store required upper-level approval to simply shift the position of sales counters (Wu 1984); in another store, management was not allowed to make discretionary expenditures over 5 yuan (roughly the equivalent of US$2.60 in 1982; Wang Shiquan 1982).

By the early 1980s, the "contract management system" (*chengbao zerenzhi*) emerged and gave a growing number of stores greater control over their expenditures, merchandise, purchasing, labor management practices, and wages and bonuses.[6] These changes, coupled with tax re-

---

[5] Autonomy trial sites were all state-owned retail outlets. Examples include the *Nanfang dasha* (the Southern Mansion) in Guangzhou, the *Baihuo dalou* (General Merchandise Building) in Changchun, Jilin province, and the *Huaihai shichang* (Huaihai Market) in Anhui province (Yang 1983; Department of Commerce 1989: 121; Wang Guisen 1984, 1987, 1988). The selected enterprises were allowed to retain a portion of their profits, though the formula for this varied widely and was negotiated on a store-by-store basis (Wu 1984; Yang 1983).

[6] The broad concept of "contract management" took many forms. The term "operation responsibility system" (*jingying zerenzhi*) was usually applied to large and mid-sized commercial units and *chengbao* (contracting) to small-scale ones (Chen 1984). The distinction was more than semantic: Changes made to larger enterprises were more modest than those implemented in small ones (Li et al. 2001). While in both cases increased autonomy meant greater control over purchasing practices and selection of merchandise as well as more retained profits, with small enterprises the unit as a whole could be held accountable for profits and losses. Often, the contracting manager was required to make a security deposit that would be forfeited in the event of poor performance. In large and mid-sized retail outlets, by contrast, "small contracting" (*xiao chengbao*) was frequently implemented, requiring internal departments to keep their own accounts, whereas previously this had only occurred at the unit level. Contracted sales targets were generally set for the internal store

forms, replaced government-allocated operating capital with low-interest loans and allowed for greater retained profits (*Harbin City Almanac* 1996). All these reforms sought to make retail enterprises more efficient economic units and more responsive to consumer demands. By the end of 1987, more than 60% of China's large and mid-sized commercial enterprises had been officially put on the contract management system, a figure which reached 80% by June 1988 (Pan 1988).[7]

At the same time, a dramatic shift in the retail ownership structure was taking place. A new policy in 1984 hastened the conversion of small state-owned retail outlets to collective and even individual ownership or management.[8] By the end of 1986, some 60% (Li Dianjia 1987) and by June 1988 as much as 90% of small state commercial outlets had been leased or converted to collective-style management (Pan 1988).[9] This

---

department (Yang and Wang 1985), while at the enterprise level, enterprise income, not manager property, could be forfeited (Solinger 1993: 183). A "small-scale retail enterprise" was a unit with 60 or fewer employees and less than 100,000 yuan in annual sales (Deng 1984). Even within the categories of "large" or "small" enterprise, a wide array of measures was implemented.

[7] The degree to which these reforms meant real change in state-run retailers is debatable. Observers expressed concerns throughout the 1980s and 1990s that state retail enterprises were not being effectively held accountable for losses, largely because they lacked the financial resources to cover their own debts and could generally count on being bailed out by the local government or bank (Dong 1987). Others expressed concern at the continued meddling of local government in business operations (Zhu 1990; Kou 1991). In the 1980s, numerous problems reduced the effectiveness of early reforms: There was chronic haggling over profit remittances and tax responsibilities, unfair selection of managers and renters of retail units (Li Xianghua 1987), and a general lack of clarity in reform policies (Yang and Wang 1985). Haggling over sales targets occurred within stores as well, as wages and bonuses were increasingly tied to achieving these targets (Wang Guisen 1986). Others have argued that even the issuing of stocks in state-run commercial enterprises rarely meant real change in management or ownership powers (Naughton 1995: 219).

[8] This important policy statement, issued by the central government in October 1984, was known as the Decision on Reform of the Economic System (*guanyu jingji tizhi gaige de jueding*) (Department of Commerce 1989: 142).

[9] There were three standard routes for reforming small, state-owned retail units. The first was termed *gai* (literally, "to change") whereby a unit remained state-owned but became collectively operated, paying taxes to the state instead of remitting profits and held responsible for its own losses; these units were, in practice, treated like collectively owned enterprises. The second, *zhuan*, or transfer, referred to change in ownership status, where small, state-owned retail units were converted to collective ownership. Finally, *zu*, or rental, represented cases where a small retail enterprise

represented a far greater shift in ownership structure than was true for industrial enterprises (Naughton 1995). At the same time, there was rapid growth in the numbers of new collective retail outlets, as local governments, street committees, and work units established shops to provide employment for the growing numbers of unemployed urban youth. In the early years of reforms, the number of collectively owned retail units more than doubled, growing from just under 600,000 in 1978 to over 1.3 million in 1984 (Table 2).

The most explosive growth, however, was within the private sector. Over the course of just five years, the number of officially registered small-scale private merchants (*getihu*) swelled from a little over 100,000 in 1978 to almost 30 times that number (3.4 million) just five years later, in 1983 (Table 2). While initially these *getihu* tended to sell small, inexpensive consumer goods or more expensive, hard-to-find, or smuggled wares (see, e.g., Schell 1984: 21, 83; Bruun 1993), over the course of the 1980s *geti* merchants became an increasingly significant segment of China's retail sector. By 1989, there were almost 9 million registered private, individual retail businesses in China, and their collective sales had risen from a miniscule 0.1% of the country's total retail sales volume in 1978 to over 18% by the decade's close (Table 1). In some cases, these private merchants actually operated from rented-out counter space in struggling state-owned stores.[10] What is more, official numbers are underestimates, given the myriad reasons these figures

---

was rented out, on a contract basis, usually to an individual operator (Department of Commerce 1989: 141). A small proportion of these units could even be sold outright, though the percentage was small. By the end of 1986, 74% of reformed small retail units had been "changed," 8% "transferred," 18% "rented," and less than 1% sold outright (Li Dianjia 1987).

[10] Numerous articles published in the 1980s express concern about the dangers of renting counter space in state-owned stores to private entrepreneurs. The fear was that *geti* merchants would bring poor business practices and excessive profit-seeking into state-owned retail outlets. The practice of renting counters to private merchants was nevertheless so widespread that some cities, like Shenyang and Beijing, issued restrictions (Qiao 1989; Liu Guanglu 1989). Concerns were greater, and restrictions tighter, for larger state-owned retail stores. In small or struggling stores, and where local governments were supportive, renting counter space to individuals was widespread (Diao et al. 1988; Qiao 1989). Counter space was not and had not been rented out to private merchants at the Harbin No. X Department Store, my state-owned field site, but the practice was found at other, smaller state-owned retail outlets in Harbin.

TABLE 2

Number of Retail Outlets by Ownership, 1978–96, in Thousands

Year	State-owned	Collective	Joint	Individual	Other
1978	357	583		108	
...					
1983[a]	606	740	0.4	3,441	
1984	211	1,305	3	5,196	
1985	229	1,362	3	6,239	
1986	241	1,296	3	6,474	
1987	248	1,298	2	7,331	
1988	261	1,292	3	7,757	
1989	267	1,726	2	6,929	
1990	280	1,195	2	7,268	
1991	290	1,175	2	7,817	
1992	324	1,277	2	8,543	
...					
1994	248	695	11	11,168	5
...					
1996	257	670	3	13,005[b]	25[c]

SOURCE: *China Statistical Yearbook*, 1985–97
   [a] Numbers for 1983 include administrative as well as business retail organizations (*jigou*).
   [b] Includes individual (*geti*) and private (*siyou*) businesses.
   [c] Includes share-holding, overseas Chinese, foreign, and "other" categories.

tend to undercount both the number of private merchants and their sales volume.[11]

The 1990s saw more dramatic changes to China's retail sector. The early 1990s were boom years for large retailers, given their relative scarcity at a time when consumer spending rose rapidly. Shuguang Wang and Ken Jones report that profit margins for China's large, traditional state-run retailers averaged 25–30% from 1991 to 1995 (2001: 30), a point confirmed by my interviewees. The promise of quick profits brought many new entrants into China's retail sector, large and small,

   [11] Susan Young argues that official data on the numbers of individual businesses in China through the 1980s and '90s are misleading because many enterprises registered as "collective" were in fact individually owned and managed (1995: 7). In addition, the categorization of certain private rural businesses as "specialized households" (*zhuanyehu*) rather than "individual households" (*getihu*) further reduces official counts of private businesses (Young 1995: 18). Official figures also fail to account for unregistered private businesses and tend to undercount the number of people employed in registered ones (see, e.g., Bruun 1993: 62). Given that taxation is (ostensibly) based on sales volume and there is no standardized means for tracking *geti* sales, reported sales volumes are likely underestimates as well.

state and private.[12] By 1995, however, overinvestment in the retail sector and changing consumption patterns caused profit margins among large state retailers to collapse to a scant 3–5%, and some were forced out of business (Wang and Jones 2001: 32; see also Woetzel 2003; _China Economic Review_ [CER], March 1999). Older, state-owned department stores suddenly found themselves faced with competition not only from small-scale _getihu_, but also from an assortment of other retailers (CER, May 1999). Glistening new private (_siying_) department stores stocked upscale goods,[13] franchises (_zhuanmaidian_) sold inexpensive brands favored by young people, and trendy boutiques run by private merchants offered up-to-date fashions. Ever-expanding marketplaces rented counter and stall spaces to _getihu_. Even specialized supermarkets and chain stores began to appear, especially in China's most cosmopolitan cities, like Shanghai, Beijing, and Shenzhen (Wang and Jones 2001; Lo et al. 2001). By 1995, state-owned retailers made up less than 30% of China's total retail sales volume (Wang and Jones 2001) and officially stood at roughly 8% of total retail sales revenues in 2005.[14]

Foreign competition was added to the mix. Starting in 1992, China's

[12] Wang and Jones report that in 1993 the Beijing city government announced plans to develop or redevelop an astonishing 100 department stores by the year 2000 (2001: 32). The plan proved overambitious.

[13] Beginning in the late 1980s, as private businesses grew in size and stature, the Chinese government established a technical division between small-scale private business (_getihu_, with seven or fewer employees) and private firms (_siying qiye_, with eight or more employees) (Young 1995; Kraus 1991: 102–7). This is the technical difference between two of my field sites—the Sunshine Department Store, categorized as a private firm, and the individually licensed merchants in The Underground, considered _getihu_.

[14] Calculated from figures in the _China Statistical Yearbook_, 2005. After 1998, official data on the number of retail outlets, annual sales figures, and the ownership structure of the retail sector become increasingly difficult to interpret. Through the later half of the 1990s government statistics began to divide retail outlets into a growing number of ownership categories, making comparisons with pre-1998 statistics difficult. Some new ownership labels—"shareholding" and "limited liability," for example—could be applied to businesses that were still very much state-controlled. (This was the case with the Harbin No. X Department Store; see Chapter 3.) Historical comparisons are made even more difficult by the fact that, beginning in 1999, official figures only report on businesses employing 60 or more workers. Table 3 provides calculations based on 1999–2005 data and reflects the shifting of retail enterprises from one ownership category to another, the growth of large-scale retailers (especially foreign-owned), as well as the questionable accuracy of the data.

TABLE 3

Percentage of Total Retail Revenues by Ownership
(and Number of Retail Units) for 1999, 2002, and 2005

Ownership type	1999	2002	2005
State	37.7% (8,581)	18.4% (6,684)	7.9% (11,296)
Collective	11.8% (4,394)	5.3% (2,979)	2.5% (7,411)
Cooperative	2.8% (717)	2.7% (794)	1.4% (1,546)
Joint	2.7% (167)	2.6% (170)	1.4% (239)
Limited liability	10.6% (2,263)	26.4% (9,109)	30.1% (24,740)
Share-holding	23.0% (1,818)	21.6% (5,479)	20.8% (10,176)
Private[a]	2.9% (440)	13.2% (2,709)	25.7% (16,029)
Other (domestic)	0.0% (23)	0.1% (82)	0.2% (236)
Overseas Chinese	3.3% (193)	3.0% (266)	3.0% (549)
Foreign	5.2% (624)	6.7% (479)	6.9% (1,552)

SOURCE: *China Statistical Yearbook*, 2000, 2003, 2006

[a] "Private" only includes "enterprises above designated size," meaning 60 or more employees and annual sales of 5 million yuan or more.

central government opened the country's retail sector to a small number of centrally approved Sino-foreign joint venture stores, projects limited to a select number of cities and Special Economic Zones.[15] Provincial and municipal governments not included in the initial list were quick to seek foreign investment in their own local retail sectors, even before restrictions were loosened in 1995 and 1999, relying upon loopholes or outright defiance of central government regulations (Wang and Jones 2001; CER, March 1999). Harbin's Sunshine Department Store is a perfect example of this local initiative in attracting foreign retailing capital, as the store was originally a China–Hong Kong cooperative venture approved by the local government. Subsequent to China's entry into the World Trade Organization in 2001, the central government removed most of the remaining restrictions on foreign investment in retailing. By 2005, the country's retail sector had opened up more fully to such international giants as France's Carrefour and Wal-Mart of the United States, both of which already have a substantial presence in China's major cities (Saporito 2003; IGD 2003; Larenaudie 2005; Datamonitor

[15] Original guidelines allowed Sino-foreign retail joint ventures only in the cities of Beijing, Shanghai, Tianjin, Guangzhou, Dalian, and Qingdao and in the Special Economic Zones of Shenzhen, Zhuhai, Shantou, Xiamen, and Hainan (Wang and Jones 2001: 33; CER, March 1999). Foreign stake in these ventures was limited to 49% or less, and foreign businesses were forbidden from engaging in wholesale trade (CER, March 1999).

2006). Most recently, Wal-Mart has sought to increase its presence in the highly fragmented Chinese retail industry by acquiring shares in a large Chinese retailer, Trust-Mart (*Asia Pulse*, Feb. 27, 2007). Nevertheless, as of late 2005, foreign retailers were still a minor economic force nationwide, claiming on average less than 10% of retail sales in the Chinese cities where they could be found.[16]

At the time of this study, cities like Harbin largely remained out of the bounds of major Western retailers, although this has since changed. With their arrival in the city in late 2002, these new foreign additions became part of what had already become a complex mosaic of retail settings, a field of players in which domestic specialty and chain stores, swank privately funded Chinese department stores, and large *geti* markets dominated clothing sales.[17] To be sure, over the course of twenty years, the business of retailing in the city, and with it the urban landscape, has been transformed. An unpublished survey of one of Harbin's busiest shopping districts illustrates the extent of change. Up to 1978 and even through the 1980s, the main commercial area in Harbin's central Nangang district was dominated by a state-owned department store whose neighboring retailers were limited to a large state food market and a handful of other shops. But by 2001, the same area had become home to over 100 different businesses, two-thirds of which engaged in some form of retailing (Wang Yanhong 2001).

It is important to note, however, that the shops in this bustling area— the authors of the survey estimated that an average of 150,000 people passed through every day—were not just different forms of retailing; they also reflected the many strata of shoppers in the city. Indeed, the field of Harbin's retailers and the market in which they competed were closely connected to broader socio-economic changes in Chinese society and especially to stratification among Chinese consumers. This

[16] Government statistics put the foreign share of retail trade revenues at about 7% in 2005 (*China Statistical Yearbook*, 2006). Shanghai is an exception, and foreign retailers claimed a 13.5% market share there in 2004 (*Asia Pulse*, April 12, 2005). Foreign market share can be much higher in specific segments of the retail sector, such as large supermarkets (*Asia Pulse*, April 15, 2005). As of the late 1990s, the bulk of foreign-invested retail businesses could be found in just two Chinese cities, Shanghai and Beijing (Wang and Jones 2001: 36).

[17] Wal-Mart opened its first superstore in Harbin in the late spring of 2002. By the end of 2004, Carrefour had arrived in the city and Wal-Mart had opened a second outlet.

stratification of shoppers, and of retail outlets, has been accompanied by equally dramatic changes to the organization of work carried out on sales floors.

NEW BUSINESS RELATIONS, NEW LABOR RELATIONS: THE FACTORY ENTERS THE STORE

Broad changes to the ownership structure of China's retail sector and the rise of a competitive business environment have been accompanied by important changes to the internal organization of retail enterprises that have affected both workers and customers. For workers, reforms have transformed labor relations on the sales floor. In particular, competitive pressures, first among manufacturers and later among retailers, gave rise to a new model of retailing that involved increasingly flexible employment arrangements. Given the retail settings that are the subject of this study, here I focus on changes to labor relations in large retailers, especially state-owned and privately operated department stores. A brief look at how a new retail business model emerged reveals how much employment practices in China today are the direct result of the particular way in which economic reforms unfolded.

Ironically, the origins of the current system in all large department stores lie with state-owned retailers. In brief, enterprise reforms begun in the early 1980s led to circumvention of the old state-run wholesale distribution system and to the rapid expansion of direct links between retailers and manufacturers.[18] The consumer goods industries supplying urban retailers saw large numbers of new entrants in the 1980s, a result of preferential government policies and the consequence of Chi-

---

[18] The establishment of direct links between retailers and manufacturers began to occur as soon as reform measures granted store management greater autonomy. As early as 1982, 40% of manufactured consumer goods were being directly ordered or selectively purchased by retailers from manufacturers (Naughton 1995: 116). Published accounts and "surveys" of retail units provide numerous examples of growing direct factory-store relations (Xu 1985; Yang and Wang 1985; Department of Commerce 1989: 121), and a 1989 publication reported that some large-scale stores were buying "factory-direct from up to 1000 factories, representing some 60 to 70% of their total sources of merchandise" (Department of Commerce 1989: 119). By 1990, factory-direct sales had basically shut state wholesalers out of some lines of business: in Beijing, for example, factory-direct sales of bicycles (85%), color TVs (73%), and textile products (53%) had all reached high levels (Guo et al. 1992).

na's shift from a planned economy (Naughton 1995: 135–38, 162–63). As competition heated up among manufacturers in a progressively more saturated consumer goods market, factories anxious to get merchandise to market preferred going directly to stores to promote their merchandise, a trend that only accelerated through the 1990s (Yang and Zhu 1998).

New business arrangements between factory and store emerged, with commission sales (*daixiao*) being the most important during the 1980s and early 1990s. With commission sales, manufacturers would supply merchandise on a sell-first, pay-later basis, with accounts cleared on a monthly or even tri-monthly basis and stores earning a percentage of sales (on clothing, usually 23–25%). This arrangement also allowed retailers to expand with little capital investment. Manufacturers retained ownership of the goods until sold and were responsible for taking back any unsold merchandise, considerably reducing for retailers both the amount of operating capital required and the risks of being saddled with slow-moving or poorly selling merchandise. Every informant questioned was in complete agreement that competition among manufacturers was the key factor behind the proliferation of commission sales arrangements in Chinese retail enterprises in the late 1980s and 1990s. "The factories were knocking on *our* doors, wanting to get their goods into our store," one sales department manager explained. Interviews also revealed that, in Harbin, the city's largest department store procured about 90% of its merchandise in this way by 1992, and by the mid-1990s most of Harbin's major retailers were conducting business primarily on a commission sales basis.

The shift to commission sales did not immediately spell dramatic change for salesclerks. Wages for these workers were paid by the retailer, though this period saw changes to the way in which earnings were calculated. The introduction of sales commissions for salesclerks, on both an individual and group basis, became increasingly widespread. This was accompanied by a general criticism of the "levelism" (*pingjun zhuyi*) that had characterized the Mao years, when all store workers were paid roughly the same wage, regardless of work duties or performance. As one Harbin No. X worker recalled, salesclerks went from jockeying for the easiest jobs (which required selling very little) to those commission jobs offering the most money—which usually involved selling the largest volume of goods.

Through the 1990s, intense competition not only among manufacturers but also among large retailers would soon bring about changes to commission sales arrangements. As noted above, the early 1990s were boom years for major urban retailers. Existing stores made major investments in expansions and physical upgrades, and new department stores, viewed by investors as surefire moneymakers, were constructed at a rapid pace (Li et al. 2001). In Harbin, the central city's four large state-run department stores were joined by at least six competitors (representing state, private, and joint-venture investments) between 1993 and 1995, and another three by 1997. At the same time, other new entrants into the retail sector, especially small-scale private entrepreneurs, began eating away at what had once been a state monopoly on market share and department store profitability. Between 1991 and 1993, the number of retail outlets in China grew by an average of 7.7% annually, and between 1993 and 1994 alone there was a 12.4% growth in the number of stores (Wu 1997). By the mid-1990s, department stores both old and new, state-owned and private, faced greater competition, shrinking market shares, stagnating profits, and, for some, burdensome outstanding loans. In many cases, expansions had proved overambitious and excessive, and anticipated profits were slow in coming. As noted above, 1995 marked a turning point, and profits start to drop (Wang and Jones 2001). As one informant bluntly stated to me, in the early 1990s "We poorly forecasted future market developments."

It was in this intensely competitive environment that privately owned department stores began to shift their operations to the factory-in-the-store model in an effort to make themselves even more competitive. "Bringing the factory into the store" (*yinchang jindian*) required manufacturers to pay salesclerk wages and commissions as well as shoulder set-up and maintenance costs for storage, sales, and display areas. Borrowing a retailing practice that had been pioneered in large state-owned department stores in the early 1980s,[19] powerful private department stores now expanded the model to serve as their primary mode of business. Within stores, business, information, and central management departments (*zhaoshang bu, xinxi bu, zongheguanli bu*) controlled access to much-sought-after sales spaces, carefully tracked the sales performance of existing brands in the store, and evaluated the merits of new manufacturers petitioning for access to the sales floor.

---

[19] Factory-in-the-store arrangements, where manufacturers have a greater presence in the store and are responsible for salesclerk salaries, were much less common than commission sales but are first mentioned in written accounts of SOE (State-Owned Enterprise) reforms as early as 1984.

The factory-in-the-store practice would soon spread to competing retailers as competitive pressures helped propagate this retail model. Under conditions of declining profits, more conservative (usually state-owned) department stores began to seek ways to reduce operating costs in the late 1990s. They did so by emulating private competitors, replacing commission sales with the factory-in-the-store model. Suppliers of merchandise went along with these changes, faced as they were with even fiercer competition from other manufacturers of clothing and consumer goods. One sales manager for a clothing manufacturer noted that by the mid-1990s, "There was an unbelievable amount of merchandise" (*chanpin duo de bu de liao*) competing for space in department stores. Observers and industry participants argue that throughout the 1990s supplies of consumer goods grew much faster than Chinese consumers' ability to buy (e.g. Wang and Jones 2002), and today competition to enter prime retail stores remains fierce. According to one observer, by the late 1990s large stores, and entry into them, had become "like battlefields" (*shangchang ru zhanchang*) (Guan 1998). Anxious to create brand names and sell their goods at considerable mark-ups, manufacturers filled waiting lists at popular, high-end outlets and respectable state-owned stores.

The scramble among manufacturers to enter reputable department stores is related to the increasingly stratified nature of China's retail sector and its relationship to the development of product branding. Large retail outlets like department stores still act as key sites for retail, despite growing competition. There are regional variations, but in the northeast in particular large department stores stand in stark contrast to *getihu* market environments, offering return policies, quality guarantees, and the promise of customer-oriented service. These stores offer a degree of trust and respectability—and class status—that is absent from other settings. For high-priced and luxury items, these stores often provide the only suitable access to customers.

So, hastened by jockeying among suppliers and manufacturers for sales space, factory-in-the-store arrangements first began to dominate in the most successful department stores. But by 2000, all of Harbin's major department stores, regardless of ownership form or organizational history, procured the majority of their merchandise (often over 80%) this way. When I conducted my field research in 2001–2, industry analysts I interviewed in Beijing estimated that 60% to 70% of all merchandise in the average Chinese department store was sold on a factory-in-the-store basis.

The widespread use of the factory-in-the-store business form is likely to persist. Despite the fact that industry experts and retail managers in China today often characterize Western forms of retailing (such as chain stores and computerized inventory systems) as the future shape of the country's retail business, many expect the factory-in-the-store model (often referred to today as factory-store "cooperation," or *hezuo*) to remain stable and dominant in China's urban department stores for some time to come. As one informant emphasized, this model of business has simply "become accepted practice" (*bei shehui renke*) in China.[20] The practice is even found with increasing frequency in the modern supermarkets springing up across China's cities, stores that generally purchase their merchandise outright but where new, promotional goods are often supplied on a factory-in-the-store basis and where the use of factory-paid salesclerks is extensive.

For salesclerks, the rise of the factory-in-the-store system has ushered in a new set of labor relations and flexible employment (Hanser 2007). With wages paid by manufacturers or distributors, clerks find themselves now answerable to two sets of bosses—store managers and "factory" ones. Indeed, intense competition was not the only factor behind manufacturer acceptance of the factory-in-the-store system. The ability to more closely control and monitor salesclerk behavior was one of the most attractive aspects of *yinchang* arrangements, and today both retailers and suppliers agree that shifting the responsibility for sales staff salaries and bonuses from the former to the latter was hardly controversial. "Manufacturers were happy to do this," one department store manager insisted, "because it meant they have a lot more control over the people selling their goods." Merchandise suppliers concurred, not-

[20] This form of retailing has gained an even more solid footing with the rise of middleman distributors, *dailishang* or *jingxiaoshang*, who contract with a manufacturer for sole distribution rights in a given region. These distributors purchase merchandise outright from the factory and then contract with large retailers for sales space and staffing. In effect, both manufacturer and retailer are insulated from market risks by these distributors, who by virtue of their position as middlemen are forced to seek out both a manufacturer from whom to procure merchandise and existing retail outlets in which to sell their goods. Because the mark-up on retail goods like brand name clothing can be substantial—retail prices are almost always at least twice wholesale prices even for unbranded merchandise—there is hot competition to become a distributor. Store managers I interviewed estimated that about half their contracted sales areas are with factory sales offices and half with distributors or suppliers. "Factory-in-the-store," then, is something of a misnomer, for it is just as likely that a distributor, not a factory, has entered the store.

ing that paying salesclerks wages makes them "easy to manage" (*hao guanli*). Said one, "If someone isn't doing her job, you fire her . . . before we couldn't do that. And besides, compared with the impact of a good or a bad salesperson on sales, the cost of paying wages is really quite small." On the sales floor, manufacturers and suppliers have become a daily presence, checking up on sales, managing inventories, and even supervising sales activities.

At the same time, in many stores these workers are not considered full-fledged employees by either set of bosses, and department store sales work is less and less likely to provide health insurance or other benefits. And although the factory-in-the-store system had dramatically altered employment relations in only one of my field sites—the private Sunshine Department Store—nevertheless it represents an influential pattern of labor relations that has the potential to affect salesclerks working in all large, urban retail settings. New labor relations have shaped the conditions under which distinction work is organized in some of the most prominent retail settings.

INEQUALITY, CONSUMPTION, AND THE RETAIL FIELD

While the introduction of economic reforms was restructuring the retail sector and reorganizing labor relations, these same policies initiated dramatic changes to the sphere of everyday consumption. For urban residents, the shortage economy is increasingly a thing of the past, and for growing numbers of young urban Chinese it is an entirely foreign experience. While working in one of my field sites, The Underground, older merchants would sometimes try to remind younger market workers how much things had changed. When a young salesgirl in The Underground purchased some bread from a peddler, the middle-aged Mr. Zhou told her, "It used to be, no one was able to eat that stuff . . . if you had enough rice to eat, that was pretty good." The young woman, only about 18 years old, giggled as the older people in the room began to reminisce about the old days. TV's were small and only a few people had them. "Most people just listened to the radio," Mr. Zhou continued. "That was considered pretty good entertainment!"

Certainly, televisions only became a commonplace item in urban homes as a result of major changes to China's light industrial sector. When resources were redirected to light industry in the 1980s in an effort to jump-start China's ailing economy, the increased production of consumer goods was explosive. For example, between 1978 and 1985, annual bicycle production swelled from roughly 8 million to 32 million. The figures for the growth of television production are even more striking: between 1978 and 1985, annual output rose from 500,000 to 16 million (*China Statistical Yearbook* 1986).

Incomes also rose rapidly. Real incomes rose at an annual rate of roughly 5% through the 1990s (Khan and Riskin 1998). Between 1985 and 2001, the average urban Chinese saw food expenditures drop from 54% of total spending to 38%; spending on "entertainment, leisure, and education" rose from 8% to 13% (*China Statistical Yearbook* 2002).[21] Not only did people find themselves with more money in their pockets, they also had more free time in which to spend it: Shaoguang Wang (1995) has calculated that the amount of daily leisure time enjoyed by the average Chinese grew from a little over 2 hours to 4.5 hours between 1980 and 1991.[22] And, as detailed above, a plethora of settings where people could spend their time and their money began to appear (Davis 2000b).

Greater wealth has also meant greater inequality. As noted in Chapter 1, researchers engage in vigorous debates about which social groups are benefiting most from China's economic reforms, but the growth of inequality itself is not in dispute. Other research suggests that income disparities translate, not surprisingly, into stratified consumption patterns, with the rich purchasing higher quality food, branded clothing, and much more spacious housing (Li and Zhang 2004; Croll 2006). Studies of the rich[23] in China argue, for example, that luxury consumption,

[21] Inflation and deregulation of food prices complicate this picture (Chai 1992), though a general trend in consumption patterns away from necessities still holds (Sun 2003).

[22] Wang attributes this growth in leisure time to various social changes, including the decline of compulsory participation in political campaigns, greater use of time-saving devices in the home (e.g. washing machines), improved commodity supplies, and, notably, a more efficient service sector (Wang 1995: 157–58). In addition, since the early 1990s official work weeks have been reduced from six to five days.

[23] Definitions of who constitutes China's "rich" or "very rich" strata can be surprisingly vague. In Buckley's (1999) 1994 survey conducted in Beijing, he defined those earning incomes of 1,000 yuan or more per month as "rich," representing the top 6.5% of his sample. (Buckley's survey was unable to capture the city's more elusive "very rich.") A 1997 survey, also conducted in Beijing, defined the well-to-do (*fuyu*) as people with a monthly income of 1,000 yuan or more *or* with family assets

including "highly visible [status] items" (Buckley 1999: 225) form a key part of an evolving elite culture (see also Goodman 1995; Li 1998). Consumer settings for the elite, such as restaurants, entertainment clubs, and high-end retail settings, play a critical role (Gu et al. 2004: 277; Larenaudie 2005).[24] Eileen Otis (2007) has demonstrated how exclusive surroundings and elaborate service offered by luxury hotels in Beijing symbolically recognize the status of wealthy elites. Luigi Tomba (2004) has similarly argued that the emergence of a self-conscious middle class in cities like Beijing hinges on shared consumption patterns, especially housing (see also Fraser 2000). While there is much dispute about the size of these two affluent groups, the rich and the middle class, they nevertheless continue to represent a small segment of China's population, even in most cities (Croll 2006).

In a society in which increasing inequality is accompanied by greater levels of social mobility than in China under Mao (Bian 2002), consumer goods become an important avenue for communicating social position and readily convert into markers of social status (e.g. Hamilton and Lai 1989). Expensive and elaborate weddings once again act as testaments to family wealth (Siu 1993), and the "three bigs," the three status-enhancing purchases considered a necessity by urban newlyweds, escalated from televisions, washing machines, and refrigerators in the 1980s to VCRs, microwaves, and other expensive household electronics in the '90s. For the affluent, computers, private cars, and apartments are becoming *de rigueur* purchases (Lu 2000; see also Croll 2006). One newspaper article even predicted the "retirement of the wristwatch," as "what was once *the* status symbol" is replaced with the increasingly ubiquitous cellular phone.[25] The size of one's phone, in inverse proportion to the size of one's wallet, serves as a marker of purchas-

---

of 200,000 yuan or more *or* families owning a car (Gu et al. 2004: 265–66). Croll cites the income cut-off for the affluent in China as 2,000 yuan per month, though she notes that monthly salary often represents a small proportion of total wealth or even total income (2006: 83). Gu et al.'s study found Beijing's wealthiest residents tended to be enterprise managers, employees of foreign-invested companies, individuals with advanced technical training, and private businesspeople (2004: 269). In other studies, these same groups might in fact be considered "middle class" (e.g. Tomba 2004).

[24] Gu et al.'s (2004) study of the very rich in Beijing used a shopping center to recruit survey participants.

[25] "The wristwatch approaches 'retirement time'" (*shoubiao linjin 'tuixiu shijian'*), *Harbin New Evening News*, Oct. 1, 2001, p. 18.

ing power and status: the smaller, the better. Some young people even wear their phones on their wrists, suggesting a higher-tech, and higher status, consumer good has indeed displaced the wristwatch. Based on survey data, Stanley Rosen has identified a growing sense among Chinese youth that wealth is "a key indicator of [social] worth" (2004: 160). Rosen has also found growing social divisions among college students according to consumption patterns (ibid.). Wang Jing characterizes this as the rise of a "social economy based on emulation" (2001: 76), one often promoted by new urban lifestyle magazines (Zhao 2002). As Elisabeth Croll notes, it is lifestyle and consumption patterns as much as income that differentiate "elite earners" from other groups (2006: 83).

In fact, for many Chinese—especially for groups less secure about their position in the new social order—consumption provides a way to feel included in a modern, urban culture. In interviews with rural migrant workers, Eileen Otis (2003) found that these women, legally excluded from urban citizenship, tried to become urban by participating in the urban consumer economy, spending limited wages on clothing, makeup, and sometimes jewelry in an effort to acquire the look of modern femininity and attain a degree of dignity (see also Lee 1998; Pun 2003, 2005). Maris Gillette (2000), who studied a Muslim Chinese community in the western city of Xi'an, found that the consumption of frilly, Western wedding dresses was one way a marginalized ethnic group asserted their own modernity. But as the following chapters will demonstrate, Chinese urbanites are divided both by what they can buy and also by how they buy: low-income consumers shop in largely informal markets selling cheap merchandise and must haggle over consumer goods that are of poor quality and may be dangerously substandard. The well-to-do, by contrast, shop in "risk-free" shopping complexes that carefully screen merchandise and offer explicit return policies.

In cities like Harbin, crowded shopping districts have become a testament to China's dramatic new consumerist face—and an increasingly visible gap between rich and poor. During the peak of the winter shopping season, pairs of young women in short, stylish down coats coupled with snug jeans share the sidewalks with middle-aged women in practical woolen coats. Middle school students snacking from packages of potato chips or cookies jostle against rakish men in leather jackets and baggy trousers. Chic women in a knee-length fur coats step daintily from private cars. On the curb might sit a beggar wearing the traditional cotton-padded jacket that not long ago was standard winter attire for everyone in China's north.

In many ways, stratification of consumption and of China's retail sector have gone hand-in-hand. And, as I argued in the previous chapter, one of the concrete social spaces in which people "do" class and enact class entitlements is the service setting. Retail venues, as spaces of consumption, are important and particularly public venues for such class performances by both customers and workers (Benson 1986; Miller 1981; Winship 2000; Young 1999; Zukin 2004). In Europe and North America, the rise of such stores was tied to notions of middle- and upper-class respectability and distinction (Benson 1986; Miller 1981; Zukin 2004). As Susan Porter Benson points out, American department stores were pioneers in cultivating customer expectations of deferential service that were tied to "new standards of gentility" sought by the middle and upper classes (1986: 134). Even the catchphrase "the customer is always right" was coined by Philadelphia department store giant John Wanamaker (Benson 1986: 93).

In China today, aging state-owned department stores have been joined by sleek new private and even foreign-invested department stores that target China's new economic elites with high-end, luxury goods and claims of solicitous service. At the other end of the spectrum, large numbers of small-scale private merchants have appeared in China's urban marketplaces, selling cheap and inexpensive wares to an often money-strapped clientele. In the end, the distinctions made among retailers are also distinctions among customers, and *those* distinctions are laden with class meanings (Benson 1986; Cohen 2003; Miller 1981; Winship 2000; Zukin 2004; Zukin and Kosta 2004). Changes to China's retail sector also hold important implications for salesclerks, shaping the conditions under which they labor.

While this chapter has traced the political and economic context for changes to retailing, sales work, and consumption in urban China, the rest of this book will explore how China's retail sector is as much a symbolic field of cultural meanings as it is a field of economic competition. As I will show, the construction of new service work regimes, and the gender- and class-coded cultural meanings they produce, draws upon understandings of both the recent past as well as aspirations for the future. Ultimately, these changes entail the rise of distinction work and the production of inequality in the service settings of urban China. For while service work may no longer be viewed as a "site of class struggle," there is much contention and negotiation over what kinds of people should be performing service work for what kinds of customers—struggles that involve understandings of gender, of class, and of what a "modern," market-oriented China should be like.

CHAPTER THREE

Service Work with Socialist Characteristics

 ⌒⧹

Rising up in the heart of the city, the Harbin No. X Department Store was easily associated with socialism. The store was a prize of the revolution, once a foreign-ow`ned store that was nationalized even before the formal founding of the People's Republic in 1949. As a physical space, the department store imparted a distinctly proletarian, even revolution-era, feel. Its material form was vast, a ring of eight towering floors of cement covering an entire city block. On an inner wall, a colossal mural of a hard-hatted worker reminded store employees to be vigilant against fire as they crowded through the back entrance every morning. Each day the store opened its doors to an operatic broadcast of the store song, steeped in revolutionary fervor and sung in CCTV military chorus style, entitled "Soar, Harbin No. X!"

> Great ambitions to expand, like the surging ocean!
> The spirit to engage struggle, like the lofty mountain!
> Genuine smiles win the customers' love!
> Exquisite merchandise is exchanged for a golden reputation!
> Glorious Harbin No. X! Glorious Harbin No. X! . . . Go create
>   a splendid new era!

Although composed for the opening of the store's new building in the early 1990s, the song was infused with the language of the Chinese revolution and extolled the contributions of China's workers to a glorious future.

Harbin No. X's socialist atmosphere and the organization of sales work in the store raise a number of questions about service work, the production of class distinctions, and inequality. As this chapter will show, service interactions at Harbin No. X push us to ask about the conditions under which service work becomes distinction work. In particular, when do managers of a service organization like a department store structure their hiring and labor control practices to produce social distinctions? When, in other words, do these businesses become invested in the production and reproduction of a culture of inequality? When does recognition of customers' social position and class entitlements become part of what workers produce and what customers consume?

In the introductory chapter, I suggested that market competition and an organizational field in which competition over customers takes place are key factors behind the appearance of distinction work. In this chapter, I examine the organization of service work at the state-owned Harbin No. X Department Store, demonstrating that management at this department store did *not* choreograph the production of class distinctions at the organizational level. I argue that because service work at this state-owned department store was originally organized under the conditions of a centralized, planned economy, it does not bear the characteristics of distinction work. That is to say, the store, its managers, and to a lesser degree its workers, were not invested in cultivating a new, differentiated structure of entitlement among urban consumers.

As Chapter 2 has detailed, retail outlets and consumer goods were scarce under China's centralized planned economy, and customer patronage was a non-issue. Retailers instead directed their organizational energies toward the state and its bureaucratic distributive hierarchy, almost the exclusive source of material resources and other benefits. In this chapter, I demonstrate that this "state socialist" mindset continued to guide many managerial activities at Harbin No. X. Consequently, top managers at the store, in contrast to managers at Sunshine, did not seek to organize service work to convey class distinctions.

On the sales floor, the result was a workplace bearing many of the hallmarks of a socialist labor process. With managers focused on local state agencies, salesclerks self-organized their work activities relatively free from managerial intervention. The resulting work culture was characterized by a critique of managerial authority and assertions of worker expertise and control on the sales floor. As a result, service interactions were constructed on a basis of customer-worker parity and, unlike at Sunshine, did not require the subtle recognition and legitimization of inequality. This chapter explores these three elements: a socialist managerial mindset, a socialist work culture critical of inequality between workers and managers, and egalitarian service interactions.

I should emphasize that I am not arguing that service work at Harbin No. X was the same as in pre-reform China—it was not—but rather that the organization of work and the quality of interactions in the store were clearly shaped by pre-reform, state-socialist ideology and social relations. In fact, Chapter 6 will show how change was occurring in the form of distinction-marking practices innovated by store workers in the face of market challenges. It is important to first recognize, however, the important legacy of state socialism inside the store.

ORGANIZATIONS AND CULTURE

Organizational distinction-making, I have argued, involves managers making hiring and labor control decisions that distinguish their own service setting from other, usually less "distinctive" ones. These organization-level distinction practices are mirrored in the service interaction, where salesclerks are expected to recognize customer claims to class position and entitlements to deferential treatment. But managers are only invested in this production of class meanings when such meanings are a key aspect of how their organizational field is structured—in this case, when customers, faced with a range of retail options, respond to and are attracted by the class meanings that service settings and service workers convey.

I have borrowed the concept of "field" and more specifically "organizational field" to argue that organizational culture and orientations are very much a product of the environment in which an organization operates (Fligstein 2001b; Schoenberger 1997). At the same time, both managerial and worker cultures are also structured by the broader political-economic organization of society (e.g. types of capitalism, or forms of socialism), as Michael Burawoy has argued in *The Politics of Production* (1985). In this chapter, I attempt to show the crucial connection between organizational fields and the broader political economy, and the importance of both factors in shaping life at Harbin No. X. In the first case, the organizational field recognized by Harbin No. X managers was not the stratified marketplace understood by Sunshine managers but rather the administrative hierarchy of state socialism. Both managerial and worker practices and strategies also reflected the broader structuring of life and work under reforming state socialism, leaving Harbin No. X with the indelible marks of a socialist work unit.

In the introduction, I suggested that culture functions as an integral part of organizations. As this chapter will show, culture can structure a durable (though not fixed or permanent) set of dispositions embedded in the practices of the managers and workers who make up a service organization (cf. Schoenberger 1997). In contrast to studies of work organizations that focus on managerial ideologies and strategies for control (e.g. Bendix 1956) or even explicit managerial attempts to engineer workplace culture (Kunda 1992), I point instead to a more subtle but important role of culture in structuring social life within organizations. Bourdieu pointed to the "harmony" between objective structures and subjective orientations in social settings, what he called a "coincidence of habitus and habit" by which institutions are made real by actors inclined to fill their roles within those institutions. An organization only comes to life if, "like a garment or a house [it] finds someone who . . . feels sufficiently at home in it to take it on" (Bourdieu 1981: 309, cited in DiMaggio and Powell 1991 [1983]: 26). In other words, the role of *habitus*—which is made up of largely unspoken values, dispositions, and practices—helps explain why social structures, housed in institutions, are so enduring and are readily reproduced. Institutions are, in many ways, products of the daily practices of individual social actors who feel "at home" in them.

The Harbin No. X Department Store, with a history strongly shaped by the social and economic organization of pre-reform China, offers an opportunity to consider questions of cultural durability within an organizational setting. In particular, Harbin No. X represents a retail organization in which important elements of a state-socialist organization have proved resilient through the course of economic reforms—certain managerial attitudes, for example, and on the sales floor prominent features of what I characterize below as a socialist work culture. These culturally guided attitudes, values, and practices all made up the "tool kit" (Swidler 1986) that Harbin managers and workers relied on to structure their daily work activities in the store. For managers at the store, their state-socialist mindset operated largely through accepted power relations and unstated assumptions—assumptions managers often only made explicit when pressed, by me, to do so. In this sense, managerial orientations were evidence of a "socialist" habitus that resided in a doxic, or accepted, realm of habit and disposition (Bourdieu 1977).

Like managers, workers at the store also expressed dispositions strongly associated with a traditional, socialist work unit. To some degree, the repeated and *explicit* assertion by workers of their work culture hinted at less coherence between circumstance and culture than the concept of a largely unconscious *habitus* suggests. There are two reasons why this might be so. Following Burawoy and Lukács (1992), I suggest that the explicitness of this work culture was in part a product of the organization of work and life under state socialism. But also, as Ann Swidler (1986: 278) has argued, in unsettled cultural periods strategies of action become more explicit, and "culture's role in sustaining existing strategies of action and its role in constructing new ones" becomes more apparent. This chapter is primarily concerned with how both circumstance and culture have operated to sustain existing strategies of action at Harbin No. X, as store leaders maintained many of their pre-reform managerial orientations and workers continued to cultivate a socialist work culture. Culture and practice were nevertheless not static; Chapter 6 will explore the construction of new strategies of action (and practices of distinction) by these same workers. Ultimately, the consequences of distinction work for organizations, workers, and customers become especially clear when we examine a service setting *not* structured by the dictates of distinction work.

A SOCIALIST (SERVICE) ORGANIZATION

Despite numerous organizational changes and reforms, the Harbin No. X Department Store in 2001 retained many important institutional orientations rooted in China's pre-reform, planned economy era. In particular, managers directed their attention and energies not toward the market and consumers but rather toward the local city government and party offices that sat directly above them in the administrative hierarchy of the local party-state. Having enjoyed a privileged position within the state hierarchy prior to 1979, Harbin No. X's links to and its dependencies upon the local city government and party organs continued through the reform period. This fostered a "socialist" managerial mindset, one *not* geared to produce class meanings in the service setting.[1]

---

[1] This argument contrasts with Doug Guthrie's (1997) findings for Shanghai's industrial sector. Guthrie found that firms located at higher administrative levels—for example, under the jurisdiction of a municipal bureau—were *more* likely to experi-

In the pre-reform era, location in the Chinese party-state's bureau-cratic hierarchy was a key determinant of an organization's status, in-fluence, and access to material resources (Bian 1994; Li 1993), a situation compounded by the economics of shortage characteristic of command economies (Kornai 1980). China's planned economy was marked by an especially tight monopoly on commerce and more severe shortages of consumer goods than was true in Eastern European countries (Naugh-ton 1995: 45–46). In this context, Harbin No. X enjoyed an advantaged position within the city of Harbin and in Heilongjiang province more generally. Prior to 1979, it was one of only two retail outlets in the city directly managed by the municipal commerce committee (*shi shang-wei*) and not the state-run dry goods corporation (*baihuo gongsi*), as was more typical.[2] This gave merchandise procurement officers (*caigou yuan*) at Harbin No. X direct and differential access to provincial-level state distribution centers possessing scarce consumer goods that rarely made it down to lower-level distribution stations. When restricted dis-tribution channels were opened in the aftermath of the Cultural Revo-lution (Solinger 1984), Harbin No. X was one of the first retailers in the province given permission to directly procure merchandise from outside Heilongjiang province (*Harbin City Almanac* 1996). Historically, a privileged relationship to the state was the most valuable resource at the disposal of the store's leadership.

The store's special relationship with city leaders remained strong through the course of economic reforms in the city, and in the early 1990s loans from the municipal government financed the construction of a massive new eight-story structure. In the process, Harbin No. X swallowed up a less prestigious state-owned marketplace, absorbing personnel from the old organization into its own, more dominant en-

---

ence the pressures of market reforms. Guthrie shows that in the 1990s, highly placed industrial firms were likely to cope with risk by investing in the service sector. There is no evidence, however, that *service sector* firms located high in the administrative hierarchy were under similar pressures. Nevertheless, I do not mean to suggest that Harbin No. X's relationship with the Harbin municipal bureau is representative of China's large service sector firms, though the pattern *was* representative within Har-bin. My intention here, rather, is to explain the enduring "socialist" nature of man-agement and work at this particular store.

[2] As noted in Chapter 2, the actual organization of retail between 1949 and the 1980s fluctuated between control by the centralized state commercial system and control by local authorities (Solinger 1984). Harbin No. X, however, was always un-der the control of local (city) leaders.

tity. Store management claimed (in revolutionary fashion) that at the time the new building was completed in 1994, Harbin No. X had become, square footage-wise, "the largest department store in China."[3]

Economic reforms had, of course, dramatically altered the way the store engaged in the business of retailing. By the late 1980s, for example, Harbin No. X was no longer procuring merchandise through state-run wholesalers, opting instead for the direct producer-retailer links that had been proliferating throughout the decade. In the early 1990s, the store shifted from turning over all its profits to the state and instead was taxed at the standard rate for state-owned enterprises.[4] From the 1980s, workers were shifted from flat monthly wages to a commission sales system. In 2001, workers' health and retirement benefits also underwent change. Store workers were enrolled in social welfare programs sponsored by the city government and into which they were required to make individual, monthly contributions. As a result, the store no longer shouldered the full social welfare burden for its workers. All these changes represented important and real organizational impacts of economic reforms.

Ironically, Harbin's municipal commerce committee had largely mandated these responses to new market conditions, increased competition, and declining profits. Reforms had done little to truly separate store from state, and nominal ownership changes had left the enterprise under the thumb of municipal commerce officials. In the late 1990s, store ownership was converted to stock, yet the government maintained a formal 33% stake in the enterprise and controlled roughly another 33% informally (the remaining shares were owned by staff and management), giving municipal commerce officals *de facto* control over any major organizational decision. As one store manager pointed out,

[3] These managerial claims are laden with the tones of Chinese state socialism. Franz Schurmann, in his study of organizations under Chinese communism, notes the "love of 'gigantism'" that motivated the development of massive industrial complexes in the early years of the Communist regime (1968: 300). Schell (1984: 6) also notes the Chinese Communist Party's fondness of doing things "in a big way."

[4] Given that China introduced business taxation in the early 1980s, Harbin No. X seems to have moved to the system relatively late. In 2002, a "stock company" like Harbin No. X, unlisted in the stock exchange, was technically taxed at a rate of 33% of profits, but the store's chief accountant explained that the city actually returned 18% of profits to unlisted companies, such that the city's listed and unlisted companies were taxed at the same 15% tax rate.

what was nominally a "stock company" (*gufen gongsi*) managed under a stockholder system (*gufen zhi*) was in fact a *state-owned* stock company (*guoyou gufen gongsi*) subject to the directives of the local party-state.

In other ways Harbin No. X remained financially tethered to the local city government. The mid-1990s, when Harbin No. X completed the massive new shopping structure built on funds borrowed from the city, was also a turning point in China's retail sector. As the previous chapter described, retailing, so profitable in the late '80s and early '90s, had attracted large numbers of new competitors, and as a result Harbin No. X saw its profits slide. In 2001, the store still owed loans exceeding 500 million yuan (over US$60 million) to the city government (Ji 2002), placing the store's financial fate in the hands of city officials.

City officials also controlled the store through its general manager, who was not an internal selection but an external party cadre appointed by the municipal commerce bureau and expected to approve every managerial decision of any importance. As a result, the managers below him, many of whom had worked their way up the store hierarchy from salesclerk positions, expressed little sense of control over, and often little interest in, the major business affairs of the store. "Store management doesn't have a say" (*bu shuo de suan*), one manager explained to me after I witnessed her tell another manager that an important store matter could not be decided until the general manager returned from a business trip. "The city commerce committee still sends down a plan" (*xia jihua*), another manager commented. "We basically have to respond to the demands of those above us."

This sense of lack of authority or control also characterized managers' relations with workers. In particular, store managers frequently reminded me of their inability to fire workers. The store did have an institutional process for firing workers, involving a large meeting of workers' representatives (*zhigong daxing daibiao hui*) and, if approved, a meeting of managers. But firing workers was viewed as impossible, unless the individuals were involved in corruption or other illegal activities, and managers could not recall a single instance of having let a worker go. As one top manager at the store explained, "When people enter a state enterprise, it is [still] expected to be a lifetime relationship. If you try to fire someone, the labor bureau [*laodongju*] will probably intervene. . . . You might tell someone they have to leave, and they'll say back to you, 'Well, I'm just not leaving.'" Managers believed that, given the high rates of unemployment in Harbin due to lay-offs in the state industrial sector, the city government would not allow the store to add to the pool of unemployed.[5]

All this suggests that Harbin No. X inhabited an organizational environment peculiar to state socialism. Despite the competitive pressures of a newly crowded retail sector—pressures of which managers were certainly aware—the most important set of relationships, for almost all store managers, continued to be those with municipal government and city-level party organs and officials. This was amply demonstrated by the endless political activities, meetings, and events that managers either organized, at the store level, or attended, at the city or provincial level. At one such event, a manager at my elbow pointed out all the important *guar*, or officials, in attendance, including leaders of the Communist Youth Leagues for both the city and the city's municipal commerce office.

The socialist state, then, with its array of interlocking government and party organizations and units, was the primary organizational field in which store management recognized themselves as operating.[6] This understanding dictated the issues and relationships managers focused on, turning their attention away from workers and customers in favor of local state officials. In the minds of store managers, Harbin No. X's position in the cosmos of Chinese retailers was dictated not by the market, ultimately, but by the Chinese state. Even store management's reaction to my desire to work and conduct research in the store serves as a case in point, for they took a foreigner's interest in them to be yet further evidence of the store's exalted position in the city of Harbin and within China as a whole.

A SOCIALIST WORK CULTURE

Fixed upon reaping the benefits of the store's relations with the local state, managers and especially upper-level management felt little need

[5] Managers also expressed the view that Harbin No. X had a *duty* to employ people. Guthrie found similar expressions of managerial loyalty to workers, which he attributed to socialist ideology and its sense of equity and fairness (Guthrie 1998: 484–87).

[6] The store's relations with merchandise suppliers made up a somewhat distinct field in which store management also operated. However, those store-supplier relations, which I will not address here, were strongly shaped by perceptions of the store's close links with the city party-state.

to engineer Harbin No. X as space for the production and consumption of class meanings. Instead, the sales floor claimed sparse attention from mangers on a day-to-day basis and was primarily the domain of workers and customers. In this relatively autonomous space, workers cultivated a work culture infused with the stated, if not realized, egalitarian values of socialism. So, not only was service work *not* structured by management to produce class distinctions, as I have argued service work organized under a market system is, but this socialist workplace in fact fostered an egalitarian ethic and critiques of inequality.

Work culture in a service setting can provide workers with the resources to assert their autonomy and challenge managerial control on the sales floor. In a study of early twentieth-century American department stores, Susan Porter Benson (1986: 228) defines work culture as "the ideology and practice with which workers stake out a relatively autonomous sphere of action on the job." Work culture incorporates collectively held values as well as the practices through which these beliefs are enacted, and, as Barbara Melosh has argued, work culture "guides and interprets the tasks and social relations of work," becoming "an inextricable part of the work process itself" (1982: 5–6). Benson describes how in American department stores, autonomy on the selling floor fostered a work culture shaped by the "complicated triangle of saleswomen, managers, and customers," and overlaid with gender and class issues (1986: 240). The sales floor became a space where workers asserted themselves, collectively, through the self-organization of work, a sense of professionalism and selling skill, and strategies to handle both managers and customers (Benson 1986, chapter 6).

Many of these aspects of the work culture among American saleswomen could be found at Harbin No. X as well, ranging from the flouting of managerial rules to the collective development of selling skills and techniques. However, the work culture I found at Harbin No. X also bore the clear marks of China's experiences with state socialism. Most strikingly, workers maintained a sales floor culture that frequently invoked socialist values and included an explicit, almost Marxist, critique of inequality in the workplace and of managerial authority over workers. Much like managerial attitudes and practices, the work culture at Harbin No. X could be linked to the organization of work under state socialism. (In Chapter 6, I explore how this work culture served as the basis for new sales strategies that might rightly be label distinction work, and therefore should not be viewed as fixed in the past.)

Ethnographic studies of social life under state socialism have found that daily life was often characterized by a critical consciousness grounded in both the ideology and material relations of the state socialist system. For example, Michael Burawoy and Janos Lukács (1992) have argued that the transparency of state power under state socialism required an explicit legitimating ideology that produced "a heightened consciousness of the discrepancy between ideology and reality" (82). Whereas under capitalism the sale of a worker's labor power takes place through the obscuring mediation of the market, under socialism labor and its products are clearly appropriated by state. This results in a kind of "negative class consciousness" that enables people to criticize the state and social reality for failing to live up to ideological claims (Burawoy and Lukács 1992: 114).[7] In Eastern Europe, the lived experience of state socialism, and the political rituals and ideology that punctuated it, formed the basis for a highly skeptical orientation toward the state (Verdery 1998; Drakulic 1991). In the Hungarian steel mill where Burawoy labored as a furnaceman, for example, farcical political performances—such as the "cleaning" of a dirty industrial workplace for the prime minister's visit—highlighted for workers how much everyday reality departed from state propaganda (Burawoy and Lukács 1992).

There was evidence of a similar orientation in pre-reform China, where decades of state-orchestrated class struggle and revolution-making—and the Cultural Revolution in particular—generated an extensive, and explicit, toolkit with which to critique authority relations in the workplace. Andrew Walder found that workers used work hours to conduct personal business, do laundry, or just sleep, and pilfering of work unit goods for personal use was pervasive, behaviors that were all "designed to reclaim time and material goods from the enterprise in a situation where compensation was perceived to be insufficient" (1986: 215). This was a reversal of the usual power relationship between the socialist state and its subjects (what Katherine Verdery has termed the "etatization of time" [1998]) and the creation, in the words of Mayfair Yang, of a "sphere of oppositional tactics" that "*redistributes* what the state economy has already distributed" (1994: 205, 204).

In China, anthropologist Lisa Rofel has situated this negative class consciousness, which she labels a "politics of authority," in the cohort of Chinese workers who came of age during the Cultural Revolution. For

[7] Burawoy and Lukács label such class consciousness as "negative" because it is only critical of the existing system; a "positive" class consciousness would include an alternative vision of social organization (1992: 114).

this group, Rofel argues, "the radical questioning of authority as well as the politicization of everyday life became the commonsense knowledge that ineluctably shaped their aspirations, insights and actions" (1999: 166). In Rofel's study, this politics was most clearly expressed on the factory shop floor, where workers resisted attempts to impose new, production-oriented controls by taking extended cigarette and rest breaks and disregarding managerial attempts at stricter discipline. She contends that workers asserted a degree of control over their daily activities and movements, conducting domestic and personal tasks at the workplace and during work hours and resisting efforts to intensify and revalue labor (1992: 97). Rofel holds that this mindset was historically contingent, tied to the era in which a specific cohort of workers came of age, rather than the result of a general, state socialist organization of production as Burawoy and Lukács argue.

But at Harbin No. X it was clear that an oppositional consciousness was not only or even primarily embedded in a particular generation. Younger workers as well as the seasoned Cultural Revolution generation could present an almost structural understanding and critique of their relationship to store management and the socialist state more generally. Workers demonstrated an acute understanding of the inequalities created under China's socialist planned economy and even maintained a less elaborated critique of new reform-induced inequalities on the sales floor. Much like the Chinese industrial workers described by Ching Kwan Lee (2000, 2002, 2007), Harbin No. X salesclerks drew upon cultural resources cultivated by state socialism to critique the state's building (or even un-building) of a failed or compromised socialism. But unlike laid-off industrial workers, the socialist and egalitarian strains to the work culture at Harbin No. X were neither nostalgic nor repressed; rather, they were grounded in daily work practices, discussions among workers, and interactions with managers. The result was a set of deeply held dispositions—a socialist *habitus*, if you will—from which workers actively endeavored to make Harbin No. X an organization in which they felt at home—bending it, with their practices and habits, into something that matched their work culture and its values.

Politics of Authority on the Sales Floor

The Harbin No. X sales floor served as a crucible of "negative class consciousness" that was forged daily through the concrete organization of work and the work culture that accompanied it. This space of autonomy and worker self-direction enabled salesclerks to engage in a "politics of authority" that both challenged managerial power and asserted worker competence and authority on the sales floor. This was certainly true of the down coat counter in the women's department to which I was assigned.

The women's clothing department at Harbin No. X occupied about half of the store's second floor, stretching away from the main escalator in aisle upon aisle of blouses, skirts, and pant-sets. In the winter, a large down coat area sprung up in the center of the department, where clerks worked in two- or three-person sales teams selling a single brand of merchandise. I found myself assigned to the Ice Day counter, where I joined an existing team of three: Big Sister Zhao, an exuberant woman in her early 40s; quiet Big Sister Lin, in her late 30s; and the obstreperous Little Xiao, in his late 20s. We worked from behind a set of glass counters that formed one end of a long, unbroken stretch of counters: to our left, the neighboring sales team of three sold Winter Weather coats and beyond them another team of three sold Snow Lion down coats. All told, the nine workers with whom I worked most closely were typical of the store's workforce: Two of the nine clerks were men, four clerks were in their mid- to late 20s, three in their 30s, two in their 40s. All but two clerks had worked at the store for at least ten years.

Big Sister Zhao was fairly typical of the older clerks in the store. Her first job had been in construction work when she was a teenager, having left high school early to help support a poor family. At the age of 19 she transferred to Harbin No. X, where she had worked ever since. Her husband also worked a state-sector job, and Zhao and her husband lived with a daughter and Zhao's mother-in-law in housing allocated by his work unit. Little Xiao was typical of younger workers: like many of his age cohort, Xiao had trained at the city's local vocational school with a specific program for sales clerks and which had channeled him directly into a department store job. Many other younger workers had parents who had worked at the store and retired, passing their position on to their children (a practice termed *dingti*) like a state-socialist form of inheritance. Big Sister Zhao, still unready to retire, was contemplating this option for her teen-aged daughter, a recent graduate of the vocational school.

The store that Zhao's daughter might enter was in many ways not the same one that Zhao herself had begun her career with. Starting from the early 1980s, reforms had gradually altered the wage system at Har-

A Harbin No. X sales counter. Photo by the author.

bin No. X, such that stagnant wages and storewide bonuses had been replaced with monthly base pay and team-based sales commissions. My co-workers earned a 1% sales commission on their monthly sales, an amount divided equally among the sales team and which could double, triple, or even quadruple the basic monthly wage of 400 yuan. These wages were issued by the store, though the suppliers of our merchandise actually paid these costs. Given the low basic wage, workers actively pursued sales commissions, and on the sales counters I worked I never witnessed workers restricting sales upon reaching a collectively recognized sales limit (contrast Benson 1986: 248; Dalton 1974).

A department manager and two assistant managers were in charge of daily operations in the department, and upper-level managers would conduct periodic, though infrequent, inspections. Workers could be subject to fines—for being late, for a sloppy work space, for chatting with one another—but in practice such penalties were infrequently applied. In fact, management was a rare presence on the floor, and when a manager did pass he or she was likely to focus on superficial and incidental problems like a forgotten bucket of soapy water or a sloppy work area. Workers could run errands, visit friends at other counters, or even take a nap (if well concealed) without ever being discovered. This high level

of autonomy also gave workers the freedom to organize their work activities, work space, and merchandise as they saw fit. The result was an
idiosyncratic, but highly efficient, self-organization of work activities.

In a sense, the rhythms of work were similar to those Christopher
Warhurst (1998) observed in an Israeli kibbutz factory. Warhurst identified high levels of worker self-direction and autonomy as a key element of this "alternative socialist work setting," revealed by the flow
of people about and even in and out of the workplace.[8] While Harbin
No. X's salesclerks were certainly not free from managerial evaluations
and control, they claimed many of the privileges that Warhurst ascribes
to the socialist labor process. Salesclerks' self-direction also enhanced
their sense of expertise and competence, heightening their disdain for
a seemingly ineffectual management, much as Burawoy and Lukács
(1992: 197) have shown for industrial workers under state socialism.

High levels of worker autonomy on the sales floor made salesclerks
especially skeptical of managerial power, so it is perhaps unsurprising that open critiques of authority were most frequently roused by
the relatively rare appearance of upper-level management. When upper management *did* appear—commonly in some formal "inspection"
sense—workers were likely to denounce the power relation between
workers and management, in the process revealing the politicized nature of work and authority on the sales floor.

Just such a critique came out quite unexpectedly one day when I was
quizzing Little Xiao about management service inspections. A group
of men from "upstairs," where management offices were located, had
just passed through the sales area. "Is the store more strict about inspecting service than when you first came here?" I asked Little Xiao,
who at age 28 had been at the store for almost ten years. "This matter
. . ." Little Xiao's voice trailed off. Then he launched the conversation
in another direction. "You know, there are about 3,000 people working
at this store, but only about half of them are actually salespeople who
produce anything of value. We are just carrying along the rest of them.

---

[8] Burawoy and Lukács similarly identify high levels of autonomy with the industrial labor process found under state socialism, though the sources of that autonomy are different from those that either Warhurst or I identify. Burawoy and Lukács
(1992) contend that the uncertainties of a shortage economy necessitate high degrees
of worker autonomy, as shop floor autonomy becomes the only way to cope with
supply and production uncertainties while still endeavoring to fulfill the plan. Service workers, by contrast, deal mostly with the *demand-side* of the economy—consumers—which is not generally a source of uncertainty in a shortage economy.

Those folks upstairs, they simply don't have anything to do, they're just whiling away the time" (*tamen xianzhe*). Xiao's comments pointed to the injustice of non-producing members of the store asserting authority over those who were truly productive. This critique was quickly directed against the realities of life under state socialism. "Those people are just where they are because they have *guanxi*, whereas the rest of us don't and can't really do anything about it. It's because of how things worked under socialism," Little Xiao continued. He used his hands to indicate that organizations that should be pyramid-shaped are instead structured like straight-sided buildings. Xiao criticized both domination by bureaucrats (who are not themselves productive) and the social realities of state socialism.[9]

I got an earful of complaints on another occasion when, once again, a few members of upper management appeared on the sales floor. I was chatting with Xu Li-mei and Snow Lion Wang, salesclerks at neighboring counters.[10] Suddenly, two women wearing Harbin No. X's blue blazers appeared from the stairway opposite and moved onto the sales floor, passing near our counter. Li-mei and Wang straightened up, making it clear that these women were upper management inspecting salesperson behavior. Wang joked that since I was present, he and Li-mei probably would not be fined. "This isn't chatting" (*lauker*), he pointed out, "it's cultural exchange" (*jiaoliu*).

"How much do they fine you, anyway?" I asked. Snow Lion Wang explained that the fine issued by upper management for chatting was 40 yuan. When upper management "writes you up," a slip of paper is filled out and then the next day when you come to work they hand you the slip and expect you to pay on the spot. "It's pretty brutal" (*can*), Wang noted, "seeing as we don't earn that much money." According to Wang, he once was fined 70 yuan for being "one minute" late for work.

---

[9] There are two ironies here. First, service work was frequently considered "unproductive" by the Chinese Communists, and in some cases (as during the Great Leap Forward [1958–60] and the Cultural Revolution [1966–76]) commercial workers such as store clerks were sometimes expected to engage in factory work since commerce by itself was not considered "productive" (Solinger 1984: 235, 241). The second irony is that the only way upper management could visibly demonstrate their own "productivity" was through the assertion of authority, usually in the form of the inspections that prompted Xiao's claims that they were unproductive.

[10] "Snow Lion" was in fact the name of the brand of coat that Wang was selling; the two-syllable brand name was jokingly tacked onto Wang's surname, resulting in a plausible Chinese name.

"I decided after that to get up earlier in the morning so I won't be late again, even if I have to come in running, huffing and puffing."

"Seventy yuan is really quite a lot of money, given our salaries," Wang continued. "I used to sell regular clothing, and my base pay was only 400 yuan per month, maybe 500 or 600 with bonuses." Selling in the down coat department, Wang claimed he could earn about 1,000 yuan a month with bonuses, but, he added, for a man with a family, that was still not enough. (Wang was single.) "It seems like wherever you go, it's not too easy for men to earn money."

Wang continued with his comments, his voice rising in volume. "Everyone has a say over us" (*shei dou guan women*), he said, and started rattling off a list: the department management, the store management, the human resources department, customers, newspaper reporters, Setting Sun Red (*Xiyang Hong*, an organization for the retired). "It seems like just about everyone but the traffic police!" he quipped. At this point, Little Xiao arrived and joked that Wang was "telling the bitter history of a revolutionary family" (*tongsu geming jiashi*). The reference was to a Cultural Revolution-era opera, "The Red Lantern" (*hongdengji*), that relates the vicissitudes of a family during the War of Resistance against the Japanese invasion of China (1937–45).[11]

That the rhetoric of the Cultural Revolution—along with the analytical concepts of Marxism—continued to find critical, if at times ironic, usage on the sales floor hints at the close connection between workers' critiques of authority and the legitimating discourse of Chinese state socialism.[12] As Burawoy and Lukács (1992) argue, critiques of state socialism made from *within* state socialism are often based on a notion of justice and democracy that is promised, but not delivered, by the socialist state itself. Ironically, socialist ideology provides the bar

[11] The actual imposition of fines was less frequent than Wang suggested, and generally much smaller—being late to work garnered a 5 yuan fine from the department management, with heftier fines imposed only by infrequent store-wide inspectors. Nevertheless, store discipline and monetary fines were a real threat and a sorely resented expression of managerial authority.

[12] Even customers might tote the politicized language—and the implicit critical perspective—of the Revolution into the store. For example, when Big Sister Lin told one young man that our coats used fabrics imported from the United States, the man scoffed, "*Chongyang meiwai!*" (My little red dictionary translates this phrase as "worship foreign things and toady to foreign powers.") This slogan was a recurring theme under the Gang of Four—thanks to Tom Gold for pointing this out.

against which to measure reality—and criticize that reality for coming up short.

Workers' skepticism was heightened by the increasingly anachronistic political rituals in which Harbin No. X's management still engaged. The emptiness of these rituals was apparent by my third day on the job. That morning, the entire store staff was required to attend an hour-long political education meeting in their respective departments. I arrived to find the clerks of the women's department streaming over to a large staircase where they set up small, army-green folding stools that had been issued for such political meetings. The gathering felt more like a party than a political education session, however. A group of women behind me joked raucously among themselves until Manager Zhang dispatched Assistant Manager Yu to the top of the staircase. As Yu climbed the stairs with a sour expression on her face, workers whispered warnings to the troublemakers. Despite Yu's presence, workers paid little heed to the speaker, a woman salesclerk reading out a prepared document. At times the chatter rose to a level that made the speaker almost inaudible. Some of the women massaged each other's backs or chatted quietly, others tried to get down a little breakfast. For most of the meeting I could distinctly smell cigarette smoke. No one took notes. Upstairs on the third floor, a similar meeting was being held, and the volume of their address system was set so high that it was difficult for us to hear clearly what was being said on our own floor.

As a result, the content of the meeting was hard to follow. Manager Zhang first announced that this was a political theory (*lilun*) study session. The document read aloud had been prepared by the store's propaganda department and covered a large range of things: Jiang Zemin's "three represents" (*sange daibiao*) and its basis in Marxism-Leninism, as well as exhortations to maintain the country's socialist spirit. There was also some discussion of market issues and China's coming entry into the World Trade Organization. Wal-Mart was explicitly identified as a threat.

Big Sister Zhao took out her pen and carefully wrote out this list of issues on the palm of her hand. The people sitting around her chided, "Why are you bothering to write this down?" "For fun," she replied, unruffled, but her co-workers were offended that Zhao was taking any of this seriously.

On one level, workers and management alike recognized that these events paid lip-service to ideals and principles that the state and the

Chinese Communist Party had, in practice, largely abandoned. At the political meeting, Manager Zhang appeared bored, adding a few more random comments at the end about how "everyone has a responsibility to fight terrorism." (This meeting took place in late September 2001.) He seemed to be trying to stretch the meeting out so we would finish exactly at 9 A.M. Yet the visibility of management in orchestrating these events made them seem like co-authors of the charade. These events slotted neatly into workers' negative opinions of their "higher-ups" (*shangji*), feeding a critique of managerial authority that drew in part upon experiences of the inequalities of state socialist society.

This ethic was especially evident in criticisms of managerial favoritism and the use of personal connections, or *guanxi*, to secure good positions or promotions within the department store. When I asked Little Xiao if workers could request or apply for a specific sales position, Xiao said, "You can, but it's no use. Unless you have *guanxi* or money, you won't be able to influence the decision." For this reason, salesclerks' earnings were not perceived to be a good measure of ability or effort, but rather a sign of the attractiveness and salability of the merchandise and, by extension, the strength of one's connections with store or department management. *Guanxi* can be viewed as an oppositional force, acting counter to universalizing forces of the bureaucratic, socialist state (Yang 1994), but for that exact reason the existence of *guanxi* practices makes the state vulnerable to criticisms based on notions of impartial fairness. Workers perceived the use of instrumental ties in the workplace, rather than skill or merit, to be *part* of the socialist planned economy, and not in opposition to it. The use of *guanxi* served as yet another basis upon which to critique store management.

The failure of the store to fully realize an effort-based system of rewards, coupled with the legacy of China's "virtuocracy" (Shirk 1982) which demanded deliberate and instrumental expressions of revolutionary zeal and loyalty to the party-state (Walder 1986), could make overt displays of hard work laughable, much as the lingering rituals of the socialist state (such as political education meetings and model worker ceremonies) seemed pro-forma and devoid of real meaning. For example, one morning after shuffling back to our counter from the daily group meeting (itself more form than content), Little Xiao started working on our "books," our records of daily sales. As Xiao sat working over the numbers with a calculator, other salesclerks passing by repeatedly joked at what a hard worker Xiao was. "Just got here and you are already poring over the books," said one woman, and when Snow Lion Wang passed he quipped, "So hard at work, you really are a model worth studying [*zhide xiang ni xuexi*]!" In fact, much like the Chinese state that originally promoted the image of the model worker (Chen 2003a), management and their priorities at Harbin No. X were the targets of a steady flow of worker criticism that was part of daily life on the sales floor.

Worker Autonomy and Authority

Challenges to managerial authority had a flipside on the Harbin No. X sales floor, namely a powerful assertion of *worker* authority, expertise, and selling skill. Much as Burawoy observed in Hungarian industrial settings and Rofel reported for state-owned Chinese light industry, worker autonomy at Harbin No. X fostered a sense of competence among workers that inflected their relations with both managerial staff and, as I will show below, customers. The long tenure of workers at the store, and to a lesser degree their greater age (relative to Sunshine's clerks), also enhanced high levels of worker authority and provided a space in which Harbin No. X's sales floor culture could flourish.

Admittedly, I witnessed no open challenges to store management on the sales floor, and workers recognized the formal hierarchy that allowed management to fine them and allocate their sales positions. All the same, scarce managerial presence meant salesclerks would regularly flout store rules and regulations.[13] On my counter, Little Xiao would periodically light up a cigarette, stepping out from behind the sales counter so customers would not know he was a clerk. On one occasion Xiao even performed this maneuver in front of a floor manager.[14] And on my very first day on the Ice Day counter, Big Sister Zhao handed me a stick of mint gum, a common after-lunch procedure, saying as she did

[13] There are parallels between these forms of salesclerk resistance to managerial authority and James Scott's descriptions of everyday forms of resistance in *Weapons of the Weak* (1985). However, I wish to emphasize that Harbin No. X salesclerks were much more assertive, and carried a greater sense of entitlement, than the impoverished Malaysians who people Scott's field accounts.

[14] The cigarette maneuver was not only an assertion of Xiao's freedom and autonomy on the sales floor; I believe it was also an assertion of his masculinity in a strongly feminized workplace. Chinese women are much less likely than men to smoke, and in Harbin women were infrequently seen smoking in public.

so that we were not supposed to eat anything behind the counter. The trick was to pretend that there was nothing in our mouths. A customer lingering by the counter interjected, "Is that a good thing, pretending not to be eating? What if we see you?" Zhao replied slyly, "Well, then we're not pretending not to be eating, are we?"

The prohibition on food was perhaps the most frequently flouted rule, and my co-workers and I were constantly squatting down behind the counter to consume fruits, cakes, and other collectively shared snacks; smaller items, like nuts, could be eaten surreptitiously and while standing. Every Sunday I would empty the bulging pockets of my uniform of all the edible presents I had received in the course of the week.

Workers even resented any reminder of the numerous rules that could be enforced upon them. When Little Xiao handed me a whole pack of gum after lunch, I asked him if it was okay to eat behind the counter. He gave me a funny look and asked me who had told me that. Xiao then pointed out with irritation that chewing on a stick of gum was "not the same thing as eating." And when Xu Li-mei, a young woman at the neighboring counter, explained to me that cellular phones and beepers must be turned off while working the counter, a clerk listening in on the conversation immediately interjected, "But it's not *that* strict!" Workers engaged in calculated rule-breaking activities that acknowledged management authority largely in the breach.

However, workplace autonomy at Harbin No. X extended far beyond the freedom to circumvent formal store rules and even beyond flexibility in dealing with customers—the kind of autonomy we might expect with service work (Leidner 1993; Sherman 2006). Salesclerks exerted considerable degrees of control over aspects of service work frequently not controlled by salesclerks in other settings in Harbin, from tasks such as the organization and management of merchandise stocks to arrangement of the sales area.

Stock in particular—as both Francis Donovan and George Lombard have noted in ethnographies of American department stores—is a key element of department store work (Donovan 1930; Lombard 1955). In many ways, stock *is* the work environment for salesclerks, and familiarity with the range and availability of merchandise, and the ability to access it quickly, is often crucial to making a sale. At Harbin No. X, the organization of merchandise served as an important way for workers to adapt their work environment to their individual or group work styles and preferences. It was also a matter over which salesclerks expected not only store managers but also manufacturers and suppliers to defer to their authority. As such, it is an excellent example of how salesclerks conceived of themselves as knowledgeable professionals with decision-making authority on the sales floor.

Salesclerks were keenly aware that well-organized stock could greatly enhance their ability to sell. This was especially true of merchandise sold from behind counters, such as down coats. The bulkiness of down coats also demanded an efficient and regular system of storage with which clerks were thoroughly familiar. An impatient customer might not be willing to wait while a clerk laboriously sifted through piles of coats. Each sales team tailored their stocking arrangements to their own needs, habits, and preferences.

Stock issues also highlight another set of relationships within the store: that between factory sales representatives (*changjia daili*)[15] and salesclerks. In a technical sense salesclerks in the store had two bosses—the store management, who loosely monitored their daily work and service performance, and representatives from manufacturers, who actually paid commissions and salaries, funded advertisement campaigns, shouldered the costs for outfitting a sales area, and, importantly, supplied merchandise. Manufacturers would naturally seek to channel the best and most popular merchandise to venues where they believed it would sell the fastest, and as a result they did not treat all stores, and did not supply all sales counters, equally. Harbin No. X workers recognized that in this respect they were highly dependent on the manufacturers of the goods they sold.

But in striking contrast with the clerks at the Sunshine Department Store, the salesclerks at Harbin No. X repeatedly asserted themselves with *changjia* reps in ways that reflected their authority and expertise on the sales floor. The issue of stock was one about which Harbin No. X salesclerks were constantly exerting pressure. It was, for instance, a regular practice for salesclerks to make lists of the merchandise we hoped our manufacturer would re-supply us with, though when new shipments arrived we were never certain what we would find. If dissatisfied, clerks might hassle the "*daili*," or sales rep, when he arrived on his daily rounds. On one occasion, Big Sister Zhao was particularly

---

[15] Sales representatives could also be from a "middle-man" supplier (*daili shang*), but in our case merchandise was supplied to the store factory-direct.

stern with our sales rep, an affable, middle-aged man from the company headquarters in Jiangsu province. Zhao informed him that on the previous day, her day off, she had visited a wholesale clothing market in Harbin and found a wholesaler there selling Ice Day coats. She had discovered that the wholesaler was selling a style of men's coat our counter had never carried and another style of which we had only received a single box. Big Sister Zhao even quoted to the sales rep the prices of the coats and their product numbers. The sales rep seemed a bit surprised but asked her to note this information down for him, assuring her that he would try to make sure we got these goods. Zhao did not conceal her annoyance at his oversight.

Later that day, several boxes of merchandise arrived. When the sales rep returned the next day, Big Sisters Zhao and Lin enthusiastically informed him that the new styles were selling very well. The sales rep handed over a master list of prices due to the new items. Big Sister Zhao examined the list closely and found a number of items that we lacked; she immediately grilled the sales rep about this. He defended himself by explaining that not all these products had been sent to the Harbin sales region.

My fellow salesclerks understood very well that having the right merchandise was crucial to maintaining sales levels, and maintaining brisk sales was the basis for healthy commissions. When the various sales reps from the down coat company would stop by, Xiao, Zhao, and Lin would discuss popular colors and styles with them in the hope that more of these items would be channeled our way. It was from one of these conversations that we incidentally learned that our counter had the best Ice Day sales in the city. This provided more ammunition in our haggling for more and better stocks. "We have hardly anything left, and we were still able to sell 23 coats today!" Little Xiao exclaimed one day to the sales rep, who immediately agreed that we needed to restock but noted that there was little left in the company's own Harbin storage facility—new shipments were on the way. "Whatever I can get I'll send to you," he assured us.

In the course of the same conversation, Xiao and Big Sister Zhao passed on some advice that they hoped would be communicated to those in charge of designing and producing the coats: women's coats, they explained, should include one size larger, because many older women were unable to squeeze into our largest size. And long coats, they added, should be made a little longer—many people had been asking for longer coats.

Salesclerks recognized that they served as a vital source of current market information and often the only source of information about how well competitors' merchandise was selling. Passing that information back to the manufacturer was both a self-interested move—clerks wanted to improve sales by getting better merchandise—but it was also an assertion of expertise, professionalism, and authority. Salesclerks at Harbin No. X were so confident of their expertise that they would routinely offer up marketing advice to manufacturer representatives. One afternoon, for example, Little Xiao began lecturing a young sales rep on the company's publicity campaign, complaining that advertising had been too thin. "I've never heard of Ice Day before, and I'm selling the stuff!" he exclaimed.

This sense of authority enabled workers to assert themselves in other ways, such as resisting attempts to impose new routines or work practices on them. For instance, Ice Day coats were all labeled with a cardboard tag. At the base of each tag was a detachable stub on which the color, style, and size of the coat were listed. The manufacturer had devised this system as a means for tracking which coats were selling best. Because this was a new procedure, we frequently forgot to rip off the stub before a customer walked off with his or her purchase. One afternoon, our sales representative pressed Big Sister Zhao and Little Xiao over our failure to regularly rip off the stubs from the tickets on the coats we sold. The sales rep said, "How can we calculate your wages if we don't have the tabs?"

"You have to pay us!" exclaimed Zhao. "What do you expect us to eat if we are to sell your coats, the Northwest Wind [*xibei feng*]? You can't live off the Northwest Wind, you know!"[16]

Little Xiao joined in. "Sometimes we are simply too busy to have a chance to rip off the tags."

Zhao added, "Some customers dislike it [*you fan'gan*] when we rip

---

[16] The term "northwest wind" (*xibei feng*) has been used to refer to a Chinese cultural trend in the 1980s that engaged in "multiple modes of nostalgia" (Anagnost 1997: 154). As Ann Anagnost explains, China's northwest region is variously associated with China's cultural origins, the Chinese Communist Party's land reform and early class struggles, as well as with crushing poverty (this last shaping a critique of the state). Big Sister Zhao's reference was probably to the region's poverty, in this way incorporating an implicit critique of the powerful letting others languish in hardship. Zhao's choice of words reflects some level of anxiety at the sales rep's talk, even though workers were in fact paid *through* the store and it would have been difficult for a manufacturer to withhold wages.

off the tags, they don't like it." The harried sales rep eventually left for another sales counter, and though we all made a greater effort to collect the tabs, no one seemed overly concerned about doing so.[17]

AN EGALITARIAN SERVICE ENCOUNTER

Work culture at Harbin No. X, then, was composed of not only a critique of managerial power but also a sense of authority, expertise, and professionalism among workers. The dignity this generated carried over into interactions between these salesclerks and their customers, producing a set of worker-customer interactions strikingly different from the distinction-producing and distinction-recognizing service interactions found at the Sunshine Department Store. Instead of an aura of luxury, moneyed privilege, and deferential service, at Harbin No. X a working-class ethos dominated service interactions. Shaped by new market incentives and salesclerks' work culture, both clerks and customers at Harbin No. X participated in encounters marked by high levels of parity and mutuality.

Service Encounters Among Equals?

As noted above, because economic and enterprise reforms had not substantially altered the store's orientation to the bureaucratic hierarchy of the state, managers did not cultivate either the physical space of the store or the workforce itself to convey a class-specific market position. Instead, the store was an open, permeable, and even democratic space, in the sense that the world "outside" would frequently spill in and was subject to little, if any, filtering: people visited the store not only to shop, but also for a bit of exercise, to socialize, or even to engage in a little social activism. A senior citizen's group called Setting Sun Red would parade through the store on weekends carrying signs warning customers of pickpockets, while they chanted "Take care, take care!" Rural families in town for a day of shopping and working-class urbanites in blue or white work smocks enhanced the store's populist and proletarian feel. Many people carried on other, non-store business

---

[17] This is not to deny that manufacturers did successfully impose all sorts of work routines and procedures upon salesclerks. In fact, every separate counter operated along slightly different systems that were an amalgam of store, manufacturer, and the workers' own protocols and practices.

activities inside the store as well—fruit sellers, telephone card peddlers, even a roving tailor and a friendly pornography salesman. Workers extended their hospitality to animals, which customers might deposit atop sales counters, their pets' doggy antics a form of public entertainment.

Workers themselves were not so distinct from "the masses." Lax policies governing uniforms meant that through the winter months, workers were only required to don a blue blazer, allowing them to adapt their work clothing to individual tastes and comfort. Permed and dyed hair sat piled atop heads, and women salesclerks skittered about in impossibly tall high-heeled shoes and stylish, tight pants. This diversity of appearance allowed the streets of Harbin to be reproduced within the store walls. As one store manager pointed out to me, the store was very *dazhonghua*, or massified.

Without management dictating the contours of the customer-clerk relationship, Harbin No. X clerks and shoppers performed one of parity. The store's customer base fell into the low- and middle-income ranges among urbanites, meaning that customers and workers came from similar socio-economic strata and earned similar incomes—between 400 and 1,000 yuan a month, on average—and could consume many of the same things, be it clothing, food, or entertainment.

In fact, workers and customers would often make explicit the *lack* of social distance between them. For example, when trying to sell a man's down coat to a young Southern man, Big Sister Zhao urged him to purchase navy blue, explaining that it had *laoban qi* and would give him the "air of a boss." The young man joked with us that he was not a boss at all, only a *dagongzai* (slang for "male employee"). In another instance, a customer complained to us about how his son wanted a new winter coat every year in order to keep up with fashion. Zhao diagnosed this as *guizu bing*, or "aristocracy syndrome," to which the man immediately replied that his own economic situation was not so good. "You folks aren't so bad off," he continued, gesturing to my colleagues. "You can earn a bit more [than basic wages] in this line of work." At times, workers would point out their own wages to customers as a way of establishing a sense of empathy or rapport. One clerk joked that if there were a problem with a coat after the customer washed it, she would give the customer the money for the coat. "Out of my wages!" she exclaimed, adding that she only earned 400 yuan a month (this being her pre-commission base wage).

If rough social equals with customers, sales staff was nevertheless able to establish themselves as both experienced and expert regarding the products they sold.[18] Clerks and customers did not, of course, enter into these interactions as complete equals, especially as salesclerks' salaries were closely bound to customer purchases. However, while customers expected salesclerks to respond to their requests and needs, they did not expect clerks to enact extreme deference to customer wishes (though they also did not anticipate pre-reform levels of surliness). Instead, salesclerks constructed a knowledge hierarchy that elevated them above customers, and from that elevated position clerks could and often did issue judgments and pronouncements on customers' tastes, choices, and product knowledge.

For example, Little Xiao chided a customer who was being fussy about a loose thread on a coat. "It is impossible not to have a loose thread or two on these coats! The coat isn't made with a single length of thread!" Clerks could also be quite aggressive about redirecting customers' choices (often to fall in line with what we had in stock), and customers were sometimes cowed into accepting these authoritative instructions. For example, Big Sister Zhao exclaimed to a customer who wanted a smaller-sized coat that if the woman wore a size smaller her bottom would be hanging out (*lou*) and it would be unattractive (*bu hao kan*). The customer relented and purchased the recommended size. In many cases, clerks would guide customers' choice of color or style, instructing them as to which colors were appropriate or inappropriate for their size, age, or skin color. Zhao put a woman customer through an elaborate series of inspections, having her put on different coats and step back from the counter so Zhao could get a good look. Zhao then told her light brown was the right color given the woman's age, and suggested that she should wear a black sweater under the coat for the best effect. As the woman made the purchase, Big Sister Zhao continued to enthusiastically lecture her on how dark brown was not an appropriate color for middle-aged women.

Clerks would repeatedly resort to such tactics, and customers rarely challenged clerk interpretations of consumption norms. In fact, those who did not conform to clerk standards of customer and consumer behavior were sometimes described as deviant or even "sick-in-the-head." An amusing exchange occurred when Little Xiao was introduc-

[18] Pei-Chia Lan describes how cosmetics saleswomen in Taiwan use an aura of professionalism to exert control over their interactions with customers (Lan 2003: 33–34; see also Sherman 2006).

ing a coat with netting sewn into the lining to an older customer. The customer, unfamiliar with this innovation to allow for better ventilation, was suspicious. Xiao forcefully scolded her. "You don't understand!" he exclaimed with exasperation. "But won't dust get into the coat then?" the woman worried. "How much dust can you possibly have on your body?!" Little Xiao cried. "The coat does not have a problem, it's your ideas [*gainian*] that are the problem [*you wenti*]," he concluded. In another case, Little Xiao became irritated with an elderly man who was confused by the distinction between down and feathers. After Xiao attempted a detailed description of the physical distinction between down and feathers, the customer was still baffled. Xiao threw up his hands in defeat and exclaimed, exasperated, "I don't know how else to explain it to you, unless I pull out a dictionary and show you the words!" As the man shuffled off Little Xiao turned to me and complained loudly, "That guy is sick-in-the-head [*you bing*]! He understands less Chinese than a foreigner!"

Another example was a clerk's response to a customer, a tiny woman, on whom the sleeves of every coat she tried were too long. In this case, Big Sister Zhao explained that the woman had narrow shoulders and told her to consider other styles, but the woman insisted she liked that particular style. After the woman had wandered off, Big Sister Zhao turned to me and complained that the woman's arms were *bu biaozhun* (non-standard) and suggested the woman had a problem acknowledging this fact. In line with the "mass" character of the store, clerks often engaged in enforcement of "universal" standards against which customers' behaviors (and bodies) were judged. Failure to conform was a mark of stupidity or perhaps "old ideas," but not of relative class location per se. The irony, of course, was that these "universal" standards had become class-specific—that is, specific to the middle- and low-income urbanites who shopped at, and were employed by, the store.

Mutuality on the Sales Floor

If service workers' expressions of deference are a key means of signaling class difference and recognizing customer claims to class entitlements (see Chapter 4), then service interactions at Harbin No. X were especially notable for the *lack* of deference expressed by either side. In fact, the level playing ground upon which clerks and customers engaged one another was exemplified by the degree of give and take between actors and the doses of disrespect—mutual disrespect—they served up to one another. On the part of the clerk, disrespect at times took the form of gruff dismissal of fussy or troublesome customers. One time some customers responded with suspicion to Little Xiao's claim about merchandise quality. Xiao rejoined, "Go have a look around! [*Liu yi quar ba!*] I tell you there is no need to doubt the quality and you don't believe me. Go look elsewhere and if you find better, then buy that."

Customers, of course, dished out such disrespect as well as they received it. The most common way of doing this was to simply ignore a clerk who was rattling off a sales pitch, but customers might do other things, like ask to see an item and then leave while the clerk went to fetch it. Sometimes they would even have us write out a receipt and package up the item and then never return.[19] Sometimes this disrespect was expressed as distrust in the clerk's honesty. For example, one customer cut a sales pitch short by exclaiming "Give it a rest [*La dao ba*, local dialect]!" Big Sister Zhao responded evenly, "Do you mean that you think that what I said is incorrect?"

Ironically, it was clear to me that both sides felt they should be treated with respect. For example, in response to a customer who had just described our merchandise as *ke'chen*, local dialect for "extremely ugly," Little Xiao turned to me and said with gravity: "With the steady improvement of people's quality [*suzhi*], this kind of language will disappear." He continued: "Our treatment of customers is already very friendly. There is no need for customers to use such language with us." At the same time, customers also expected a degree of respect from clerks (and likewise might attribute bad service to the poor "quality" of the individual). For example, when Big Sister Zhao muttered something under her breath in response to a particularly difficult customer, he wheeled around and confronted her. "What was that?" Zhao then repeated what she had said: "I said, I wasn't able to explain clearly to you." The man, satisfied that he had not been insulted, moved off, at which point Zhao turned to me and said with irritation that the man was a *waihang* or "non-expert."

My claim that salesclerks at Harbin No. X did not engage in judg-

[19] In most department stores and other retail settings in China, clerks must write out a receipt for customers, who then go to a separate cashier location to pay and return, with a stamped receipt, to collect their merchandise.

ments of class is subject to an important caveat, however. For while urbanites could expect to shop in the store free of status anxieties, clerks' treatment of rural people was colored by pronounced urban-rural status distinctions. It was not uncommon for people who were clearly from non-urban backgrounds, especially migrant workers, to be summarily categorized as outside "the norm." For example, the relation between a middle-aged man accompanied by an attractive young woman, both of whom were definitively labeled "peasants" by my colleagues, was debated intensely after they left. "Certainly not father-daughter nor husband-wife relation, and not relatives," Little Xiao decided. "*Er hun guanxi*," said Big Sister Zhao, "'second' marriage [meaning extra-marital] relations." "Whatever their relationship," replied Xiao, "it is not normal [*bu zhengchang*], and they've just come to Harbin to piss all of us off [*chou de'se*, local dialect]." In another case, a group of deeply tanned young men, probably casual laborers from the countryside, were quickly labeled deviant. "They aren't like us normal people," Big Sister Lin explained to me. "We feel uncomfortable just looking at them." These "abnormal" rural shoppers, marginalized as they are in China's urban centers, were neither directly confronted with these judgments nor did they challenge the reserved manner in which they were served.

In fact, when rural shoppers did suggest that they should receive better service, their rural origins could be used to discredit these demands. For example, on one occasion I dealt with two fussy women customers who carefully inspected coat after coat. One of the women praised my "service attitude" (*fuwu taidu*), noting that (as a foreigner) I was very patient. She even said directly to Big Sister Lin and Little Xiao, "If a customer takes a long time, *you* get annoyed." This comment drew funny looks from Lin and Xiao, and after the women finally left with their purchase Little Xiao came over to me and asked pointedly, "In the United States, do you have the concept of '*nongmin*' [peasant]?"

"What exactly did you mean?" I asked, baffled.

Little Xiao then replied, "In China, you can tell country people from city people." He explained that it was partly about dress, but the differences were also apparent in other ways.

"Were those two women *nongmin*?" I asked, surprised. Little Xiao said yes, noting that it was their pickiness, in part, that gave them away. This explanation left me even more surprised, given that such levels of pickiness—as Chapter 6 will show—were common among Harbin No. X's customers. Rather, it was clear that by labeling these women "peasants" (which they may or may not have been), Little Xiao was discounting their demands for better service.

Indeed, as the presence of rural customers shows, the egalitarian nature of customer-clerk interactions in this "socialist" department store was to some degree class-bounded. It is important to note that the department store itself made few efforts to impose a set of class-recognizing relations upon its workers and customers—service encounters were thus not organized as forms of distinction work. As a result, clerks did not dole out deference to most customers because deference recognizes class or status difference and differentiated entitlements to respect. In most cases, clerks and customers occupied similar socio-economic positions in Harbin society. But when clerks were confronted with customers with whom there *was* a social gap—rural people—the give-and-take of the clerk-customer relation was disrupted. As urbanites, clerks felt distinct from and distinctly elevated above these rural shoppers, and the mutuality of the interaction could be converted into one-sided disdain.

CONCLUSION

Harbin No. X was, in many ways, a "socialist" department store. Managers operated the store by drawing on strategies that focused primarily on the local state, not the local market. On the sales floor, workers sustained a vibrant work culture characterized not only by a politics of authority that critiqued managerial power but also by active assertions of worker authority, professionalism, and skill. The sales floor was also a space of relative parity between customer and salesclerk, and egalitarian service interactions predominated. In a sense, both managers' and workers' cultures served as durable repositories for values and practices linked with social organization under state socialism and the ideology that sought to legitimate it. And while Harbin No. X was far from a static site as workers began to innovate new sales practices (see Chapter 6), the features of work life described in this chapter served to identify the store and its workers, in the minds of Harbin residents, with state socialism and the planned economy.

But in the context of economic reforms and the shift to a market economy, a critical worker consciousness and egalitarian work culture have come unhinged from the larger historical framework that marked them not only as oppositional but even as vanguardist. In China today, a workplace culture that maintains a perceived continuity with the socialist past is marked, and marks itself, as belonging to the past. Like the "straightforward" Polish workers associated with socialism in Elizabeth Dunn's research (1999), Harbin residents frequently described the salesclerks at Harbin No. X as "honest" and "frank" (*laoshi*), characteristics that also marked them as belonging to the simpler, less sophisticated socialist era. In an increasingly marketized society, being *laoshi* also differentiated these working-class clerks from more "modern" and prosperous groups.

In the course of China's economic reforms, certain groups of people, and certain spaces, have been temporalized. Lida Junghans (2001) argues that the terms "plan" and "market" are special distinctions in China that "linguistically capture modes of economic coordination . . . [but] also evoke distinctly temporal categories" (185) with different moral valences. The positive forces of "progress" have, of course, come to be associated with the market. Junghans contends that these temporal distinctions have come to settle on different Chinese bodies, positioning them in an imagined timeframe that also maps their locations in contemporary Chinese society—some advantaged, some disadvantaged.

These temporal values were the raw material for the kinds of distinctions produced in new service settings such as the Sunshine Department Store. Workers like those at Harbin No. X provided the perfect foil against which elite retailers like Sunshine could define themselves as modern and high-class. As the following chapter will show, managers at Sunshine mobilized a "modern" notion of sexualized femininity that both disciplined their young female workforce and distinguished their store from working-class retail settings like Harbin No. X and its middle-aged, women salesclerks.

CHAPTER FOUR

Distinction Work and the
Gendered Production of Class

A glistening structure rising up from Harbin's bustling streets, the Sunshine Department Store dominated a downtown shopping plaza where the city's rich and style-conscious shopped. Inside the luxury department store, the floors were laid with marble and punctuated by mirrored pillars. Like Harbin No. X, Sunshine was constructed in a ring, but here the center formed an atrium into which customers could gaze as they glided up and down on crisscrossing pairs of escalators. Sales areas offering brand name goods were designed in boutique style, and many offered seating at which weary shoppers might rest while clerks tended to their wants.

The goods arrayed across Sunshine's sales floors were the trappings of a lifestyle of wealth and luxury. Imported men's suits and women's cosmetics could be found on the first floor, and a vast selection of stylish domestic and foreign shoes occupied the second. On floor three, swank women's fashions commanded shoppers' attention. But it was on the fourth floor, where I worked, that much of the most luxurious—and most expensive—merchandise was displayed. Extravagant fur coats cost upward of 11,000 yuan (about US$1,300), while nearby customers could browse through another marker of wealth and prestige—sumptuously soft cashmere sweaters. In the lingerie department, set discretely at the back of the floor, one boutique offered custom-made bra-and-panty sets for an eye-popping 900 yuan (over US$100). These goods were clearly not targeted at the average Harbin consumer, who in 2000 reportedly earned only 580 yuan per month (*Statistical Yearbook of Harbin* 2001).

This aura of wealth and privilege was borne upon the bodies of the shoppers who visited the store. Many arrived in stylish fur or fur-trimmed coats. During the winter months, many shoppers' clothing made it clear they had arrived either by private car or taxi; their high-heeled shoes or boots and light-weight or light-colored clothing were no match for Harbin's sub-zero temperatures, brown, slushy winter streets, and crowded, grimy public buses.

Customers' privilege was similarly conveyed through the bodies of Sunshine salesclerks. In the mornings, store workers stood at military-style attention along the isles as customers entered the store to Bizet's theme from "Carmen." Attractive uniforms, youthful women sales-clerks, and attentive, deferential service were all hallmarks of new, elite consumer spaces in urban China.

Service work at the Sunshine Department Store was distinction work. Management in the luxury store saw themselves as situated at the top of a competitive market hierarchy in which they must distinguish themselves in order to attract Harbin's most elite customers. Certainly, the store's luxurious sales floors and expensive merchandise set it apart from proletarian shopping environments like Harbin No. X. But as this chapter demonstrates, the production of organizational distinction at Sunshine relied on a relational organization of service work at the de-partment store. In fact, when I started work as a salesclerk at Sunshine, a store manager stated outright that I would find *his* store much better than Harbin No. X, the state-owned department store I had also stud-ied. He suggested that the undisciplined salespeople at Harbin No. X delivered poor service, whereas Sunshine upheld specific expectations about how clerks treated customers. "You will have to spend a long time at Sunshine to understand the culture here," he added.

Sunshine's distinctive culture was laden with class meanings ex-pressed through the actions and bodies of its sales force. This chap-ter explores two levels of distinction work at Sunshine. At the level of the service organization, managers enforced a class-coded femininity through which Sunshine workers were expected to distinguish them-selves from service workers in less prestigious settings. At Sunshine, a new, naturalized conception of gender combined with the imagery of economic transition to powerfully convey class meanings. The carefully policed bodies and dispositions of Sunshine's uniformed young sales-women distinguished the store from its less exclusive competitors.

At the level of the service interaction, Sunshine culture involved acts of class recognition. In China's newly stratified retail sector, acts of deference performed by salesclerks, and organized by elite department stores, have become visible rituals that recognize customers' class-based claims to esteem and respect. This symbolic recognition of customers' social position and their entitlement to deferential service simultaneously produced the markers of social distinction for both store and customer.

Combined, these two levels of distinction work put Sunshine in a direct dialogue with the city's other retail settings and the work routines found in them. The Sunshine Department Store was recognized by managers, workers, and customers alike through contrasts with what it clearly was *not*. For if Harbin No. X was regarded as a relic from the socialist past, replete with an aging, undisciplined workforce, Sunshine by contrast endeavored to represent a new China populated not by the "masses" but by a newly rich and upwardly mobile class served by an obedient army of attractive young women. Sunshine's management was equally anxious to distinguish both its workforce and its merchandise from the chaotic, morally suspect Underground, the subject of Chapter 5. At Sunshine, discourses of gender, post-socialist transition, and constructions of "good service" converged on the sales floor to delineate the symbolic boundaries of class and status.

Luxury Service and the Market for Social Distinction

As earlier chapters have suggested, distinction work emerges with a competitive market for distinction-seeking customers. The previous chapter argued that because retail outlets and consumer goods were scarce under China's planned economy, customer patronage was secure, and retailers instead directed their organizational energies toward the state and its bureaucratic, distributive hierarchy. At state-owned stores like Harbin No. X, this organizational orientation has persisted well into the reform period. Luxury retailers, by contrast, actively orient themselves to a field of competition in which the wealthiest customers are the prize. High-end retailers lure well-heeled shoppers by offering a shopping environment that affirms claims to privilege and entitlement. The Sunshine Department Store, generally acknowledged by shoppers and retail industry specialists alike as one of Harbin's most exclusive, and probably most successful, department stores, serves as a prime example of how service organizations stake out territory in the emerging class landscape of contemporary China.

SUNSHINE AND THE RISE OF LUXURY RETAIL IN HARBIN

The Sunshine Department Store, as a privately owned-and-operated luxury retailer, was born of China's economic reforms. The store first opened its doors in the early 1990s as a joint venture (*hezuo qiye*) between a local real estate company and a Hong Kong–based retailer. One of the city's first luxury retailers, from the start Sunshine sought to distinguish itself from the dour state-owned stores and surly, proletarian service interactions that once dominated Harbin's shopping environment. The department store explicitly catered to Harbin's wealthiest consumers: in 2000, its target market was the top 3% income bracket in the city (Wang 2001: 11). While a growing number of new department stores encroached on Sunshine's claim to offer the most modern shopping experience in Harbin, Sunshine remained more devoted to city and provincial elites than any other retail setting.

Under the original joint venture agreement, Sunshine's Hong Kong partner had independently operated the first four floors of the store, hiring local managers who were sent to Hong Kong for specialized training. When a conflict between the two sides caused the joint venture to collapse in 1997, the Harbin firm took full control of the store. The majority of the store's Hong Kong–trained managers stayed on, pulling Sunshine through an uncertain period. The store quickly proved successful—so much so that in 2000, Sunshine opened a second branch in the city. By 2004, a third store was operating in yet another city district.

Maintaining an array of exclusive merchandise was fundamental to management's strategy for organizational distinction. Like many high-end department stores in China, Sunshine's business recruitment department (*zhaoshang bu*) made careful decisions about which brands would occupy the sales floors. Offerings ranged from internationally recognized brands to domestic ones, some widely known and others seeking to make a name for themselves. Sales contracts enabled Sunshine to ensure minimum sales levels, and the store quickly ejected the suppliers of poorly selling merchandise from the store. The market research department (*xinxi bu*) conducted regular analyses of sales figures to ensure Sunshine's merchandise enjoyed sufficient popularity with the store's elite customers.[1]

---

[1] The most prestigious products—for example, Christian Dior cosmetics—were usually purchased outright by the store. Most other goods were sold on a *baodi koulii*

The store's reputation as a luxury retailer made it a magnet for merchandisers. Merchandise sold at Sunshine promised a high mark-up, and the scramble among clothing suppliers to gain access to the store reflected the business advantages they believed Sunshine's prestigious reputation could bestow. In 2001–2, when I conducted my research, access to Sunshine's sales floors was in such high demand that the department store could pick and choose among product options. The store maintained a lengthy waiting list of companies, and a distribution agent told me that a fellow distributor had been waiting for over three years to enter the store.

One store manager explained that in general Sunshine only contracted sales space out to large manufacturers or their distribution agents in order to maintain a clear distinction between Sunshine products and those sold in clothing bazaars like The Underground. The manager noted that department stores that opened up sales space to individual merchants (*getihu*)—and here he explicitly named a main competitor—exposed themselves to the threat that their merchandise might also be found in the *geti* clothing bazaar. Rather than stake its reputation on providing the latest fashions, Sunshine supplied its loyal clientele with an array of widely recognized and easily identifiable high-status designer and brand name goods often unavailable elsewhere in city.

Not only did Sunshine offer exclusive merchandise, but managers also believed the store was home to distinctively modern managerial practices. They claimed that the most significant legacy of their connections with Hong Kong could be found in Sunshine's personnel practices, which had propagated a new style of management in Harbin's retail sector. As one manager explained, Sunshine's employment practices sharply distinguished the store from the outdated lifetime employment schemes at state-owned retailers like Harbin No. X. Sunshine hired and retained (or fired) staff based on experience, skill, and performance, well before this practice became common in Harbin. Aside from a few top positions, which were occupied by well-connected elites or expe-

---

basis, by which the supplier would contract for a guaranteed minimum of sales. This meant that a suppler might, for example, guarantee 400,000 yuan minimum sales of its merchandise over a given time frame. The store would be promised a 23–25% cut, and even if actual sales fell below this figure the store would collect its 100,000 yuan. For sales above the contacted minimum, the store would still take a 23–25% cut. More prestigious domestic brands were generally sold on a simple *koulü* basis, with the store taking a cut of sales without requiring a guaranteed minimum.

rienced managers, managerial staff was college-educated, young, and specially trained in business management. All management staff took their work very seriously, eating in the store's employee cafeteria so they could quickly return to their work stations and often discussing work matters as they ate. (At Harbin No. X, managers could frequently be found playing animated card games during their hour-long lunch.) Not only did Sunshine cater to Harbin's most elite customers, but the store's managerial staff was careful to convey that they themselves formed a kind of managerial elite characterized by exceptional levels of professionalism and expertise.

Salesclerks at Sunshine were also hired under a different system from that in place at Harbin No. X, though this had little to do with the store's previous connection with Hong Kong. Rather, on the departure of Sunshine's Hong Kong partner in 1997, the store began adopting distinctively reform-era employment policies. This involved the "factory-in-the-store" retailing model described in Chapter 2, which shifted responsibility for salesclerk wages from the store to merchandise suppliers (see also Hanser 2007). The consequence was that not only did Sunshine salesclerks not enjoy the lifetime "iron rice bowl" still expected by many Harbin No. X workers, but in fact they had no formal employment relationship with the store at all. Instead, potential workers were filtered through the store's personnel department, which maintained a "human resources warehouse" (*rencai ku*) from which they generated lists of potential salesclerks for merchandise suppliers. Suppliers would then select their clerks from these vetted lists, negotiating wages and commissions directly with clerks and sometimes requiring workers to attend company training sessions and sales meetings. At Sunshine, the store set no minimum pre-commission wage, and monthly pay was handed over, in cash, directly from the supplier sales representative to the clerks who worked under him.

Despite the fact that Sunshine had effectively shed the financial costs of its sales force, clerks were still bound to the store and its managers, who continued to exercise great control over their work lives. As discussed below, the store issued uniforms (rented by manufacturers) and set regulations and parameters for service interactions (including standardized greetings, product introductions, and farewells). Top management enforced these standards through the floor managers and their assistants who patrolled the sales areas, helping to resolve difficulties but also monitoring salesclerk performance. Management was committed to "quantifying" (*lianghua*) responsibility in the store, and had plans to issue each salesclerk an individual sales goal. And even though salesclerks had no direct financial relationship with the store itself, they were still subject to fines for misbehavior, which they might be required to pay on the spot. Salesclerks signed a "service contract" with the store, which outlined the store's service expectations, and they attended store-sponsored training classes as well as other meetings and events.

In fact, salesclerks served as one of the department store's key resources in the production of distinction. Despite their seemingly attenuated relationship with the young women staffing Sunshine's sales floors, managers regulated the sales force as carefully as they did the luxury goods arrayed throughout the store. The rest of this chapter will explore the nature of the store's relationship to its workforce and how service work at Sunshine was organized to produce the class meanings appropriate to a luxury retail setting. Workers were integral to the production of those meanings, for only a particular type of woman—young, attractive, and deferential—was suited to staff a department store servicing the upper echelons of Chinese society.

SELLING LUXURY: THE GOAT KING SPECIALTY COUNTER

Cashmere is a true luxury good in China, and genuine domestic demand only emerged, along with China's "new rich" (Buckley 1999; Goodman 1995), over the course of the 1990s. One cashmere company sales representative described it as the "top of the pyramid" of consumer goods. Because its high price tag is widely known, cashmere's *hanjinliang*, or "value content," is substantial, and wearing cashmere is a powerful claim to social status. "People wear cashmere not because they think it looks good, but because it looks expensive," explained Manager Song, a sales manager for Goat King, a leading brand in China's cashmere sweater market.[2] Given its prestige, Goat King had negotiated prime real estate just opposite an escalator that deposited shoppers onto Sunshine's fourth floor. It was here that I took up a post selling sweaters, thanks largely to the diplomatic efforts of Manager Song.

[2] Studies of luxury consumption characterize this as a good or service's "conspicuous price," which can, as the discussion of bargaining below suggests, be distinct from its real price (LaBarbera 1988: 183).

Selling cashmere sweaters at Sunshine. Photo by the author.

As with Harbin No. X, I joined a three-person sales team in Sunshine's Goat King sales area. Zhang Xin, in her mid-20s, was our senior salesclerk, having worked at the store for several years. Married and in the early stages of pregnancy, Zhang expected to leave Sunshine in the spring. Wang Lihua, a single woman in her early 20s, had worked in Goat King's Sunshine sales area the previous winter season; given the high turnover of salesclerks at the store, this made her a veteran salesclerk.[3] Finally, there was Xiao Hong, also single and in her early 20s. She had worked for Goat King in another store, but at Sunshine she was considered a rookie. Both Zhang and Wang earned a base salary of 500 yuan a month, Xiao earned 450 yuan, and the three split a 1% commission on monthly sales. Goat King set this pay arrangement, and a company sales rep handed wages, in cash, directly to the salesclerks once a month. With commissions figured in, wages during peak

[3] Sunshine experienced considerable turnover among sales personnel. The personnel manager I interviewed declined to specify how many positions, on average, the store needed to fill every month, though she acknowledged that turnover was high. She suggested that the average worker might stay two years at the store, though some worked for many years and many worked much shorter stints. She explained that some left to continue their education, while others hoped to start their own (small-scale) retail businesses. Many also left to have children.

months ranged from 1,200 to 1,400 yuan a month. For such respectable wages, these young women labored long hours, rotating three daily shifts (morning, day, and night) with no scheduled rest days.

Because sales areas at Sunshine were organized according to brand, they were domains controlled by both store and merchandise supplier, and as a result Sunshine floor management and Goat King sales representatives were both a daily presence in our salesclerking lives. Floor manager approval was needed for merchandise returns and other routine matters, and the floor manager and her two assistants would regularly inspect sales areas for compliance with store policies and standards. Upper-level store management would make periodic inspections of the store, wearing white cotton gloves to test for dusty surfaces. Goat King sales representatives, on the other hand, supplied us with merchandise and monitored sales. Our main sales rep, Little Wei, would closely supervise Goat King salesclerks, insisting that sweater displays be rearranged to his specifications. A bit like a cross between a bully and a mischievous little boy, Little Wei would bang his hand on the counter when sales were slow and yell at the clerks, "Why don't you sell something!" When in a bad mood, Wei would threaten all sorts of fines (for lateness, for slowness, for bookkeeping mistakes), threats that he usually would forget by the next morning.

It is hard to convey how much anxiety all this close supervision caused me when I first arrived at Sunshine. In contrast to Harbin No. X, I found Sunshine highly regimented, and opportunities for mistakes abounded. A workday at Sunshine began in the dimly lit basement locker room where clerks jockeyed for space as they changed into their uniforms. We would then trudge up cold stairwells to our sales floors. The doors to each floor were briefly unlocked from 8:15 to 8:30 A.M. The doors were again locked between 8:30 and 8:45, when each floor manager held her daily "morning meeting" (*zao hui*) for salesclerks. Because a partial roll call was conducted each morning, locked-out, tardy clerks risked discovery and a fine of 10 yuan. The store opened its doors to customers at nine o'clock.

Following the morning meeting, when store policy changes were announced and workers exhorted to improve sales, clerks would tidy their sales areas and chat with one another. Promptly at 9 A.M., music would broadcast over the store's public address system, and clerks would line up along the aisles, their feet neatly pressed together to form a "Y" and their hands delicately folded. Stern-faced managers would sometimes inspect this "morning greeting" (*zao ying*), and unsuspecting salesclerks who dared to chat with one another across the aisles might find themselves soundly scolded.

Naturally, dealing with customers—introducing merchandise, tracking down desired styles and colors, negotiating discounts, and trying to fend off returns—punctuated the day. This aspect of work at Sunshine will be considered in the context of distinction work later in the chapter. But I found my fellow salesclerks were often preoccupied with other matters that could eclipse the actual selling of merchandise. They would constantly calculate and recalculate daily and monthly sales figures, for example, working out sales commissions in their heads or on paper. They would ceaselessly compare their sales with those of other cashmere brands in the store (something the store strongly encouraged by posting monthly sales rankings on each floor's bulletin board) or other Goat King counters across the city, and they regularly visited neighboring sales areas to try to pry sales figures out of other clerks. In addition, my co-workers engaged in what seemed to be the endless counting of the merchandise in our sales area—sometimes as often as three times in a single day—in order to ensure that not a single sweater had gone missing. Theft-prevention was considered the responsibility of salesclerks, and the cost of a lost or stolen item would be deducted from monthly wages, either collectively, or, if the negligent salesclerk could be identified, individually.

Given that the cost of a sweater was worth a month's wages (or more), the possibility of lost merchandise was a source of great anxiety.[4] On one occasion, Xiao Hong arrived at work looking pale and wan; she explained that she had hardly slept the night before. Her last count of merchandise the evening before had come up one short, and she spent the night worrying about the consequences of a lost sweater. It turned

---

[4] During my time in the Goat King sales area, no sweaters were lost. But the theft of merchandise was a real threat, and while I was at Sunshine a fur coat was stolen from another boutique. The clerks split the cost of the coat, which must have run several thousand yuan. (They were asked to pay the manufacturer for the value of the coat, not the retail price—the latter could represent a mark-up of 50% or more.) News of this theft traveled quickly among salesclerks. By contrast, when a down coat was stolen off a mannequin at Harbin No. X, the involved salesclerk was not fined. When I asked the salesclerk if she would have to pay for the coat, she tossed her head and huffed, "I'd like to see them try!" The coat had been stolen because it was displayed behind a pillar, making it impossible for the clerk to see while working at her counter. As such, she was not deemed responsible for its loss.

out that the miscount resulted from a recording error, not a lost sweater, but sorting out the situation consumed much of my co-workers' energy that day. These fears about stolen merchandise complicated my relations with my co-workers at the Goat King counter. When I first arrived, Zhang Xin and Wang Lihua in particular saw me as a burden and potential liability, fearing that they would be penalized for merchandise I had lost. It was only after I had established myself as trustworthy in this regard that they relaxed with me.

As a result of such tensions, salesclerks at Sunshine were a far less cohesive group than the workers at Harbin No. X, and the various types of "responsibility" and competition on the sales floor resulted in an atomized workforce. High turnover among clerks also meant that there were no extensive and long-standing social networks like those among salesclerks at Harbin No. X. Perhaps the strongest indication of fragmentation among workers, however, was the way in which the threat of fines for a lost item or deductions from one's pay for mistaken discounts led to scapegoating within sales teams. To my indignation it was the exceedingly kind Xiao Hong who, as a newcomer, was the target of such tactics by her co-workers Wang Lihua and Zhang Xin.[5] It was in this tense and competitive environment that management pursued its disciplinary regime.

Organizational Distinction and the Rice Bowl of Youth

As discussed in Chapter 1, conceptions of gender and sexuality have become integral to the organization of elite service work regimes in contemporary China. In particular, essentialized conceptions of gender and sexuality have come to powerfully communicate class distinctions in service settings through imagery associated with China's shift from socialism to a marketized society. Elite service organizations like Sunshine rely upon these new gender norms to choreograph the behaviors and dispositions of their female workforce, in the process distinguishing themselves from other service settings located lower down in the social hierarchy. As Pun Ngai has argued of labor control in China's southern factories, "To construct new capitalist industrial subjects in the work-

---

[5] In one such case, I found my field notes identified the perpetrator of the mistake, but I also knew it was inappropriate to intervene. To my relief, the matter was clarified without my input.

place, the old socialist and rural identities are constantly devalued and downgraded" (1999: 18). This is often done in conspicuously gendered ways, and in the service sector gender becomes a strategic resource for the production of organizational distinction among class-stratified service settings.

At Sunshine, managers implicitly referenced the "rice bowl of youth" imagery as they sought to secure a position at the top of the retailing hierarchy. The good worker was a young, well-disciplined, and attractive woman distinct from both the "blue collar" middle-aged service workers described in the previous chapter and the highly sexualized young women employed in street markets and clothing bazaars, subject of the following chapter. She was, in other words, a woman whose embodied and classed gender performances aided the store and its management in their own bid for distinction in China's retail sector. A "distinctive" workforce was as important as the array of goods for sale.

Managers at Sunshine deployed two forms of control designed to produce and maintain clear symbolic distances between the store's workforce and other women service workers. The first was an intense level of bodily discipline, which was aimed at standardizing bodies, and the second was exposure to what might be called managerial practices of "subjectification," which sought to make workers manage themselves. Here my analysis draws particularly from the work of two sociologists, Pei-Chia Lan and Leslie Salzinger.

From Pei-Chia Lan (2001, 2003) I borrow the concept of "bodily labor" and the idea that employers seek to control not only *physical* labor activities but also the *symbolic* images or messages workers can produce. Lan argues that disciplinary power (Foucault 1995 [1977]) is one means of extracting bodily labor. By deploying a set of practices that locates bodies precisely in space and then dictates, monitors, and coordinates their movements, disciplinary techniques make individual bodies intelligible to power (Foucault 1995: 167). The body that results is a "docile" one, subjected not only to scrutiny and surveillance but also to the forces of normalizing judgment that differentiate individuals from one another by holding them to a standard, "an average to be respected or . . . an optimum towards which one must move" (1995: 183). At Sunshine, the rice bowl of youth served as the disciplinary norm used to measure a woman's value as a worker.

Leslie Salzinger (2003) has termed this relationship between production and gendered meanings "productive femininity," whereby workers are understood, and understand themselves, through notions of femininity that shape both hiring and labor control practices. But as Salzinger points out, productive bodies are not simply docile bodies. The construction of productive femininity involves a process of "subject-making," in which the individual actively shapes the self (Foucault 1988, 1990 [1985]). Indeed, in the workplace, gender, sexuality, and femininity form the basis of regimes of workplace control, which, as Aihwa Ong noted in her study of women factory workers in Malaysia, revolve not only upon direct control of workers' bodies but also upon "the ways young female workers come to see themselves" (1987: 4). In China, studies of women industrial workers (Lee 1998; Rofel 1999; Pun 2005) as well as service workers (Otis 2007) suggest that the deployment of gendered frameworks for worker identities is a key managerial technique, and the ways in which workers take up and craft gendered subjectivities that conform or challenge managerial expectations is central to power struggles and inequality in work settings.

At Sunshine, managers used a seductive image of youthful femininity to encourage workers to become individuals who did not just appear to be, but in fact *were*, good workers and good women. Much like the luxury hotel staff Eileen Otis (2007) studied, workers at Sunshine were invited to recognize in themselves the qualities that management desired, qualities that were cast as a proper and desirable form of femininity. Management's goal was to create a corps of salesclerks who embodied the youthful, obedient beauty that the image of a modern, luxury department store demanded, linking class meanings to configurations of femininity. Below, I explore both the disciplinary and subjectifying processes present in the store.

DISCIPLINE AND THE SALESCLERKING BODY

Store disciplinary routines aimed to control workers' bodies through a norm of youthful femininity that was expressed in rules and regulations focused on appearance, posture, physical deportment, and demeanor.[6] I first encountered the rice-bowl-of-youth norm when, to my surprise, Sunshine's human resources staff applied their standards to

---

[6] These rules applied primarily to salesclerks and not to the considerable numbers of women managers in the store, who dressed in gender-neutral suits and ties.

my own body. They carefully measured my height (1.6 meters required) and scanned my personnel form (high school education required, no previous work experience necessary). The store required workers to be Harbin residents, a key means for barring rural young women from these jobs, and easy to enforce given the large number of applicants.[7] The upper age limit of 25 for entering salesclerks was graciously waived, yet I wondered if the store would have done so had I deviated from the rice-bowl-of-youth norm in more visible ways—if, for example, I had been deemed ugly or fat, or had looked older than age 30, the standard age at which salesclerks were retired from the sales floor.

These basic requirements were expanded upon during the store's initial, pre-work training session. At the class I attended, the instructor devoted over a quarter of her lecture to issues of bodily deportment and conduct, reinforcing the connection between a disciplined body and a worthy body, valued as sufficiently high-class, Sunshine salesclerk material. The instructor did this by labeling incorrect bodily practices disgusting or immature. She produced elaborate descriptions of outrageous salesclerks who had blown snot from their noses directly onto the floor or who had arrived at work in wrinkled or soiled uniforms. These same behaviors were often acceptable in other settings—The Underground, in particular—and are closely associated in the urban mind with rural laborers and the urban working class's less refined segments.

Proper salesclerk behavior was also explicitly linked to proper feminine deportment and disciplined sexuality, highlighted through more examples of "bad" clerk behavior. For example, at one point the instructor suddenly and dramatically performed a woman plucking her eyebrows. "Oooo! Ow! Ei!" she cried, twisting her face with each imagi-

[7] Store personnel managers insisted that a Harbin municipal policy required them to hire women holding Harbin residence permits, or *hukou*. These policies are found in the service sectors of many Chinese cities, especially large ones like Beijing, and are meant to alleviate unemployment pressures among urbanites by protecting them from competition with rural workers. To my bafflement, an official I interviewed at Harbin's labor bureau was adamant that no such regulation required large retailers to hire Harbin residents. And in fact, I was aware of at least a handful of salesclerks at Sunshine who were *not* holders of Harbin *hukou*. All these women had procured their jobs either through the use of social connections (*guanxi*) or through deception, however. They were also all urbanites from smaller cities in Heilongjiang province. As far as I am aware, there were no women of rural origin clerking at Sunshine.

nary pluck. She then informed the class that once a male customer had spotted a salesclerk plucking her eyebrows while at her workstation. The man immediately complained at the service desk. Another example, which illustrated the importance of doing up all the buttons on your uniform, involved a young woman who exposed her chest when bending over, to the delight of some male customers but to her own extreme embarrassment. On another occasion, a salesclerk who bent over instead of demurely crouching down in her short-skirted summer uniform reportedly caused a male customer to exclaim, "That young woman is quite interesting—she's wearing strawberry underwear!" In the latter two cases, the reported male gaze disciplined sexualized female salesclerks through humiliation: Sunshine salesclerks were not "that" kind of girl.

These gender norms were meant to make distinctions among groups of women service workers. The guidelines produced by the instructor suggested that a salesclerk's role was to be overtly feminine and subtly sexual—a configuration that involved an explicit rejection of unappealing older women workers as well as an implicit rejection of hyper-sexualized, gaudy femininity. Store regulations addressing physical appearance sought to purge the store of both. Hair and nails, of a specified short length, were to be natural in color. Eyebrows must be real, not penciled in, and stick-on eyelashes were discouraged by way of a cautionary tale about their dropping off at inappropriate times. The instructor also warned the students against using makeup "in colors that make you look like you've just been beaten up," a not-so-veiled reference to the young women of The Underground. The store, the instructor continued, sought "natural beauty" (*ziran mei*) in its salesclerks (for parallels in China's hotel industry, see Otis 2003, 2007; for a U.S. parallel, Loe 1996).

This so-called natural beauty formed a key aspect of salesclerks' value as workers. The instructor suggested that a loss of "natural beauty"—even if superficial—would render workers unproductive. Both beauty and productivity were defined relationally. For example, the instructor explained that a permanent wave could make a 20-something young woman look like a 40- or 50-year-old matron. "Everyone wants to look at young, beautiful people," the instructor noted. "So what would happen if everyone permed their hair? We'd have a store that looked like it was filled with 40- or 50-year-old women, and who wants to see that?"

Older, state-owned stores, of course, were in fact filled with 40-year-old female salesclerks. The presumption, then, was that *Sunshine's* customers would be scared off by middle-aged salesclerks. In all these cases, restrictions were calculated to maintain an easily visible distinction between Sunshine's workers and women selling merchandise in retail settings serving lower echelons of Harbin society. Workers' carefully policed bodies and their embodied performances of femininity served as a clear conduit for communicating distinctions among retail organizations and, by extension, their customer bases.

PROPER WOMEN, GOOD WORKERS, AND PRODUCTIVE FEMININITY

Bodily discipline, however, was always incomplete. The sheer extent of managerial claims on workers' bodies meant that noncompliance was widespread and frequent. As a result, management engaged in practices that called upon workers to govern their own behavior, not out of fear of managerial reprisals but rather because such behavior accorded with their own sense of self, in the process also distinguishing themselves from undesirable female bodies. Much like the organization of work in the *maquiladoras* in Salzinger's study (2003), Sunshine's management structured the image of a productive worker in accord with a trope of sexualized femininity, such that youth and beauty became the badges of a good salesclerk (see also Pun 2005). As Michel Foucault has noted, sexuality operates as an expansive realm of behavior where individuals construct identities and actively govern themselves (Foucault 1990 [1985]: 6). At Sunshine, a kind of sexualized femininity became the measuring stick by which women workers were evaluated and evaluated themselves, "an ongoing evaluation in which desirability and productivity are indistinguishable" (Salzinger 2003: 67). In this way, store managers were able to enlist workers' active participation in the production of organizational distinction.[8]

One way the store did this was to appeal to workers' sense of them-

---

[8] This kind of ethical focus on the self (Foucault 1988, 1990 [1985]; Rose 1998) finds distinct echoes in China traditional culture and history (Bakken 2000) and is especially apparent in both the political practices and social organization of the Chinese Communist Party (Whyte 1974) as well as in moral education today (Bakken 2000).

selves as stylish, physically attractive young women possessed of the self-discipline necessary to work in a luxury department store. On a number of occasions Floor Manager Lu called for salesclerks to be more "self-conscious" (*zijue*), requiring less supervision and managerial direction. "The point is not to regulate (*guan*) you, but to create a good work environment," she explained. Failure to live up to managerial expectations was cast as a lack of "self-control." Self-consciousness extended into salesclerks' non-work lives as well, especially practices involving care of the feminine body. Before the store opened each morning, management would use the public address system to broadcast store news and short reports, including mini-lectures on subjects such as wintertime skin care (since "all young women are fond of being beautiful [*ai mei*]").

Fulfilling these managerial mandates required workers to devote attention to the sexualized, feminine body. This was dramatically illustrated for me through a set of encounters with a fellow salesclerk. Miao Yun worked at an underwear boutique and stopped to chat with me one morning. While we talked she started to examine my body and placed her hands under my breasts. "You're not wearing a bra?" she exclaimed with surprise. "I am, I am," I insisted, embarrassed. Miao Yun explained that a woman's breasts were not supposed to hang lower than such-and-such a position, otherwise she was suffering from some kind of disorder. She noted that I was drooping a bit and encouraged me to come for a bra fitting. A few days later she stopped by again. To my chagrin, this time she examined my buttocks, warning me that my "flesh is a little loose" (*rou you yi diar song*). "Feel my butt," she offered. "See, mine isn't as soft as yours. Don't Americans worry about this? You should stay fit [*bao jian*]. Sometime I'll give you some tips on how to firm up your butt."

In retrospect, I should not have been surprised at Miao Yun's fixation on another salesclerk's breasts and bottom, for these were the same body parts that were the subject of cautionary tales during salesclerk training. The salesclerk's body was subtly sexualized, obliged to maintain breasts and buttocks in a desirable condition. At the same time, the Sunshine salesclerk must also reflect the level of propriety appropriate for a luxury store, hence the modesty of our neatly buttoned uniforms. Clerks were asked to tread a fine line, and could be reprimanded for replacing the store-issued trousers with their own, either too baggy (and hence dowdy) or too tight (and so too sexy). And often, as with

Miao Yun, young women working in the store adopted this viewpoint as their own (see Pun 1999, 2005 for parallels with young women factory workers).

Ultimately, these distinctions identified the proper kind of young woman to work in the store, rejecting the alternative version of young womanhood exemplified by the young women who worked in Harbin's clothing bazaars. This was a distinction about which management expressed considerable anxiety. During one morning meeting, Manager Lu cautioned salesclerks against leaving the store during their lunch period. Salesclerks had even been spotted in places like The Underground, "doing what, I don't know." (They were, of course, shopping for clothing, since they couldn't possibly afford the goods sold at Sunshine.) Workers were not, the manager added, to leave the building in uniform. Management was as intent on drawing a clear line between its salesclerks and The Underground's unruly hawkers as it was concerned to distinguish its expensive merchandise from the knock-offs sold in such markets.

Perhaps most importantly, workers themselves drew such distinctions. One morning Auntie Chen, a sales manager from Goat King, stopped in, complaining that a salesgirl in The Underground had been rude to her. Auntie Chen exclaimed, "Such a pretty girl, who would guess that such nasty words would come out of her mouth!" Zhang Xin comforted her: "It's not worth getting upset about. The Underground and upstairs [the department store] are just different. Most of the girls [in the bazaar] are from outside the city, the quality [*suzhi*] of the people is of two different levels."

Sunshine's sales floor was recognized by salesclerks themselves as the domain of relatively well-educated, urban young women with the poise and level of civility demanded by such a high-class institution. Sunshine's high prices—and the relatively high wages of its workers—rested in part on the distinction between Sunshine and The Underground, which was often portrayed as tainted by the influence of rural China. Salesclerks like Zhang Xin seized upon distinctions that garnered them an elite position within China's urban working class. It was for this reason that Xiao Hong became very uncomfortable when another store worker asked her where she lived. "Out by the university?" "Beyond that," Xiao Hong said. "By Huafeng road?" "Beyond even that," Xiao Hong answered, her face reddening. Afterward, she explained to me that she did not like to be asked about her address. Her family lived in a village that had been re-zoned from rural to urban in the course of Harbin's economic reforms. Though now a bona fide urban *hukou* holder, Xiao Hong feared her co-workers would look down on her as countrified.

Within the burgeoning urban service sector, salesclerks at Sunshine tended to view themselves as elite. Much like the women data entry clerks that Carla Freeman (2000) studied in Barbados, the "blackcoated" English office clerks in David Lockwood's (1989) research,[9] or even the Cantonese women factory workers in Pun Ngai's (2005) work, Sunshine's salesclerks occupied a curiously intermediate position between more traditional forms of working-class employment and middle-class jobs, and this ambiguous position encouraged them to actively engage with the distinctions Sunshine management cultivated. Their comfortable, clean work environment and smart uniforms not only set them apart from the factory employment young urban women might once have aspired to but also distinguished them from workers in less luxurious service sector venues. Employment at Sunshine was, to some degree, a "Cinderella of occupations" (Benson 1986: 178). At the same time, these young women's wages did not lift them securely above other women workers. As Freeman suggests, the symbolic, if not structural, facets of service work can make class "an embodied identity" that operates through "particular notions of femininity" (2000: 61), carving out hazy spaces of what Lockwood terms "status ambiguity" that fragment social groups. It is critical to remember that this differentiation within the working class was tied to organizational strategies directly linked to the creation and maintenance of spaces of entitlement and privilege for China's new rich.

In the end, managerially enforced discipline was to be buttressed by the appropriate moral and cultural character of its workforce. Both workplace discipline and worker dispositions operated to distinguish the store, through its workers, from other market settings in the city. In an effort to secure its profitable position at the top of the city's retail hierarchy, Sunshine cultivated class distinctions that marked its youthful workforce as a working-class elite, young women whose access to Sunshine jobs ensured them monthly earnings often double those of Harbin No. X workers and Underground sellers. Within the store, the construction of a particular form of sexualized femininity marked Sunshine salesclerks as distinct from both the aging workers in failing

[9] Thanks to Brian Elliot for directing me to Lockwood's study.

state-owned businesses and the morally suspect—and possibly rural—young women in open-air markets and clothing bazaars. The high-class position of Sunshine's customers was to be mirrored by its workers, whose disciplined, obedient performances of sexualized femininity represented China's bid for capitalist modernity.

EXCLUSIVE SERVICE IN A LUXURY DEPARTMENT STORE AND THE PRODUCTION OF CLASS MEANINGS

Sunshine's workforce produced an aura of organizational distinction that was recognized and consumed by customers. But as I have argued in Chapter 1, distinction work operates at two levels, the organizational and the interactional. At the level of service interactions, service work produces social distinctions among *individuals* through salesclerks' acknowledgment of customers' claims to class entitlements. In a newly stratified retail sector, this acknowledgment took the form of acts of deference performed by salesclerks and organized by department stores; deferential service became a visible ritual that recognized customers' class-based claims to esteem and respect.

Deference, Service Work, and the Performance of Class

Deference, Erving Goffman suggested, is a symbolic act conveying "appreciation" (1967: 56). Expressions of asymmetrical deference—where one side defers to the other, and deference is not reciprocated—recognize unequal social positions. Goffman labels such acts "status rituals" that "guarantee that everyone acts appropriately and receives his due" (1967: 55). Service interactions that involve asymmetrical acts of deference become practical enactments of relative social locations, a "doing" of social hierarchy.[10]

Asymmetric deference can be viewed as one way economic and cultural capital (class position) converts into what Bourdieu termed "a capital of recognition" (Bourdieu 1998: 102) or "symbolic capital."

---

[10] My use of the term "deference" makes no assumptions about links between performances of deference and levels of "class consciousness" (see Newby 1979). Deference is a social action that conveys meaning, whether the author of that meaning be the worker herself or the organization that enforces certain patterns of behavior upon her.

Symbolic capital gives individuals and social groups the power to both portray and receive recognition for their way of life as worthy of esteem (Bourdieu 1990: 135). Dominant groups tend to be the recipients of one-sided expressions of deference that both recognize and legitimize their elevated social position.

Existing studies of capitalist societies point to the connections among service interactions, acts of deference, and social class. In *Human Relations in the Restaurant Industry,* for example, William F. Whyte found that waitresses in working-class restaurants, unlike the servers in restaurants serving middle-class diners, were not expected to enact deference to customers (Whyte 1948: 92–93; see also Hall 1993). As one waitress in a "lower-class" restaurant informed Whyte, "In this place the customer is always wrong, and he knows it—God bless him" (Whyte 1946: 142). In service work settings, deferential recognitions of social class also assume highly gendered patterns. Arlie Hochschild's (1983) influential work on service work, *The Managed Heart,* argues that the predominance of women in service jobs means they must publicly perform deference more than men, with the result that women are less respected and command less authority in all public contexts. Hochschild's framework and her concept of emotional labor suggest that acts of deference carried out as a part of service work are expressions of, and help reproduce, both class and gender domination.

Rachel Sherman dubs this class-recognizing aspect of service work "recognition work" (2006). Part of what service workers do, Sherman demonstrates in her study of luxury hotel workers in the United States, is to *recognize* high-class consumers as entitled to luxury service, which is a marker of class privilege. "What appears as recognition of the individual," Sherman notes, "is in fact a recognition of class entitlement" (2003: 273).

It is crucial to remember how deeply invested service organizations like department stores are in these acts of class recognition and the legitimization of class entitlement. As I suggested in Chapter 2, department stores have long been associated with notions of middle- and upper-class respectability and have served as important sites for the production of class distinction in Western societies (Benson 1986; Miller 1981; Zukin 2004). Indeed, service organizations have an interest in choreographing unequal service interactions that recognize customers' claims to elevated class positions and elite social status. In a department store setting, demands for deference are acts of power that both enact and constitute relations of inequality, exerting what Judith Rollins has called a "system-supporting psychological function" (1985: 156). Acts of one-sided deference do not simply reflect symbolic capital and relative class positions; they also reproduce structures of inequality. At Sunshine, deference was an integral part of what the store's salesclerks were expected to produce and what customers expected to consume, in the process delineating new lines of an unequal structure of entitlement in urban China. It is in these interactions that we get a sense of what, to borrow a phrase from Arthur Stinchcombe, "powerful people can get others to do" (1965: 180).

A SPACE OF DISTINCTION

Sunshine not only offered customers an environment of luxury and comfort, the store also engineered an atmosphere of attentive, deferential service as the mark of social distinction. As described above, Sunshine managers closely monitored staff appearance, in part to distinguish the store, through its workers, from competitors. But managers also ensured that the store's workplace disciplinary regime produced the proper markers of class privilege for the store's customers. Strictly regulated uniforms accentuated the distinctions between customer and worker to create a formal environment that clearly delineated staff duties and customer privileges and emphasized gaps between the two (cf. Paules 1991: 135; Benson 1986: 235).

At Sunshine, security officers who policed the store wore green, army-style uniforms, and store management was clad in professional blue suits and gray button-down shirts. Floor sweepers wore crisp white overcoats, a departure from the proletarian blue work smocks that similar workers wore in more modest retail settings. But given the centrality of the service interaction to successful distinction-making, salesclerks' appearances were subject to the most intense regulation.

In addition to strictly monitored uniforms, store regulations standardized everything from hair to jewelry to the color of the soles of one's shoes. At times I felt as though store uniforms made sales staff indistinguishable from one another and almost invisible to customers (until they deemed us useful or necessary), a point exemplified by customers' reactions to me. Despite the anomalous combination of my foreign features and my store uniform, passing shoppers would regularly ignore me even after I had spoken a few polite words to them. In numerous cases, customers were well into an interaction with me before they noticed that I was not Chinese. As a number of scholars of work (Rivas 2003; Rollins 1996) have argued, the "invisibility" of service workers is a sign of their devalued labor and low status. At Sunshine, customers would regularly fail to acknowledge the presence of clerks who stood by attentively.

Likewise, restrictions on salesclerks' physical movements extracted what Judith Rollins (1985: 171), borrowing from Goffman (1967), calls "spatial deference." Clerks were expected to strike certain poses while waiting for customers, and their movement about the sales floor was theoretically limited to trips to storage areas and the toilets. Salesclerks in uniform were barred from sitting while on the sales floor and prohibited from riding store escalators (though management and security were free to do so). Management would monitor compliance with all these rules by circulating the sales floors equipped with walkie-talkies. These restrictions drew a clear line between the entitlements of customers and the constraints on salesclerks.

THE CUSTOMER IS ALWAYS RIGHT

The key opportunity for recognizing customers' class privilege, however, was the service encounter, which was typified by a lack of reciprocity between customer and clerk. Sunshine management went to great lengths to clarify for salesclerks the acceptable parameters for such interactions. In training sessions, future clerks were exhorted to take every precaution possible to avoid angering or offending the customer. Directions should be given with an open hand, not a pointed finger; when taking a drink of water, workers were instructed to turn their back to customers, lest the customer take offense. Crossing one's arms was dismissed as looking uncooperative, and at one point, the instructor dove her hands into her pockets, and asked us, "What kind of feeling does this posture give you?" She remarked that customers, on seeing a clerk introduce merchandise while stuffing her hands in her pockets, would be sure to think, "What on earth! What [lack of] class [*cengci*]!" One's body was not to smell of unpleasant things (smoke, alcohol, onions, garlic), and picking one's nose or ears, sneezing, and even yawning were all dismissed as "dirty." "These things might make you comfortable, but they are unpleasant for those around you. Sales staff should not create feelings of repulsion in customers [*yinqi guke de fan'gan*]," one instructor explained.[11]

The golden rule of salesclerking—never assert yourself with a customer—was reinforced with the iron reality that clerks who did so might lose their jobs. The Sunshine training session I attended began by progressing through a series of parables about how workers' mistakes had caused them to lose their jobs. Workers at Sunshine were keenly aware of the consequences of openly defying a customer, and as a result they felt unable to react to mistreatment or verbal abuse. As Xiao Hong told me after she had endured a customer's tirade in silence, "In ordinary circumstances, I definitely would have lost my temper with him, but in this job you can't. If they yell at you, all you can do is not respond, because if you start to get angry with them then the fault becomes yours."

Deference-extracting work routines were buttressed by "real world" differences between clerks and customers in terms of income, lifestyle, and consumption patterns. As a general rule, clerks could not afford to buy the merchandise they were selling; this was especially true of more expensive merchandise like fur coats, cashmere sweaters, jewelry, and exclusive brand clothing. Even though clerks earned good wages compared to the average city resident, they still inhabited a lower socio-economic class than the customers whose needs they tended.[12] The age difference between the women salesclerks and customers—most customers were in their 40s or 50s—as well as gendered expectations about deference (cf. Hochschild 1983) only served to heighten the gap

[11] Paules (1991) similarly reports prohibitions against "physically necessary acts" in the restaurant she researched, including rules against openly drinking water (132–33; see also Otis 2007). I attended a training session at another prestigious department store in Harbin and found the course content remarkably similar, despite the fact that there were no standardized training materials in use.

[12] Salesclerks' inability to consume the merchandise they sold was apparent in a number of ways, aside from the fact that none of them actually owned or wore cashmere sweaters of their own. Clerks would only contemplate buying a cashmere sweater when specially discounted merchandise was set out, and even then they would try to bargain down the already reduced prices through negotiations with sales reps. Invariably such purchases were for an esteemed family member (e.g. a parent) and not for the clerk herself. Clerks would, however, sometimes "borrow" merchandise—for warmth during a quick trip outside or the cold trip home—establishing their right to these luxury items by virtue of their daily proximity to them.

between worker and customer.[13] Even so, management clearly felt disciplinary measures such as fines and the possibility of being fired were necessary to ensure that the proper roles were adhered to.

Shoppers at Sunshine would freely express their expectations of deferential service, and indeed the store's promises of complete satisfaction encouraged them to do so. Customers exerted a considerable degree of authority over clerks, and some customers would brusquely issue commands and requests. One customer chastised my co-workers by noting "We [as in 'Chinese society'] still haven't realized 'the customer is God' [*guke shi shangdi*]." Another, insulted by Wang Lihua's sullenness when he returned some expensive merchandise (which affected her commission) said to me, "She has a bad attitude, I should report her. It should be warm service [*reqing fuwu*], service with a smile . . . shouldn't it?"

At times, the imbalance between customer and clerk authority took shape as outright fear (on the clerk's part) of the customer. In one instance, Wang Lihua urgently whispered to Xiao Hong to move away from the wallet that a customer had just set down on our sales counter. It was clear from this incident that salesclerks had to take great care in protecting themselves from possible customer accusations of theft or misbehavior, given that clerks had little standing with which to defend themselves against such claims. For this reason, Xiao Hong warned me when I first started working at the store never to carry money in my pockets, because it could be used as evidence of stealing from a customer. According to the store's internal hierarchy, clerks were dispensable, whereas customers were not.

A more subtle reflection of customer authority lay in the supplicating manner in which salesclerks offered suggestions and advice. As Zhang Xin, our most experienced salesclerk, explained to me, offering advice to a customer was a delicate matter that involved reacting to a customer's choice and telling them what they wanted to hear.[14] "So if

[13] We sold both men's and women's sweaters and handled both male and female customers, though women predominated. In my experience, both men and women expected salesclerks to perform deferential service for them.

[14] Lombard (1955: 177) identified a similar pressure in his study of the children's department of an American department store. One salesclerk described this as "guiding" a customer's purchase (*daogou*). "You can't get them to buy something they don't want," she said of Sunshine customers. She contrasted this with The Underground, where she characterized selling as *yougou*, involving the enticement (and deception) of customers. See Chapter 5 for more on perceptions of The Underground as a space of deceptions.

they ask you, 'Do I look stylish in this?' you tell them, 'Yes, you really look stylish in that,' and they go away feeling very good about their purchase." Xiao Hong explained to me that there was not much need to introduce our merchandise to customers. She noted that if you said too much, sometimes customers would get irritated and leave. "Many of them are kind of like experts themselves," knowing what is and is not good cashmere through their experience buying and wearing it, she added. Sometimes customers would even make a show of their expertise, announcing to friends as they entered the sales area, "You don't have to worry about [the quality of] this brand, this is 'Goat King.' It's a famous brand [*mingpai*]."

A very different sort of knowledge hierarchy existed, then, than the one constructed and maintained by workers at Harbin No. X. At Sunshine, clerks were expected to be knowledgeable, but not too expert, about merchandise, lest they challenge a customer's own expertise in the consumption of luxury goods. In some cases, customers would even challenge clerks' knowledge, especially regarding wool quality, brand reputation, and what were and were not the most current styles. In fact, much of the advice clerks dispensed was not about their *own* knowledge of consumption and the merchandise per se, but rather knowledge about how *other* people consumed such things.[15] In this way, Sunshine salesclerks produced a form of deferential service that affirmed customer expectations for class recognition.

THE CONTRADICTIONS OF DISTINCTION WORK

All this made Sunshine a highly regulated but also highly stratified space that did not make all customers feel equally welcome. This was one of the key contradictions of the luxury department store: the space was semi-public and open to all shoppers, yet it clearly catered to, and wished to focus its workers' energies on, the wealthy. Because the store had no way to separate the true store patron from the merely curious (or envious) window shopper, this task fell to the people who had the most direct contract with customers: salesclerks. Given the expensive

---

[15] This could be especially important when customers were purchasing cashmere sweaters as gifts. When clerks became aware that the sweater would be a gift they might probe the customer and then issue advice based on whether the recipient was a government bureaucrat, retired military, businessman, or the wives of one of these.

merchandise and the likelihood that many customers were "just look-ing," workers would try to judge (and then ration) how much effort they would accord each customer (cf. Donovan 1930). Efforts aimed at the "conservation of energy" were greatly exacerbated by store pric-ing and discount policies, which allowed discounts to be somewhat negotiable. Because clerks were discouraged from offering too many discounts, and also because their pay was largely made up of sales commissions, they engaged in a slippery game of judging a customer's ability and willingness to pay. The need to evaluate customers' class status in a luxury setting served as a source of anxiety for shoppers and produced conflicts over whether a class gap existed between "real" customers and any given individual.

The sheer cost of the merchandise was sufficient to make some cus-tomers sweat. The cheapest sweater in our sales area, before discount-ing, was a very simple cashmere crewneck costing 980 yuan; the most expensive item, a cashmere dress-and-jacket set, cost over 4,000 yuan. (Recall that the average monthly wage in Harbin was 580 yuan in 2000.) As a result, from the moment I began working at the store I found my-self sizing up almost every customer who entered our sales area, trying to gauge whether they were capable of purchasing one of our cashmere sweaters. I would regard a customer who went to use the payphone when considering a gift purchase to be much less likely to buy a sweat-er than someone who breezed in equipped with his or her own cellular phone. Customers who exclaimed with shock at the prices were espe-cially safe to ignore.

It was clear that my co-workers engaged in a similar calculus of evaluating customers' class positions. For instance, customers who purchased our brand of sweater from sale carts on the store's first floor were coldly received when they approached Wang Lihua in the fourth floor boutique for gift boxes. People buying sale items were clearly low-er on the customer totem pole, and my co-workers would sometimes even refuse to make eye contact with *tejia* or "sale price" customers. Another time, Zhang Xin managed to convince a customer who had just bought another brand of cashmere sweater to purchase one of ours instead. The customer, claiming that she needed to return the other sweater first, left without a purchase. When Wang Lihua expressed dis-may that the woman had not purchased a sweater immediately, Zhang Xin murmured that the woman was clearly not so rich that she could buy a second sweater without returning the first.

Store policies exacerbated the situation by institutionalizing differential treatment meant to reward moneyed customers, special treatment that some customers wore like a badge of honor. Sunshine granted "VIP" or "gold" cards to customers who spent over 5,000 yuan in a single day or over 10,000 yuan in the course of a year. These customers not only got small rebates on their annual purchases, but they were also granted a 10% discount on every purchase. Customers who were especially well connected could get even greater discounts through store management (a rare practice at Harbin No. X), and "return customers" (*huitou ke*) expected all sorts of special treatment (such as extra discounts and more solicitous service) that less moneyed or inexperienced customers never dared request. Less experienced customers clearly felt uncertain of their status in such an expensive shopping environment. On two occasions customers apologized for being underdressed, one woman even promising to return another day in better clothing so that she could try on a sweater. Most customers seemed fully conscious that they were subjected to class evaluations upon entering Sunshine.

Of course, salesclerks themselves had no intention of treating all customers equally, because customers who were not able or likely to make a purchase were, quite frankly, not worth the effort. Given that we encountered browsers as much as serious shoppers, workers would ration their energies and their deference, devoting considerably more time and effort to customers they thought would actually buy something. This rationing of effort was related to the piece-rate nature of salesclerk's pay, and clerks would disregard customers who seemed clearly unable to purchase a cashmere sweater, judgments usually based on clothing or customer remarks.

The process of evaluating a customer and gauging how much energy to invest in him or her was further complicated by the store's discounting policies and the dynamics of granting discounts, over which salesclerks had some discretionary power. For example, a customer with a VIP card could legitimately be granted a 10% discount (the cut in profits split by Sunshine and the manufacturer), but sometimes the manufacturer was willing to shave another 5% off if it meant the difference between making and not making a sale. Salesclerks also had techniques for granting regular, non-card carrying customers 10% discounts by using "borrowed" gold card numbers. This was a strategy that was only tacitly approved by the store, and so store clerks had to limit the use of such practices to cases where it would make or break a sale. Clerks could offer no discount or a 5% discount if the customer could be convinced that the clerk did not have the authority to grant something larger. The delicate balance between granting and refusing discounts obeyed another logic as well. Each cashmere company wanted to conceal discounting practices from its competitors, both to improve sales and to avoid price wars. It was also necessary to conceal discounts from scouts sent out by other department stores where the manufacturer operated sales areas, because if those stores discovered higher discounts being offered elsewhere they would demand the same discounts be granted by the manufacturer at their store as well. Discounting, then, was fraught with difficulties and required considerable negotiating skills of both clerk and customer. Most importantly, it demanded that clerks make a judgment about a customer's ability and willingness to make a purchase before entering into lengthy, often tedious, price negotiations.

Discount negotiation on a cashmere sweater in the luxury department store always began the same way: the customer would ask "*Da bu da zhe* [Is there a discount]?" The clerk would then size up the customer and either say, "No discount" or "10% off with a VIP card." If the customer remained interested, then the clerk would continue sizing up the customer—how small a discount would be enough? For example, one woman without a VIP card asked if she could get the 10% discount if she bought three sweaters; when Xiao Hong cautiously agreed, the woman thought she had received a special deal, even though it was our regular practice to grant 10% off to customers with and without cards, regardless of the size of the purchase; a three-sweater purchase regularly garnered a 15% discount. When I accidentally revealed this to a customer who *did* have a VIP card, she angrily demanded "But you'll give 10% even without the card . . . what good is the card?" The negotiating of discounts was by far the most nerve-wracking part of the job for me, and I found myself constantly concealing and revealing discounts when I was not supposed to.

In the end, the customers who looked or acted wealthy, and who could convince the salesclerk that they would only buy with a discount, were granted the most generous price reductions. For example, a woman entered our sales area and asked if there was any discount. Zhang Xin, wanting to test the customer's resolve, hesitated a moment and then said, "If you like the style, why not try it on?" The woman repeated herself somewhat sharply: "*Da bu da zhe?*" Zhang Xin responded hurriedly, "10% off with a VIP card." The customer was savvy. "I haven't brought my gold card with me," she said, and continued to pressure for a discount. The smartly dressed customer said that she wanted to buy two sweaters, and that she was leaving the city in just two hours. Zhang Xin then offered the woman a 20% discount, indicating this not verbally but with a calculator.

Given that clerks attempted to woo "real" shoppers while neglecting browsers and pretenders, some customers felt the need to lay active claim to clerk attention and deference. These customers would boldly announce to us that they had purchased cashmere sweaters before, or they would make detailed comments about the previous year's styles. Claims of class status could be delivered icily if the customers felt the clerk had already failed to grant them due deference. A clear example was a pair of customers who wished to exchange one sweater for another. Wang Lihua was initially quite sharp with them, refusing to look at them and demanding to see their receipt. The man then said forcefully that there was no need to be in such a hurry, let the woman first choose the item she was going to switch the sweater for. Wang quickly altered her tone, and in the course of the interaction it became clear that this couple was, despite their casual appearance, quite wealthy. The woman spoke some English to me, and then revealed to Wang that she already possessed some "20 or 30" cashmere sweaters, one of which she was wearing. "I wear them for a while and then I don't like them anymore," she said lightly. The couple had forcefully established themselves worthy of Wang Lihua's attentions without resorting to open conflict.

But a clerk's perceived misreading of a customer's class status was not always settled so peacefully, and this was when clerks might find themselves subject to a barrage of verbal abuse. In a case I observed closely, it was clear from the customer's behavior that he felt both wronged and disrespected. He wanted to exchange a sweater he had purchased over six months before. The sweater had developed a hole, he claimed, and therefore should be replaced; he was from outside Harbin (a source of status anxiety in itself), and this was his second trip to try to resolve the matter. Xiao Hong, acting on manufacturer instructions, told him she could only offer him a repair. The customer exploded.

"I paid more than a thousand yuan for this and all you will do is re-stitch [*bu xian*]? Look at this, what's the difference if you do it or I do?" He then accused Xiao Hong of being insolent with him and told her that he had a mind to report her bad behavior. She hurriedly made a phone call to the manufacturer's representative, who arrived almost immediately. The customer continued to rant until the sales rep led him off to the floor manager's office. After he left, Xiao Hong, whose only response to the abuse heaped on her had been to cower in a corner of the sales area, turned and said to me, "I didn't think I'd been short with him. I'm so angry! [*Qisi wo!*] You can tell how low status this job is when people treat you that way."

That same day, another argument broke out in the neighboring underwear area. A woman customer, feeling the salesclerk had treated her rudely, began yelling angrily at the clerk. This clerk exchanged a few sharp words with the customer, and soon a manager arrived to lead the clerk away. The customer, now being tended to by a different clerk, hollered after the departing worker, "*Sai lian! Sai lian!*" (A local term used to scold misbehaving children). In another case, in the neighboring sales area, a woman customer erupted when the salesclerk informed her that she would not be allowed to exchange an item. The woman suggested the clerk was trying to take advantage of her (and that she was not familiar with store policy) and fetched a manager. A compromise was reached, but as the customer left she yelled, "That salesclerk's attitude is the worst, I tell you!"

In an environment where clerks were constantly engaged in judgments of customers, some customers received less deferential treatment than they believed themselves entitled to claim. Usually a customer outburst, buttressed by store policies, was sufficient to restore recognition of the customer's demands for deference. Customer outbursts were potentially destabilizing in cases where the dissatisfied customer was not a high-class customer but rather a low-class one, revealing the accepted link between extraction of deference and class difference. One last conflict illustrates this. In this instance, the angry customer was a Chinese translator for a group of Russians. He had given a salesclerk money to pay for an item and then claimed she had shorted him 50 yuan on his change. The clerk was lividly angry at this accusation, and the two shouted heatedly at each other. A manager came to deal with the situation, and it became clear that the worker would be forced to pay for the "missing" money. I passed this clerk when I got off work, and she stood sullenly in her sales area, her face burning with anger.

This conflict is instructive because the clerk *did* dare to stand up to the customer. The customer, a translator who worked in a subterranean wholesale market, was of undeniably low class status and worked in a retail setting of equally low status. Such men were almost universally viewed with distaste and suspicion by Harbin residents and even by merchants in the wholesale market itself—there could be no misreading of his social standing. In such a case, then, the clerk felt she could justifiably stand up for herself—and deny the man deference.

The irony is not that the clerk defended herself, but rather that because of store policies she lost the dispute, even against such a suspect character. The presence of a clear gap in social class between worker and customer usually buttresses the legitimacy of service regimes that demand workers to display deference (Gold 1952; Sherman 2003; Whyte 1948). By the same token, unclear status gaps can destabilize performances of deference (Gold 1952; Hochschild 1983; Paules 1991; Rollins 1985; Shamir 1980; Whyte 1948). As Whyte noted in his restaurant study: "If it is hard to be pushed around by those of higher status, it is doubly hard to be pushed around by one's equals or inferiors" (1948: 94; see also Sherman 2003: 204).

The incident described above challenged the service model of granting deference to the customer, because deference was in fact also recognition of the customer's broader class position and not simply of having enough money at the time to make a purchase. Given the distinction-producing nature of service interactions in the store, the irony is not that the clerk defended herself but rather that because of store policies she lost the dispute. Indeed, although explicit store policies appeared to make customer claims to deference reducible to purchasing power, in fact the extraction of deferential service was only sustainable when symbolic or cultural class boundaries were upheld.

Keeping the Rice Bowl Youthful

It is important to note that the class project of Sunshine management, in the shape of a stringent workplace discipline and efforts to get young women to identify personally with the image of an obedient, attractive, and deferential Sunshine salesclerk, was not as airtight as I perhaps have portrayed it to be. Salesclerks did not always find the extraction of deference acceptable or reasonable. Over time, I learned that clerks had numerous strategies aimed at circumventing various rules and regulations. They would wear long coats over their uniforms and then ride the forbidden escalators anyway. They would don a sweater or jacket over their uniform so that they could unobtrusively sit down for a rest, and they were quick to warn one another of an approaching manager. When a co-worker slipped out on a personal errand, we would tell management that she had "gone to the toilet" and would be "right back." Perhaps more tellingly, when a customer was mistreating a salesclerk, other clerks would quietly draw near to watch, a silent but disapproving audience.

Given the fragmented nature of worker relations and Sunshine's large "human talent warehouse" of ready replacements, the salesclerk resistance I observed was limited to these circumspect tactics of concealed rule-breaking.[16] In practice, the deeply gendered nature of workplace control and the feminized subjectivities it called forth could make the line between personal preferences and managerial dictates a fuzzy one (cf. Pun 1999). This is perhaps best illustrated by the main mechanism through which Sunshine was able to keep the rice bowl of youth youthful. As Lisa Rofel (1999) has noted, new "modern" constructions of femininity in China are accompanied by ideas about marriage and women "fulfilling a biological desire for motherhood" (246). At Sunshine, salesclerks would usually marry by their mid-20s (sharing wedding photos was a popular early-morning activity among clerks), and they would very likely leave their sales positions some time afterward to have a baby. When these young women were prepared to re-enter the labor market, most would be over 25 years of age—the age limit for entering salesclerks. Indeed, during an interview the head of the personnel department explained that one of the main reasons workers left Sunshine was to have a child.

In this sense, Sunshine's workers were "maiden workers," like the young women factory workers of whom Ching Kwan Lee (1998) and Pun Ngai (2005) write, expected to eventually marry and leave their jobs. But many of Sunshine's clerks hoped, indeed needed, to continue working once wives and mothers. This was just the position in which my pregnant co-worker Zhang Xin expected to find herself, and one day I discovered her looking over a job application for another, somewhat less prestigious department store in the city with less stringent age restrictions. So in contrast to the silk factory Rofel studied, where women's desires to devote themselves to motherhood could wreak havoc with workplace demands, at Sunshine modern femininity and the preservation of a distinctive service setting were very much in sync.

Conclusion

In this chapter, I have outlined the extensive disciplinary and subject-shaping projects engineered by management at the Sunshine De-

---

[16] Rule-breaking at Sunshine was more akin to James Scott's (1985) notion of "weapons of the weak" than was rule-breaking at Harbin No. X. See Chapter 3, note 13.

partment Store, and in which workers participated, with the ultimate aim of producing social distinctions. Managers at this high-end service organization recognized themselves in a competition for customers who themselves sought distinction in the service setting. In urban China today, the wealthiest customers, and by extension the most elite retailers, practice the most vigorous distinction-making as they stake out their positions at the top of a reconstituted social hierarchy.

The marking of social distinctions, I have shown, occurred at two levels. Managers at Sunshine produced organizational distinction by engaging in a symbolic conversation with other, less prestigious retail settings in the city and identifying their store as modern, high-class, and exclusive by comparison. Managers hired, trained, and monitored their salesclerks' work activities in order to ensure that these clerks successfully distinguished themselves from other service workers. To do so, managers drew upon discourses of gender and post-socialist transition, as class distinctions within the working class and across the broader class hierarchy in urban China are spoken through the "naturalness" both of gender and of the progression from failed socialism to a prosperous and modern capitalist society.

I have also shown that relations between workers and customers in this luxury retail setting were engineered to produce social distinction at the level of the service interaction. Service interactions, dominated by acts of deference and stripped of most forms of reciprocity and mutuality, were recognitions of class difference. Ultimately, the Sunshine Department Store served as a space where class entitlements were enacted—by the wealthy—and class recognition extracted—from working-class salesclerks. The service work regime at Sunshine and the social interactions it structured sat nested in a wider context in which wealthy elites are viewed as the legitimate and appropriate recipients of esteem, respect, and deference. The class meanings produced by distinction work served as a powerful public buttress to broader social inequalities: she (or he) who pays is always right, and always respected. She who serves (and it *is* a she) may not dawdle in the bathroom, must turn away when she takes a sip of water, and must never talk back.

CHAPTER FIVE

The Underground and the
Counter Strategies of Distinction

⌁

Just below the surface of central Harbin stretched the city's largest clothing market: *dixia*, or "The Underground." Stairwells, immediately adjacent to or even inside stores like Sunshine, drew shoppers down into the marketplace, a disorienting subterranean space where artificial light and piped-in air obscured the seasons, weather, and time of day. Its passageways sprouted rooms off to the sides, each lined with counters and the walls clothed in merchandise. Overcrowded tunnels hopelessly confused one's sense of direction. The Underground drew large numbers of shoppers: merchants buying wholesale, local people shopping retail, as well as mere passers-by and passers-through. The wholesale/retail market provided an alternative to the sidewalks above, allowing people to avoid the bitter cold of winter, the stifling heat of summer, and the man-woman-and-child-eating buses that hurtled through busy downtown intersections. With so much to look at, crowds would slow and swell: small pockets of interest would form, small crowds would beget larger ones, and navigable space would shrink. At stairways and narrow points, the crowd sometimes would come to a halt as people struggled to shuffle forward. The Underground was unspeakably crowded almost all of the time.

But the space was, first and foremost, a market. Merchants lining the passageways tantalized passing customers by calling out rock-bottom prices while dangling merchandise in front of them. The market was also heavily populated by roving merchants peddling everything from tissues, gum, and ice cream to boxed lunches, popcorn, and chicken necks. A little old man with a bright red nose (I privately named him

Rudolph) would come through with soymilk every morning (hot) and afternoon (cold), and a cookie-and-bread lady worked the counters in the mornings, saying things like, "The actual price is 3 yuan, but I'll sell it to *you* for 2 yuan 5."

The Underground provided a stark counterpoint to the retail settings overhead. Upon entering the market, shoppers traveled from the realm of closely regulated, uniformed salesclerks to a dramatically different space where young saleswomen spent the days in languorous poses modeling the sexy clothing they offered for sale, their faces thickly painted and eyebrows carefully plucked. Here, shoppers were expected to engage in vigorous bargaining with salespeople and merchants for goods whose quality, origin, and value were never clear. The mixing of people in the market—rural and urban people, locals and "outsiders" (*waidi ren*), respectable city residents and less savory free-market characters—created difficulties in distinguishing who was who and made The Underground a particularly anxious urban space. The Underground harbored the specter of disorder that many residents of China's cities associate with the negative aspects of economic reforms. One of the most common words used to describe the market by local people was *luan*, a term that refers to chaos and confusion and resonates with traditional cultural anxieties (Dutton 1998: 61). By extension, the people working in the market—both the merchants and the young women who were their hired help—were widely perceived as unscrupulous and disruptive people.

The Underground was not economically marginal, yet it occupied a strongly stigmatized location in the city's retail field. Early on, its associations with *getihu*, small private merchants, marked it as a disreputable space. By the early 2000s, however, the market was more closely associated with the large numbers of young women working in the market, young women whose gaudy appearances represented a deviant femininity that simultaneously signified their marketplace's low social position. As Chapter 4 argued, the young women working in The Underground provided Sunshine management with one of the counterpoints against which to cultivate their own, elite corps of saleswomen. The stigma borne by the women of The Underground was both classed and gendered.

However, the women of The Underground were not passively defined by their low position in the city's retail hierarchy. Indeed, in this chapter I argue that The Underground was a space where the distinctions produced in elite service settings that marked the economically successful clothing bazaar as a low-class and even dangerous space were actively challenged by the women who worked there. The Underground was not a chaotic space, but one of contest and confrontation as the saleswomen there sought to re-draw the boundaries demarcated elsewhere. Whereas Harbin's department stores traded in the class-coded currencies of either modern exclusivity (Sunshine) or socialist-era trustworthiness (Harbin No. X), the merchandise found in The Underground had been marked as both cheap and shoddy, the people selling it coarse and devious. But merchants and their sales assistants deconstructed these distinctions daily, not so much challenging the distinctions as claiming for themselves the positive side of such binaries as high quality/cheap, branded/unbranded, and authentic/fake. In the process, these sellers challenged a fundamental set of underlying distinctions: the low class position of the market and the levels of respect to which they were (not) entitled. In this sense, these women engaged in a counter strategy of distinction.

At the same time, the women of The Underground were limited by their resources—both material and cultural—as they disputed their stigma. Ultimately I will show that these challenges were largely contained within a larger symbolic order in which social and class distinctions took on moral valences. In a deep irony, the very resources and practices Underground women used to challenge their ill repute were frequently the same ones that distinguished them from mainstream Harbin society. Just as often as not, attempts to deconstruct symbolic boundaries operated to reinforce them.

CONTESTED VALUES: DECONSTRUCTING
AND RECONSTRUCTING SYMBOLIC BOUNDARIES

In a famous part of his analysis of capitalism, Karl Marx described what he dubbed "commodity fetishism," which endows the material product of human labor with a value seemingly independent of the social relations through which it was produced. Value appears as a relation among *things* (which can be exchanged for, compared with, and evaluated against one another), thereby masking the relation among *people* from which those things emerged as objects of exchange in the first place. Pierre Bourdieu theorized cultural value and social distinction in a very similar way. Writing of France, Bourdieu insisted that "good taste" is perceived to have an independent and even objective existence apart from the people who adopt it. For the upwardly mobile, for example, acquiring "culture" appears as "a 'social promotion' experienced as . . . a process of 'civilization'" governed by universal rules of beauty and aesthetics and not the dynamics of power and social meanings (Bourdieu 1984: 251).

Indeed, the nature of distinctions made within the cultural realm— the "opposition between the 'authentic' and the 'imitation,' 'true' culture and 'popularization'" (Bourdieu 1984: 250)—conceals the role such categories play in mapping out social hierarchies. The worlds of fashion, consumption, and lifestyle all appear to trade in beauty, refinement, and urbanity, not hierarchy and power. But there is no refinement and urbanity without their opposites: the vulgar and coarse. Much as physical commodities and their values are dissociated from the human labor that produced them, the symbolic values coded in the form of cultural distinctions appear to be independent of the social relations that give them meaning.

Markets, of course, are places where people buy *things*, and interactions between sellers and buyers in The Underground focused on the value, quality, and authenticity of the merchandise for sale. Shoppers characterized the clothing sold in the market as cheap knock-offs, the poor relatives of the authentic, brand name goods displayed on department store sales floors. But The Underground was a site not simply of economic but also of symbolic distinctions and struggles. In the course of sales interactions, shoppers not only expressed negative perceptions of The Underground's merchandise; they also produced a parallel and highly gendered portrayal of the young women working in the marketplace as cheap, low-class, and disreputable. The distinctions between marketplaces and the goods they offered for sale were, at heart, equally distinctions among people in those spaces and their place in the city's social and moral hierarchy.

Yet The Underground's saleswomen reinterpreted these accepted wisdoms, up-ending the distinctions cultivated by shoppers as well as by elite retailers and department stores. In The Underground, I found practices that challenged and then re-set symbolic boundaries. The distinctions among goods and among people made in department store settings, Underground women asserted, were simply false.

In this way, sales activities in The Underground fueled the distinction-making activities in other retail settings in the city, and the symbolic distinctions carefully produced in elite settings like Sunshine became subject to tampering. Indeed, as Bourdieu pointed out, "The dominated, in any social universe, can always exert a certain force" (Bourdieu and Wacquant 1992: 80). Within a larger field of distinction-making, The Underground served as a space where the idioms of distinction were deployed, but to confound existing divisions rather than to uphold them. The sales practices of The Underground women were truly a counter strategy.

Nevertheless, at the same time that merchants and saleswomen in The Underground asserted the false nature of distinctions applied to their wares and to themselves, they simultaneously invested in the class-inflected field of cultural distinctions itself. They attempted to redraw boundaries, not do away with them. If we return to the concept of "field," we might say that the women sellers of the clothing bazaar were still engaged in the game, they just were not playing by all the rules. In fact, much as Bourdieu would suggest, the very participation of dominated groups in "the game" and their engagement in these cultural, symbolic struggles provides the expressions of "popular," "low," "vulgar," and "common" against which elite culture is necessarily defined (1984: 178–79, 251). For while saleswomen in The Underground could at times credibly threaten the distinctions made between the merchandise found in the *geti* market and that sold, at a considerable mark-up, in department stores and boutiques, their counter strategy foundered upon the deeper and more profound distinctions made among people.

It was, ultimately, these women's attempts to assert their personal dignity and claims to respect that helped reproduce the boundaries between the civilized department store and the chaotic clothing bazaar. The very cultural repertoire saleswomen drew upon in the course of interactions with shoppers—their strong language, physical assertiveness, and unapologetic pursuit of profit—simply reinforced their status as marginal people. In a marketplace organized around the buying and selling of *things*, saleswomen's unselfconscious attempts to assert their dignity as *persons* were much less successful than the claims these women made about the goods for sale.

GENDER, CLASS, AND THE UNDERGROUND
IN THE RETAIL FIELD

The Underground occupied a peculiar location within the field of retailers in Harbin. It was a reform-era space that was simultaneously perceived as a backward, low-grade form of capitalism. It was a successful marketplace, generating profits for merchants and market management companies (as well as tax revenues for the local state and wages for hired help), but at the same time it was an indisputably low-status social space associated with low-class people and cheap merchandise. It was also a deeply gendered marketplace where the predominantly women sellers were viewed as human barometers of the low cultural and moral levels in The Underground.

Down Under: The Rise of a Lowly Market

Much like the Sunshine Department Store, The Underground was a product of market reforms. The large, subterranean marketplace stood as a powerful example of the dramatic changes the reform era has wrought upon China's urban landscape, both physical and social. The tunnels were originally constructed as an air raid shelter in the 1960s, when China's relations with the Soviet Union, close neighbor to the north, turned sour. Once a symbol of the country's willingness to go it alone, even within the communist world, in the 1980s the tunnels were penetrated by newly unleashed market forces, and the shelter became home to a clothing market. In 1988, Harbin's first "underground commercial street" opened for business in the converted passageways, with over 1,000 private clothing merchants, or *getihu*, renting counter space from the state-owned management company in charge of the market (*Harbin City Almanac* 1996: 55).

The marketplace proved so successful, generating rental fees for the management company and hefty profits for merchants, that it expanded rapidly through the 1990s and early 2000s, ultimately stretching from a central shopping district all the way down to the city's main railway station, over three kilometers in all. By 2002, the number of rented sales counters and stalls approached 10,000. One informant explained that the section of The Underground where he had worked as manager had produced "100 one-million-yuan" counters—that is, one hundred merchants individually accumulating 1 million yuan in as-

A sales room in The Underground. Photo by the author.

sets—between the boom years of 1993 and 1996.[1] Over time, multiple state-owned and joint venture enterprises got in on the business, and what appeared to be a continuous marketplace housing thousands of small retail and wholesale businesses was in fact developed and run by over half a dozen separate management companies. These management companies gave their individual markets such grand names as "World Trade Center" and "Gold Street." Altogether, the subterranean complex was popularly known simply as *dixia*, "The Underground."

The basic organization of business in the market had not changed dramatically over the years, although with the market's economic success the cost of renting space had risen considerably. Merchants, licensed by the local branch of the Bureau of Industry and Commerce (*gongshang ju*), signed rental contracts for counter space with the management enterprise running their portion of the market. One informant put the daily cost of operating a counter at only 30 or 35 yuan in 1992. In 2002, with

---

[1] Part of Deng Xiaoping's official political line on economic reforms was that "some get rich first" in order to pull the rest of the country into prosperity (Schell 1984: 13–14).

increased rents and growing competition for counters, the cost of maintaining a newly rented counter had risen to at least 200 yuan per day.[2] Long-time merchants in the market usually rented their counters directly from the property management company in charge of their market, their daily operating cost often just over 100 yuan. Newer entrants to The Underground usually rented their counters from merchants in possession of long-term rental contracts (often of 10–15 years), who served as intermediary landlords, charging high rents and paying low. Because of these and other factors, the "standard" cost of running a counter space in the clothing bazaar varied greatly from merchant to merchant.[3]

There was also a huge range of profitability among merchants, some making steady profits, well into the tens or even hundreds of thousands of yuan annually, others barely scraping by. Given the stiff and growing competition in the market, one experienced merchant estimated that only about 30% of the merchants in The Underground were earning profits beyond their own cost of living.[4] Yet when empty counters came up for rent, vacated by unsuccessful merchants, they were quickly scooped up by others looking for a way into the money-making of The Underground.

The daily cost of maintaining a counter included the expense of pro-

[2] Informants based these estimates on averaged rent, fees, taxes, and merchandising costs.

[3] Renting a counter directly from the management company usually meant a lower rent but involved a considerable initial outlay of money: a deposit of around 10,000 yuan and upward of 200,000 yuan to purchase direct rental rights. In the early days of the market, before its profitability was clear, direct rental of a counter was much cheaper, and contracts were usually signed for 10 to 15 years at fixed rents. By 2002, most of the new merchants entering the market did not have the capital to purchase outright rental rights to counter space, instead paying the standard deposit plus a 3,000 yuan fee to the management company in order to rent from another merchant. All merchants renting counter space also paid rent, monthly market fees (including electricity bills), and fees to the local Industry and Commerce office as well as national and local taxes. Rental costs also varied by the location of a counter in the market and within a room; two adjoining counters were more expensive to rent than two separate ones. Taxes, nominally set somewhere between 4% and 6%, were often individually negotiated and varied widely. Nonstandardized accounting practices meant it was virtually impossible for tax collectors to know the true incomes of *geti* merchants.

[4] When I returned to the room where I first conducted observations over two years later, only three of the original merchants were still conducting business there. The others had either gone out of business or moved elsewhere, presumably to lower-rent locations.

curing merchandise. In this regard, The Underground was a model of just-in-time inventories, largely due to a lack of capital. The majority of merchants had a partner, often but not always a relative or family member, stationed in the southern city of Guangzhou, where they purchased goods from large wholesale clothing markets.[5] In some cases, goods were purchased in small quantities—five of one item, ten of another—and airmailed almost daily to Harbin. This allowed merchants to be extremely sensitive to customer demands and avoid the stockpiling of unsalable goods. Younger merchants tended to rely most heavily on this approach, in part because it required a smaller initial investment to purchase stock. Other merchants received somewhat larger shipments from their buying partner on a weekly basis. The most established, usually older, merchants did not deal with Guangzhou wholesale markets at all, instead selling factory-direct for factories with whom they had established close ties over the years. A fourth strategy involved selling clothing produced locally but usually copied from Guangzhou styles, a practice I will discuss in more detail below. In all these cases merchants were selling the standard fare of The Underground: inexpensive but fashionable women's clothing.

The Underground itself served as both a wholesale and a retail market. Generally speaking, merchants made more money off of their wholesale businesses, so in many ways they catered more to their wholesale "clients" (*kehu*). Wholesale buyers, though predominantly women, were nevertheless various: some were rural merchants buying for village shops and markets, others were from cities and towns elsewhere in Heilongjiang province, and still others were based in Harbin itself, selling from fashionable boutiques or stalls in clothing markets scattered about the city. Specific sections of the market catered to different clientele, with cheaper items targeted at rural wholesale buyers and more expensive goods intended for Harbin boutique proprietors. In general, wholesale buyers in Harbin were merchants without the resources or the sales volume to buy from Guangzhou directly. The relatively small amounts of capital commanded by both sellers and wholesale buyers in The Underground was one reason many in Harbin, especially people doing business in large retail settings, considered the bazaar an "early" or "low" stage of economic development.

---

[5] The Pearl River Delta region in Guangdong province, where Guangzhou is located, has become China's center of clothing manufacture and light industry (Lee 1998; Hsing 1998).

Retail customers were mostly local residents, be they Harbin natives or recent migrants to the city. Teenaged girls of all backgrounds flocked to the market, along with young and middle-aged women of the salaried classes (working class and some professional). The Underground was also considered a sightseeing stop for visitors to the city, especially for those from smaller cities and towns, the market being known for its stylish merchandise and low prices. Two groups, however, were noticeably absent in the crush of people populating The Underground: the elderly, and elite customers of the type who possessed Sunshine VIP cards and purchased cashmere sweaters. Elderly shoppers often felt ill-at-ease in the bargain-hard environment that did not cater to their modest tastes. As one Underground merchant explained to me, "We never like to sell to old ladies. They touch and rub the merchandise, hem and haw and look for half the day, but they never buy!" For the rich, who simply did not need to bother with the hassle, there was little to attract them to The Underground. The one time I did recognize a Sunshine customer in The Underground—and she recognized me—she expressed concern to find me rubbing elbows with the disreputable people who worked in the market. Like the inexpensive and frequently poor quality goods for sale in The Underground, the merchants and sales assistants there were regarded as dubious characters by Harbin residents.

Gender, Class, and Market Stigma

Many of the people populating Harbin's Underground—ranging from merchants to hired helpers to customers—were marked in the popular, urban mindset as "distinct." Merchants were viewed as unscrupulous and dishonest. Young women hired to sell merchandise were understood to be uncultured and morally deviant. Other sundry people working in the market, such as day laborers hauling large packages, translators for Russian visitors, roving merchants selling non-clothing goods in the market, and even many of the customers, were likewise viewed as questionable, untrustworthy, and slightly dangerous elements in the urban landscape. Despite The Underground's economic vibrancy, it was perceived as a socially and morally marginal space occupied by disreputable people, locating the clothing bazaar low in the symbolic hierarchy of Harbin retailers.

This became especially clear to me the winter I worked at Sunshine. The summer before, I had spent time down in The Underground, and on one occasion I had made the acquaintance of a scruffy man who worked as a translator for Russian merchants shopping in the market. To my surprise, this same man would regularly take a spin through Sunshine—the store was open to the public, after all—and whenever he spotted me in uniform, he would stop to chat. Often, the translator was slightly drunk, and he was sometimes accompanied by a tipsy, red-faced friend. (He was also friends with the translator, described in Chapter 4, who accused a Sunshine salesclerk of stealing 50 yuan.) His presence in the Goat King sales area made me intensely uncomfortable, in part because my co-workers were so obviously repulsed by him. I was equally afraid he would scare away Goat King customers. On one occasion, my fellow clerks at Sunshine had me hide in another sales area when we spotted him.

But in The Underground, this man was a normal presence. When I returned to The Underground after my stint at Sunshine, I again ran into this translator, this time in the space where I was conducting observations, Room 28. Here, he was not shunned; merchants would chat with him about happenings in the market and discuss changes to The Underground over time. Whereas at Sunshine this man had been a walking symbol of the clothing bazaar's lowly status, in The Underground he was just another market personality.

It is perhaps unsurprising that, populated by small, independent merchants, the market was a suspect space. Throughout the early years of reforms, *getihu* were viewed with great suspicion by most of China's urban residents (Schell 1984: 20–21; Bruun 1993: 47). These attitudes meshed with more traditional prejudice against merchants in China (Mann 1987) and a negative discourse about wealth during the 1980s (Anagnost 1989; for a post-Soviet parallel, see Heyat 2002). Studies of *getihu* in the late 1980s found that they were socially marginalized and viewed as low status, in part because many were previously unemployed but also because, as private merchants, they existed outside the state's work unit system (Hershkovitz 1985; Gold 1989; Bruun 1993; Young 1995; see also Veeck 2000). In Harbin in the early 2000s, small-scale merchants continued to be objects of suspicion despite or perhaps even because of the explosion of private entrepreneurship in the city.[6] Friends and

---

[6] Through the course of the 1990s the status of private business people rose considerably (Davis 1999), in part due to an influx of high-status individuals, who had greater access to capital, higher levels of technical knowledge, and better social networks, into the private sector (Buckley 1999; Goodman 1995).

acquaintances in Harbin would frequently assail me with stories about unscrupulous price gouging by *getihu*, whom they perceived as merciless in the pursuit of profits. One elderly couple plied me with such a story one night over dinner, describing in detail an outrageous clothing merchant who asked 260 yuan for a coat that eventually sold for only 100. This was the new social reality of the *geti* marketplace, the couple warned me, a social reality exemplified by The Underground.[7]

Increasingly, however, The Underground was closely associated with the large numbers of young women working in the market who now had become emblematic of the market's disreputable aura. The more established merchants in the market were mostly middle-aged men and women, sometimes people who had never belonged to a work unit but just as frequently former state-sector workers who had been laid off over the past ten or fifteen years or who had left their secure jobs in search of better income.[8] But recent years had seen an influx of a new category of merchants into the market: young urban women, often as young as their early 20s, usually with limited levels of education but with sufficient family resources to set up a small business in The Underground. To the average shopper, these women were virtually indistinguishable from the much larger group of young women hired as sales hands and gofers.

Indeed, the majority of people actually selling merchandise in the marketplace were young women working as hired help. These women worked very long hours—usually from 6:45 A.M. until 4 or 5 P.M., often without any rest days—for about 600 yuan a month. They received

[7] Ann Veeck (2000) describes shoppers in Nanjing food markets in the late 1990s who brought their own scales to the market, so deep was their distrust of private, and in this case often rural, vendors. See Chapter 6 for a more extensive discussion of the contemporary phenomenon of distrust in Chinese market settings.

[8] Circumstance had often pushed them out of their work units early on in reforms: One merchant I came to know well had suffered an injury at the state-owned printing factory where he had worked. When his superiors were unable to find work he could perform, he began selling small household items from a cloth spread across the ground in one of the city's early free markets. As he gradually accumulated capital, he progressed from a cloth to a bicycle cart to, eventually, two counter spaces in The Underground, which he supplied with goods produced in a small clothing factory he also owned. Although he was one of the most successful merchants I came to know at the market, many others in my "room" and elsewhere in the market were former state workers who had gradually accumulated sufficient capital to go into business. Some were barely scraping by, but many were husband-wife or family teams able to support a number of people.

"Underground" women. Photo by the author.

no benefits with these jobs, no sales commissions, no bonuses. During the winter months, these workers hardly ever saw the sun, descending into the market before sunrise and emerging after sundown. The food vendors who circulated through the market ensured that salespeople would not need to leave their counter areas in the course of the day, even to eat.

Collectively, these young women had come to represent the market and its difference from the more formal and higher-status shopping spaces located above their heads. As discussed in Chapters 1 and 4, gender formulations are fundamentally linked to other distinctions (like class), and the young women of The Underground served as a crucial foil against which Sunshine workers were expected to distinguish themselves. Both Sherry Ortner (1991) and Julie Bettie (2003) have argued that working-class performances of femininity are frequently interpreted as natural expressions of sexuality that reflect "a difference of sexual morality between 'good girls' and 'bad girls'" (Bettie 2003: 93). I witnessed a similar phenomenon in The Underground, where the women selling merchandise in the clothing bazaar performed a hyper-sexualized femininity that linked them with the moral deviance of the unregulated marketplace and the lack of culture associated with rural people. As a result, the behavior and appearances of young saleswomen served as a powerful way of identifying these women's, and their marketplace's, low class location.

Sex Under the City

In The Underground, the focus on women's bodies reached new extremes, in part because the young saleswomen modeled their wares, clothing renowned for its skimpiness and sex appeal. My first day at the market, I found my host, Xiao Li, dressed to sell: she wore a sleeveless top she was selling, paired with tight jeans and a pair of red suede pumps with gold spike heels. Xiao Li changed outfits twice that day, switching her black top for a white one and then exchanging that one for a red lacy top, which she sold right off her back. In contrast to the "natural beauty" mandated by Sunshine store regulations, in the clothing bazaar young women colored their eyelids bright purple or lime green, and whenever there was a lull in business they began touching up mascara, reapplying lipstick, or redoing hair. In the mornings used cotton swabs littered the market floor, testament to daily cosmetic rituals.

These gendered performances were subtly translated into class meanings. Many Harbin residents I spoke with viewed the gaudy appearances of the young women who sold clothing in The Underground as markers of morally questionable character and low social position. This point was clearly illustrated for me during a conversation with a teenaged girl and her mother. The girl, Wang Juan, expressed her disdain for the young women working in the underground market. She asked me, "Have you noticed how much makeup they wear? Really, really thick!" She added that many of those young women were "people who've given up school . . . there isn't much else they can do." Her mother agreed, adding: "Those girls lead a bad lifestyle, all they want to do is fool around [*war*]. After they get off work they go out to party, dance, whatever, out until who knows what hour." Here, highly gendered class distinctions were shored up by morally inflected symbolic boundaries (cf. Lamont 1992, 2000).

A sales manager from a cashmere sweater company even suggested to me that working in The Underground could taint a young woman permanently. He told me that if a young woman had previously worked in the clothing bazaar he would not allow her to staff his department store sales areas. He explained that such women would be unwilling to "stay put" and would import bad habits from the market into the department store, especially the use of "uncivilized language" (*bu wen-ming hua*).[9] Indeed, many Harbin residents associated Underground women with the uncultured or morally suspect behaviors found in the market, such as shouting, swearing, and the angry verbal exchanges that were a daily occurrence there.[10] These market women dropped neatly into a popular discourse on *suzhi*, or individual "quality" (Yan 2003; Woronov 2004) that identified them as *without* quality, an issue I will return to below.

The young women working in The Underground were widely perceived as deceptive or "false" (*xu*), both within the market and by those outside. Customers claimed these women had many *shuofa*, crafty ways of speaking meant to deceive unwitting shoppers. Many merchants did not trust these young women either, spending all day at their counters in order to ensure that their hired help did not "skim" (*lao*) money off the top of the day's earnings. People working in The Underground generally accepted that the marketplace was not a space where one could afford to be honest and straightforward, and even the young women hired to work there regarded one another with suspicion. Mei, a young woman in her late 20s whom I came to know well, explained: "There is

---

[9] This concern about the lack of culture and rootlessness of young women in The Underground parallels wider discourses about young migrant women traveling to China's cities in search of work. Yan Hairong (2003) reports a similar worry that young rural women hired to work as domestic workers in private households will not "stay put," a concern cast in the idiom of low personal "quality." Zhang Li (2001) describes how urban distrust of rural migrants is tied to long-standing Chinese cultural concerns about the instability and dangers of rootless and mobile populations (see also Dutton 1998). In Harbin, newspaper reports about outdoor markets—largely the purview of rural merchants selling produce—portrayed these spaces as disorderly, dirty, and uncivilized. For example, "Liaohe Residential Area becomes a big market" (*Liaohe xiaoqu cheng le da shichang*), *Harbin New Evening News*, Oct. 20, 2001, p. 17; and "Street market crowds into residential area" (*Malu shichang jijin le xiaoqu*), *Harbin New Evening News*, April 5, 2002, p. 4.

[10] Reports appearing in local Harbin newspapers also suggested that the market was a chaotic, even dangerous, place. For example, "Two Stolen Bags in One Day at Jindi Market" (*Jindi shangcheng yitian liang qi lingbao an*), *Harbin Life Daily*, Nov. 11, 2001, p. 6.

so much false (*xujia*) stuff at the market, often it is only when you are with your family that you can be real."

Even more problematic for urban residents was the blurring of distinctions between locals and people from "outside" (*waidi ren*). To my surprise, most people were unable to say for sure who around them was or was not from Harbin. As one saleswoman explained, people from outside the city quickly learn to talk and behave like Harbin people, and then one could no longer tell the difference. While many of these women were Harbin natives—in all my time in the market I only met one young woman who admitted that she came from outside the city—many others came from smaller cities, towns, and rural areas.[11]

Portrayals of the young women working in The Underground as bad women were in fact depictions about a segment of the urban working class and rural migrant women with relatively little chance for upward mobility. These young women usually had only middle school education, a level of achievement one young saleswoman in the market described as "useless." They frequently came from families with few economic and social resources, their parents either members of Harbin's swelling numbers of laid-off state sector workers or rural farmers. All these women lacked the educational credentials or social resources to pursue better employment elsewhere.

The often unspoken association of The Underground with rural China evoked a popular discourse that connects cities with proper femininity and labels rural women as unsophisticated, unfeminine, and unscrupulous, traits "revealed by their bodily features and fashion tastes" (Lei 2003: 619; see also Otis 2003; Pun 1999, 2003; and Yan 2003). While young women working in The Underground were not perceived to have *rural* fashion sense, their deviant femininity was similarly manifest

[11] In this regard, The Underground was different from the garment markets described by Zhang (2001) and Solinger (1999), who both found that migrants dominated this economic niche in other cities. Both Zhang and Solinger describe high percentages of migrant merchants in Beijing. Zhang, however, was looking at migrant families engaged in household production and marketing of clothing. In Harbin, locals dominated *geti* clothing markets, and even in a shoe wholesale market I observed, "outsiders" were usually still people from Heilongjiang, just not Harbin proper. I suspect migrants likely dominated sales of other types of goods in Harbin—buttons, for example, or dishware—especially in cases where domestic production is concentrated in a particular region of China (Solinger 1999: 229). It is also possible that Harbin's sluggish economy and high rates of unemployment made its clothing markets less appealing to non-local merchants.

through their appearances. Likewise, rural migrants are a marginalized group in China's cities, often denied the rights and privileges of officially recognized urban residents and viewed by urbanites as a source of instability and crime (Solinger 1999; Zhang 2001). All this is part of a broader public discourse on development and individual "quality" in urban China that differentiates groups of people, classifying rural people (especially young women migrant workers) as backward and lacking cultural value (Anagnost 2004; Murphy 2004; Woronov 2004; Yan 2003). In Harbin, The Underground was associated with both unruly urban women and uncouth rural ones.

At times, the clothing bazaar was even portrayed as representing a backward, almost primitive form of capitalism. The small-scale businesses in the market and the copy-cat form of competition they engaged in (more on this below) caused people working in large businesses to characterize the market as a "low" economic form. They distinguished this *geti* environment from more reputable—and more "advanced"— private firms (*siying gongsi*, literally "privately run companies" and now sometimes called, more euphemistically, *minying* or "citizen-operated"), like Sunshine. Much as temporal distinctions pushed Harbin No. X and its workers back into a socialist past (Chapter 3), The Underground was pushed backward in the evolutionary time of capitalism. In this way, class distinctions were understood through a framework of post-socialist transition not just to capitalism but a particular, *modern* version of capitalism.

Constructions of gender held equally powerful connections to class distinctions. In this marketplace both serving and employing rural people and the lower echelons of urban society, the undisciplined, hyper-sexualized bodies of Underground saleswomen came to represent both unregulated capitalism and a low class position. Class distinctions lurked just below the surface of gender ones, distinctions that were utilized by both elite retailers like Sunshine, as the previous chapter has shown, and working-class salesclerks like those at Harbin No. X, as the next chapter reveals. The saleswomen in The Underground were, however, active participants in this web of distinction-making, practicing counter strategies of distinction that helped drive the distinction practices in other retail settings.

DISPUTED BOUNDARIES AND COUNTER
STRATEGIES OF DISTINCTION

The difficulty of making firm distinctions was, in many ways, part of the proverbial fabric of The Underground. I have outlined above how the market was a stigmatized space in the retailing hierarchy in Harbin, and the market, its people, and their merchandise were all marked as low-class. This lack of symbolic capital also shaped the selling practices and social organization of the market, causing merchants to mobilize market strategies that destabilized the distinctions between The Underground and other, more elevated retail settings. In a sense, The Underground served as a theater for counter performances of distinction, a space where merchants and their workers sallied against the symbolic distinctions engineered at the Sunshine Department Store (Chapter 4) and those improvised at Harbin No. X (Chapter 6). The marketplace was a "theater" in the dual sense used by Robin Kelley (1994) in his study of black working-class resistance in the United States. The Underground was simultaneously a dramatic "theater" where symbolic boundaries were performed as well as a kind of military "theater," a site of conflict between buyers and sellers who struggled over cultural meanings. The Underground served as a space where the idioms of distinction were deployed, but to confound accepted boundaries rather than to uphold them.

Room 28, Counter 4

My home in The Underground was Room 28, Counter 4, where a friend of a friend deposited me late one spring morning. My host was a young woman in her early 20s named Xiao Li. In many ways, Xiao Li was exemplary of the young women who worked in the market—she was young, sharp with customers, and she dressed in the tight and often revealing fashions that she sold from her counter. An important difference, however, was that Xiao Li was her own boss and not hired help. She ran her counter jointly with her boyfriend, stationed down in Guangzhou, and two friends, a pair of sisters named Wang Fei and Wang Xia. Xiao Li, a Harbin native, had not performed well in school and so had not continued into high school. With her parents' help, she and her boyfriend first opened a clothing counter in another Harbin market. Xiao Li's partners, Wang Fei and Wang Xia, also from Harbin, both got their starts in The Underground by working as hired sales help. The counter in Room 28 was a new collective venture among the four. As the weeks wore on, however, I realized that the business was not proving to be a financially successful one, in part due to the group's lack of business experience and contacts. But Xiao Li felt she had few other options, and at times she seemed to feel trapped in the market. "I'm tired of this lifestyle," she sighed to me late one afternoon, "but if you don't keep studying then you have to get busy earning [money]."

There were four counters down the sides of each room and three across the back, all displaying women's clothing. (Men's clothing was also sold in The Underground but was clustered in another part of the market.) In the middle of Room 28 was an additional sales position, run by a middle-aged couple and their friend, who sold socks, inexpensive underwear, and cheap nylon handbags from a stand-alone table. The husband, short and stocky and with wisps of hair carefully wrapped around his head, would greet me with a heavily accented but friendly "Gud-a-morning!" regardless of the time of day. Merchants claimed that The Underground's stuffy air lacked oxygen and made everyone sleepy, but the rarefied atmosphere seemed to have an especially powerful effect on this man, and his wife often berated him for quite literally sleeping on the job.

A variety of merchants and sales assistants worked in our room, selling an assortment of merchandise ranging from jeans, denim jackets, and blouses for teenaged girls to large, loose-fitting pant suits for heavier, middle-aged women. At the counter next to Xiao Li's, a pair of middle-aged women with expertly painted faces would model their wares, white linen-like pant suits and flowered trouser-and-shirt sets targeted for the middle-aged market. These "Women in White" both wore colorful scarves around their necks, samples of their wares, making them look like twins. This counter was also home to Fourth Aunt, a woman in her 50s with a spicy tongue and copious (and often unsolicited) opinions. For example, when a punkish woman with green hair passed through our sales room, Fourth Aunt remarked that the woman's hair looked "like it's past its expiration date!" Fourth Aunt was one of very few middle-aged women hired to staff a sales counter, being a friend of the boss, one of the Women in White. Fourth Aunt explained to me that women her age had great difficulty finding work in the market. At her counter, Fourth Aunt was trusted like family but often treated like hired help, working much longer hours than the Women in White, who jokingly scolded her, but scolded her nonetheless, when Fourth Aunt slipped out to have lunch with a friend one day.

On the other side of Xiao Li's counter worked Second Aunt, another middle-aged woman who ran the counter herself with the help of her brother (stationed in Guangzhou) and her daughter. Like Xiao Li, Second Aunt's daughter, Li Chun, exemplified the appearance and behavior of young women working in The Underground: her long hair was bleached blonde, her eyes heavily lined in black, her shirts cropped, and her jeans tight. Li Chun, a tiny pixie in her late teens, would swear profusely with friends and customers alike.

The other counters were run by merchants assisted by hired help. These sales people were all young women, working long hours, usually under the close supervision of their bosses. Mei, a woman in her late 20s who worked the counter opposite Xiao Li's, was fairly typical. She had started working at Mr. and Mrs. Zhou's shirt counter after divorcing an unfaithful husband; with only middle-school education, Mei had few other employment options and needed to support herself. Yu Fei, in her mid-20s, was a well-trusted saleshand who worked a counter without her boss's supervision. She and her boyfriend were saving money to rent a space in one of the city's outdoor night markets—much cheaper than permanent, enclosed markets like The Underground—in the hopes of eventually launching her own business. Another young woman in the sales room, in her early 20s, sold handbags without supervision. She had started working in the market not long after completing middle school in Harbin. At the back of the room, colorful denim outfits for young women were displayed, merchandise targeting rural wholesale buyers and rural visitors to the city. At this counter two very young teenagers with heavily made-up faces, both reportedly from Harbin, worked under the constant supervision of their woman boss, a relative of the man who actually rented the space. The trio was a formidable sales chorus, pelting prospective buyers with helpful advice and encouraging words.

The people working in Room 28 formed a small, fairly stable community. They were not open with one another about business information, and they knew little about one another's personal lives. Nevertheless, they shared snacks, chatted and joked, watched one another's counters on occasion, and recognized their common location in Harbin's retail world.

The Copycat Economy and Questions of Authenticity

The Underground was a space where everything, at times, seemed muddled: the elaborate dye-jobs sported by some young women working in the market, for example, made them appear non-Chinese to some shoppers, and once a young saleswoman exclaimed that a customer had asked her if she were "mixed blood" (*hunxue*, a term that often carries derogatory meanings in China). Customers regularly mistook sellers for shoppers or shoppers for sellers. Even the status of a "customer" was uncertain; some merchants hired *tuor*, women who posed as customers in order to attract real, paying customers. These women would gather at the market entrance before it opened every morning, like all other market workers.[12] It even became a game among some of the merchants in Room 28 to quietly alert me when *tuor* were about to see if I could spot them. I rarely succeeded.

It was part of the very nature of competition in The Underground to complicate distinctions.[13] The Underground was, in many ways, a copycat economy that revolved around rapid copying of best-selling styles and fashions. Merchandise was purchased from wholesale clothing markets in Guangzhou and shipped to Harbin for resale, either to wholesale clients or retail customers. When a "hot" item was identified, merchants would then seek a local Heilongjiang factory to copy the merchandise, producing it at lower cost. Only a few days after I arrived in the market, Xiao Li began negotiations with a factory contact from the nearby city of Jiamusi for the production of a popular style of women's trousers that Xiao Li's partner had been shipping from Guangzhou in small quantities as they tested the local market. At least a third of the

[12] The presence of these *tuor* in The Underground was significant enough to merit an article in the local newspaper cautioning customers to be mindful. "One hundred 'hired clothing customers' active in The Underground (*Baiming 'yituor' huodong zai dixia*)," *Harbin New Evening News*, April 10, 2002, p. 18.

[13] There were boundaries that sellers in the market were invested in maintaining. The most obvious was the distinction between wholesale buyers and retail customers. Only wholesale customers, who would either buy in bulk or return to the same counters day after day or at least on a weekly basis, were entitled to lower wholesale prices. Differentials between wholesale and retail prices were substantial—often differing by a factor to two or three—and this forced merchants to make judgments about buyers before quoting prices. The result was two distinct patterns of sales interactions, and the boundary between the two types of interactions was carefully policed by both sellers and wholesale buyers.

counters in my room sold some merchandise that had been copied from goods originating in the South.[14]

Copying was also a key aspect of competition among Underground merchants, and so every counter was careful to conceal actual sales from others in the market in an effort to prevent copying. "If someone knows how well your sales are going and how much you are earning, they might be tempted to copy your merchandise," Mr. Zhou, a shirt merchant in my room, explained to me. He described how the previous year he had stumbled upon an extremely popular style of women's top, a wrap-around made of stretchy, sparkly fabric. He managed to hold off the competition for a remarkable twenty days by buying up all the special fabric in Harbin. By then someone had found the same material down in Guangzhou, where Zhou was unable to control the supply, and almost immediately copies started to arrive in The Underground. The wholesale price on the top instantly dropped from 28 to 15 yuan. "It's really brutal," Zhou remarked. "Sometimes all someone needs to do is make a phone call down to Guangzhou and they can have the same merchandise as you the very next day. If they are going to copy it up here, it can take as little as three to five days for large quantities of imitations to come out." For this reason, sales figures and market information were jealously guarded.

This copycat economy, however, complicated the boundaries structuring Harbin's retail field that shoppers and other retailers often sought to maintain. For example, locally produced merchandise was considered less desirable by Harbin shoppers, and so people buying in the market were anxious to distinguish between real Guangzhou merchandise and copies of it. Much as economic reforms have produced regional disparities in China (Wang and Hu 1999), a hierarchy exists according to which southern and coastal regions are associated with modernity and development (Anagnost 1997), and so clothing manufactured in Guangzhou was assumed to be superior to local goods in terms of quality, style, and value.

Underground salespeople did not necessarily challenge the cultural

---

[14] Ultimately, Xiao Li's negotiations fell through because the Jiamusi clothing factory was unable to procure fabric sufficiently similar to the original to make copying worthwhile. Some types of clothing—denim merchandise in particular—were never copied in Heilongjiang, because the production of these items requires more sophisticated machinery than the local clothing manufacturers possessed or were able to afford given their smaller scales of production.

understandings that were used to distinguish their market from other retail settings; rather, they tried to re-position The Underground and its merchandise with respect to those symbolic boundaries. In the process, they would challenge the position of others in Harbin's retail field.

For example, one of the many distinctions that merchants and saleswomen would complicate was that between "authentic" and "fake" merchandise. The sellers I observed in The Underground commanded a large repertoire of sales pitches that asserted the "authenticity" of their merchandise. Goods had come directly from the South, they would claim, and the items were not local copies or shoddy imitations of real fashions. Xiao Li introduced her goods with a standard line: after quoting a price, she would add, "Originals [zhengban]. Brought back from Hong Kong."[15] Her neighbor, Second Aunt, regularly reminded customers that her blouses were "Guangzhou goods, we didn't have them made [bu shi ziji jia jiagong de]! It was shipped here by air! I've only added the cost of shipping! This is the real thing!" The Women in White repeatedly claimed their goods were "real made-for-export merchandise [waimao huo] . . . feel the quality of that fabric!" At other times sellers would inform shoppers that goods were "brand name," pinpai de. "One of the news announcers on Heilongjiang TV wears this brand," Xiao Li earnestly explained to one customer, asserting that a very high-status woman wore goods found in The Underground.

Many of these claims, of course, fell on deaf ears. Shoppers reacted to sales pitches with caution and often with outright skepticism. Indeed, the labeling of even true Guangdong merchandise as "authentic" was deeply ironic, given that items that really came from the South were themselves usually knock-offs of one kind or another. For example, one day Xiao Li handed me a pair of zhengban sunglasses to try on, and I noticed that the "Chanel" stamp on the lens was kind of blurry. There were signature double-C's on the sides of the glasses, but on the inside was printed "Gianni Versace." Shirts with English lettering would appear all over the market, either extra made-for-export goods or copies of them. One shirt I spotted read "Just Do Me" in the same kind of lettering as Nike's "Just Do It" slogan. I regularly saw women in the mar-

[15] When I asked Wang Xia if the merchandise really came from Hong Kong, she responded, "It's not really from Hong Kong, it's just a saying." She explained that the factory would be in Guangdong but the company might be based in Hong Kong.

ket wearing "Cucci" t-shirts, and I came to think of these "authentic" Guangzhou wares as "Cucci couture."

But just as often sellers would turn shoppers' skepticism on its head, suggesting that customers were ignorant of and unable to recognize quality merchandise and its appropriate value. Merchants would repeatedly challenge the characterization of the clothing sold in The Underground as "cheap." One of the Women in White angrily sent away a customer who claimed an item was being sold elsewhere for much, much less, saying "Go ask them how much they sell such a thing for! Go ask them!!" In another instance, when a woman considering a pair of rhinestoned, polka-dotted pants balked at the asking price, Xiao Li chided her, saying, "You're just used to buying cheap stuff . . . this is a brand name, they have it in Sunshine . . . don't you recognize a brand name?" These conversations about cultural knowledge and social status between buyers and sellers in the market were conducted through a medium of things: brand names, current styles, and the quality of merchandise.

In this way, sellers in The Underground would regularly transgress the boundaries separating their subterranean marketplace and prestigious retail settings like Sunshine. To be sure, because Sunshine was perched at the very pinnacle of Harbin's retail hierarchy, it served as the primary target of sales counter strategies in The Underground. Xiao Li would regularly invoke Sunshine in her sales pitches—asserting not the difference but the sameness of the goods sold there. "We sell these for 100 yuan retail here, and they are selling well," she informed one wholesale customer. "They cost almost 400 yuan at Sunshine and are exactly the same." On another occasion she insisted, "These are expensive trousers [*gaodang ku*]. You can find this brand at Sunshine, go take a look!" Other sellers used similar techniques. One of the Women in White snapped at a customer, "You don't know what you are bargaining for . . . these trousers would sell for 200 to 300 yuan in Sunshine or the Far East Department Store!"

These distinctions—between "real" and fake items, between branded merchandise and copycats, between quality merchandise and cheap imitations, and especially between the goods carried in department stores and those found in the clothing bazaar—were fundamental to the retail field in Harbin and positions staked out within it. And while no one would mistake the stuffy corridors of The Underground for the polished floors of a luxury department store, the appearance of department store merchandise in The Underground—be it "real" or just copied—was cause for serious concern among elite retailers in the city. To prevent such ruptures to claims of exclusivity and elite style, upscale department stores like Sunshine would dispatch management staff to The Underground on a weekly basis to survey the goods on display there. Any supplier whose goods were found pinned up on shabby Underground walls would be quickly ejected from the store's much-sought-after sales floors.

In reality, however, the boundaries between the goods tastefully displayed across Sunshine's marble floors and those tacked up behind Underground sales counters were far more difficult to monitor and maintain. Not only were there thousands of counters in The Underground with displays and merchandise changing daily, but Sunshine's elite position made it the prime target of boundary attacks by Underground salespeople. In the end, The Underground made a mockery of one of the fundamental bases for modern department store organization: Its "authentic," brand name merchandise and the high mark-ups it commands.

The women sellers in The Underground would even go so far as to borrow, or "poach" (de Certeau 1984), certain forms of buying and selling found in department stores. They would use the ironic strategy of invoking explicit rules of department store transactions to discipline Underground shoppers. This happened most frequently when customers tried to return or exchange merchandise. Xiao Li and other merchants would issue a general department store return policy almost verbatim: "You must keep the item in the original condition [*baochi yuanyang*]; there's no way we can exchange this for you." Unlike in department stores, however, in The Underground exchanges and returns were almost never granted to retail customers and only rarely to trusted wholesale clients. Indeed, this was one of the unambiguous ways in which all department stores, elite or not, sought to distinguish themselves from the risky, precarious economic transactions conducted with *geti* merchants. A large sign in one department store I visited in the wealthy city of Daqing, a short distance from Harbin, announced "risk free shopping" for its customers. *Geti* markets, by contrast, were perceived as fraught with risk.

And yet Underground merchants and saleswomen turned this distinction on its head, poaching the language of department store service and suggesting that it was the market's buyers, not sellers, who threatened to violate accepted norms and rules. In the process, Underground women like Xiao Li and her neighbors cast themselves on par with big department stores, portraying themselves as no-nonsense business people operating according to the same logic—and deserving of the same degrees of respect. This was not, however, simply a strategy of emulation. Many customers may indeed have been engaged in a form of imitative consumption and sought to purchase, in a Veblenesque manner, look-alikes of the goods found in elite settings like Sunshine (Veblen 1899 [1934]; see also Simmel 1957). By contrast, by asserting the value of their goods and, as the next section will show, their persons, Underground women threatened to rearrange the relational positions of Harbin's retail field. They did not suggest that The Underground was as exclusive as Sunshine, but rather their sales strategies suggested that luxury department stores were really just a façade. Underneath that façade—and underneath the stores themselves—things were really not so different.

BUYING, SELLING, AND THE DEFENSE OF DIGNITY

Beneath the negotiations between buyers and sellers over goods for sale, the two sides engaged in a second, more obscure conversation about social value and entitlements to esteem and respect. A closer look at the sales encounters between buyers and sellers in The Underground reveals how merchants and saleswomen in the market sought to defend themselves against the slights of customers. While struggles between the two sides usually took on a ritualized form, at times these interactions broke down to reveal both the depth of customers' disrespect for people working in The Underground and sellers' investment in confronting that disrespect. When merchants and saleswomen asserted themselves with shoppers, they demanded the full measure of respect they believed due a hard-working person. Ironically, efforts by Underground merchants and salespeople to challenge the low social position attached to their marketplace frequently served to reinforce their stigma. Ultimately, the tools with which merchants and saleswomen contested the symbolic boundaries that set The Underground apart from other retail settings—their assertiveness, in an "Underground" manner—simply marked them as distinct.

In the previous chapter, I discussed how expressions of deference can serve to recognize class difference. At Sunshine, this kind of class recognition was a crucial part of managerially enforced service interactions. By contrast, in The Underground sellers strongly resisted the extraction of deference by shoppers. But since the two sides did not approach one another as equals, these encounters were unlike the stable expressions of mutual disrespect found at the egalitarian Harbin No. X Department Store. Instead, seller-buyer interactions in The Underground could at times spin out of control as the two sides wrangled over proper recognition of relative social positions.

The above discussion of authenticity conveys some of the ways in which sales interactions in The Underground took on the form of ritualized skirmishes over quality and value. Uncertainties about merchandise sold in the market meant that finalizing a sale involved considerable degrees of wrangling between buyer and seller. Usually, clashes between the two sides were more like routine performances. The following transaction was exemplary.

Two women retail customers stopped at the back counter in Room 28 to look over the denim summer outfits on display. After the woman merchant quoted them a price, the shoppers tried to bargain down from 100 to 60 yuan. The merchant exclaimed with force, "I've never sold at that price! When you bargain, you can't be so far off [the asking price]! No one bargains like that!" Still, the merchant reduced the price to 80 yuan. The customers held fast. The hired salesgirl on the counter piped in, crying: "We're already giving you a 20 yuan discount!" The pair of women started to leave, affecting an air of disinterest. Hastily the merchant called to them, "Add 10 yuan! Will you take it for 70 yuan?" The two shoppers kept going, and the merchant slapped the merchandise in a theatrical rendition of anger and frustration. When the two shoppers reached the edge of the room, the merchant called out desperately, "We'll give it to you! We'll give it to you!" her voice rising in pitch. But the pair either did not hear, or did not care to return, because they soon disappeared from view. The merchant and her salesgirl chuckled together over this dramatic, if failed, attempt to make a sale.

A bit later, however, the two shoppers returned, and this time they argued over quality in order to lower the price below the offered 60 yuan. "I'm already not earning anything [on this sale]!" the merchant wailed. "It'll just wash out! That's not a quality problem [*zhiliang wenti*], sister!" Nevertheless, the shoppers managed to "rub" (*mo*) another 5 yuan off the price before completing the purchase.

This interaction displayed many standard features of sales transactions in The Underground. First, buyers considered prices to be highly negotiable. Customers assumed that merchants and their hired hands inflated prices as much as possible in an attempt to gouge inexperienced shoppers. Sellers, for their part, felt they had no choice but to inflate prices, allowing them to lower the asking price enough to satisfy shoppers while still earning a profit. This resulted in a series of ritualized tactics and counter-tactics deployed by buyers and sellers in order to arrive at a satisfactory sale: sellers would exclaim about how unreasonably customers were bargaining and would frequently complain that they were "earning no profit" off a sale. Buyers would inspect merchandise, pointing out any little flaw. Merchants would respond with claims about the quality, fashion, and origin of the goods (Guangzhou, Hong Kong, or even South Korea). Customers would frequently start to walk off when negotiations stalled, and sellers would act angry or annoyed. If room to negotiate remained, however, the seller would call the customer back and offer the item at a lower price. At this point, a deal could usually be reached.

These interactions were seemingly rife with disagreements and arguments, yet they were also remarkably pro forma in nature and infrequently dissolved into open conflict. But sales interactions would at times exceed the limits of daily market ritual and routine, revealing an underlying set of tensions that speaks to struggles over social position and claims to respect. Earlier in this chapter I described many of the negative opinions about The Underground—and especially about the young women working there—held by Harbin residents. It was relatively rare for shoppers in The Underground to insult or challenge a merchant or saleswoman outright, in part because the people of The Underground were perceived to be unrestrained and ferocious. A loudmouthed customer could find herself labeled a "little bitch," a "bull's penis," or worse. The few instances when customers openly expressed their distain for sellers in The Underground, however, indicated the low social position of the market and the gendered stereotypes applied to the women working there. For example, when a salesgirl angrily swore at a customer she believed was trying to return an item purchased elsewhere, the customer hollered back, "Little girl, you have quite a mouth on you! Quite a mouth!" The customer implied an incongruity between the salesgirl's gender, age, and her foul language. The salesgirl, however, stood her ground. "Well, that's just the way it is. Don't buy here! We don't welcome you [back]!"

In such cases, sellers would break from their ritualized performances to express genuine anger or offense at customer behavior. One of the most frequent sources of anger for an Underground salesperson was a shopper not bargaining in good faith. Merchants and their sales help felt that such people made light of the business of The Underground and the earnest effort to make a living there. Shoppers who treated bargaining as nothing more than a game, with no relation to the actual costs of running a business, were viewed as both ignorant and disrespectful. Saleswomen would sometimes accuse customers of being "insincere" (*bu chengyi*). "You're price is *too* low, sister," one merchant exclaimed, sticking an epithet on the end of this comment in a low voice. On another occasion, Yu Fei exclaimed that "today is one of those days," noting that she'd just dealt with a person who had finished bargaining, tried on the item, and then insisted on an even lower price. "And I had already told her I was looking after her, giving her the wholesale price!" Second Aunt agreed, adding that some people bargain for things as if it didn't cost money to produce them, they just bargain for the hell of it ("stupidly bargain" or *sha jiang*). "That's what makes you angry," she told me.

Sellers in The Underground would not hesitate to assert themselves with such customers. For example, after devoting a good amount of time to a cluster of three young women who then walked off without a purchase, Second Aunt called out after them with irritation, "What were you doing, holding a meeting?" She then muttered to herself about how they stood around looking at so many things and then didn't buy anything. On another occasion, Xiao Li and a customer engaged in the standard set of price negotiations, with Xiao Li pulling the item out of its packaging for the shopper. But the young woman walked off even after being granted the price she requested, and Xiao Li burst out with anger. "What was that all about?" she yelled at the retreating customer. "You finish bargaining and then you don't want it?" She smacked the repackaged item down on the counter with irritation.

In these cases, sellers' angry reactions to customers were genuine, not a ritualized part of bargaining but a response to perceived slights. To my surprise, sharp-tongued merchants and their salespeople could be deeply upset when they felt a customer had treated them with disrespect. In one case, after a customer had angrily accused a merchant of treating her dishonestly, the merchant complained to others in Room 28 that the woman had soured her whole morning. "Now I'm so angry!" she exclaimed. Fourth Aunt remarked that she never let such people ruffle her feathers, "Don't let that stuff bother you." "But I'm not that kind of person!" the merchant wailed.

Equally offensive to sellers were the shoppers who made specious claims about poor quality merchandise. For example, when a retail customer (the cousin of a friend of the merchant) insisted on carefully picking over a white pant suit (suggesting quality problems) even though she was getting the wholesale price on the item, one of the Women in White angrily pointed out, "The better we know you, the more irritating you are [*yue shu yue geying*]." On another occasion, Fourth Aunt's neighbor, who worked a handbag counter, took a trip to the toilet, and while she was gone a customer came and asked to see a bag. Fourth Aunt took care of this, pulling the bag down and quoting a price, 50 yuan. When the customer suggested the price was a little high, Fourth Aunt was unimpressed: "50 yuan? You think that's expensive?" When the bag girl returned, she explained that the display bag was the last of that kind, and she asked Fourth Aunt, "What price did you give her?" On hearing it, she said emphatically, "That's cut rate!" indicating that she would not negotiate any further. The customer then claimed that the bag was dirty from having been displayed, and pushed for a lower price. But the bag girl held fast, and the customer ended up taking the bag at 50 yuan. After the customer left, the bag girl made note of the old "dirty bag" ploy, and Fourth Aunt scoffed, "Dirty! That bag was cleaner than she was!"

The sellers of The Underground, then, turned negative perceptions of market people on their head, instead characterizing *customers* as dangerous, untrustworthy, and even "dirty." Like salespeople in other retail settings in Harbin, Underground sellers often viewed customers as adversaries against whom they must strategize. For example, on one occasion a saleswoman told a customer she was out of a certain stock. "*Fei hua* [nonsense, bullshit]!" the customer spat at the saleswoman. The saleswoman was taken aback. "What do you mean, *fei hua*? Can't you see that we don't have the goods? It's not even on display!" After the customer left, the saleswoman exclaimed that the woman was "uncultured" (*mei you wenhua*).

More than any other setting, the women selling merchandise in The Underground portrayed themselves as under assault and in need of defending themselves—even physically—against aggressive or unreasonable customers. At times this was done humorously, as was the case after Xiao Li angrily dispatched a customer who had loudly demanded an exchange. Fourth Aunt, who had just purchased some links of sausage from a roving merchant, joked with Xiao Li that she could have used the sausages as a weapon against the customer. Fourth Aunt swung the sausages through the air to demonstrate the proper technique. That particular customer was deemed by Fourth Aunt to have been suffering from "mental disease" (*jingshen bing*). "Have you noticed," she asked me with a twinkle in her eye, "all the people with mental diseases appear here on the weekends, because they don't have to work on Saturdays and Sundays!" Fourth Aunt seemed concerned that I, as a semi-permanent resident in Room 28, was equipped to deal with these problem shoppers. After one fussy customer had quitted the room, Fourth Aunt exclaimed, "What a little bitch that one was . . . say, Amy, do you know what 'little bitch' means?"

At other times sellers in the market would assert themselves quite forcefully with shoppers, directly challenging the notion that they were undeserving of respect. For example, it turned out that Xiao Li did not need hot sausages to defend herself. One morning, after having taken a day off, I arrived at the market to discover that Li bore the marks of a battle with a customer, three or four large scratches on her forearm with yellowy-blue bruises forming around them. Second Aunt informed me that there had been a disagreement between Xiao Li and a customer, and when Xiao Li refused to sell to the woman, the customer started cursing her out. In response, Xiao Li angrily kicked at the customer with her metallic high heels, at which point the woman attacked Li with her nails. "If that woman had gone after my face, I really would have pulled her apart," Xiao Li asserted. Later, when she discussed the incident with one of the market's baggage haulers, Xiao Li remarked on how "such people" patronized the market. "It's a segment of society we just have to deal with."

Xiao Li characterized the fight as an assault on her person and her dignity—her right to sell (or not to sell) to whomever she pleased. But physical fights and coarse language were not considered the markers of "dignified" behavior in Harbin, so ironically Xiao Li's role in the fight and her reaction to it afterward identified her *more closely* with "uncultured" and unruly people, and not apart from them. In fact, Xiao Li and her women friends in The Underground even spoke of tracking the woman down to settle the score. (Xiao Li claimed to know "where she is from.") Indeed, while Xiao Li's boldness in starting a physical confrontation (with spike heels, no less!) was frowned upon by many in the room, almost all these merchants matched her physical assertiveness with robust verbal defenses of their own dignity. Xiao Li's scratching fight was not so deviant in the context of The Underground, where merchants and hired help alike seemed to take great pleasure at the prospect of witnessing a fight. When a fight broke out nearby, Second Aunt called out to a woman across the sales room, "Go take a look! A fight! Go check out the excitement!" On another occasion, when an argument broke out in the opposite room between two neighboring merchants, one of the Women in White joked, "Why can't they actually fight? All they are doing is swearing at each other, how boring!" And the Plastic Bag Woman, a roving merchant selling plastic bags, confessed that she was fond of "watching excitement" (*kan re'nao*), being especially partial to traffic accidents and market fights.

Direct physical and verbal confrontations were simply part of life in The Underground. Merchants and workers understood this aspect of the market as a test of their abilities. My first day at the market, the people working in Room 28 remarked that "The Underground toughens a person" (*dixia duanlian ren*). "It's not like in department stores," they told me. "You really have to know what to say in The Underground." But their felicity with the tongue—and even the high-heeled foot—were exactly the behaviors that outsiders saw as evidence of their "lack" (Yan 2003). The very tools these women used to assert themselves with customers and to defend their dignity as respectable, hard-working people were the same cultural markers that set them apart from recognized, "respectable" segments of Harbin society.

CONCLUSION

Within Harbin's field of retailers, The Underground occupied a powerfully evocative, if lowly, position. Merchants and especially the young saleswomen in the market were strongly viewed as dishonest, uncultured, and disreputable people. Harbin shoppers viewed the goods sold in the market as fashionable but low quality, in contrast to department stores where managerial gatekeepers and explicit store policies ensured the quality of the wares. It was the specter of the risky clothing bazaar and its unscrupulous, unruly sellers against which new elite stores and even old state-owned ones could define themselves as a sort of haven from a heartless, at times even immoral, marketplace.

But in The Underground such distinctions became putty in the seller's hands. The boundaries between "authentic" merchandise and fakes or copies, between department store goods and shoddy market wares, even between department stores themselves and the clothing bazaar were muddled and redrawn on a daily basis. These counter strategies were in part a response to The Underground's lack of status, and merchants and salespeople there poached across the boundaries that divided their marketplace from large department stores in order to assert the value of their goods and of themselves as honest, hard-working sellers. These Underground practices of distinction were not simply reactive, however, and in many ways the market strategies deployed by Underground merchants and saleswomen drove the anxious distinction-making activities found across the glittering floors of new, modern department stores like Sunshine. Saleswomen in The Underground were especially effective at destabilizing the distinctions made among the goods sold there and the items sold elsewhere in the city as they challenged Sunshine's claims to offer exclusive, high-class, and, of course, high-priced merchandise. It is telling, I think, that at Sunshine the occasional customer would ask if, and sometimes even insist that, the same merchandise could be found, at a much lower price, in The Underground. It was perhaps in response to these dangerous boundary challenges that managers at Sunshine devoted so much energy to cultivating distinctions among *people*. Store managers sought to make their status as elite retailers more secure both by maintaining a corps of young saleswomen clearly distinct from Underground women and by recognizing shoppers as elite clientele.

Yet if the sellers in The Underground were successful at blurring the boundaries among merchandise, in the end they were much less successful in challenging the distinctions that marked them as lower-class people: uncouth, uncultured, and undeserving of respect. The very form that the assertion of their personhood took in The Underground ironically served to reinforce the symbolic boundaries that marked them as undesirables. Indeed, as they sought to redeploy the social distinctions at play in Harbin's retail field, they became deeply invested in the very symbolic boundaries that identified their market, and their persons, as the negative pole of distinction. Because the larger symbolic economy of social distinctions was also imbued with moral valences, social positions associated with The Underground and the people filling those positions were viewed as not only culturally deficient but also as lacking in moral value and personal worthiness. The linkages be-tween cultural meanings, moral worth, and social position combined to make The Underground an important space where a new structure of entitlement—such as that promoted on Sunshine's sales floors—could be expressed.

But whereas the customers shopping in The Underground were not the same people purchasing cashmere sweaters or fur coats from well-appointed boutiques on the fourth floor of the Sunshine Department Store, they *were* the same working-class and lower-salaried profession-als who might also—and at one time most certainly did—patronize the extensive sales floors of the Harbin No. X Department Store. This very real economic competition between these two lower positions in Har-bin's retail field had begun to drive a new development at Harbin No. X. For while store managers there were still oriented to a state-centered organizational field, salesclerks at Harbin No. X increasingly recog-nized the new, market-oriented field in which they operated. They also recognized that the symbolic capital their store had once commanded was threatened by their social nearness to The Underground. As the next chapter will demonstrate, workers at No. X had begun to innovate distinction-making practices themselves, seeking to distinguish them-selves from untrustworthy *geti* markets with the language and tools of a remembered state socialism.

CHAPTER SIX

Post-Socialist Distinction Work

After only a few days at Harbin No. X, I encountered a particularly difficult customer. A young woman, accompanied by her father, stopped at the Ice Day counter in search of a winter coat. She questioned me carefully about the quality of the down coats I laid out across the counter for her. In response, I parroted back the lines I had heard Big Sisters Zhao and Lin use with customers: "This is a Bingya coat, Ice Day line, new style." The Bingya Group was a famous Chinese maker of winter coats, and Ice Day was its new subsidiary. But the young woman and her father did not believe my claim that Ice Day was part of Bingya, and they carefully examined the tags on the coat looking for some mention of Bingya as parent company.

"It must be a different company," the father said. He carefully examined the seams of the coat while zipping and unzipping the pockets.

"This isn't last year's left-over merchandise, is it?" the young woman challenged.

Certainly not, I assured her. New this year.

The young woman then insisted she wanted the coat she was looking at, but a "newer" one—that is, one that had not been taken out of the box yet. I informed her that we did not have two coats in this particular size, style, and color.

"If this is a new product, and not leftovers from last year, then how is it you don't have another coat in this color and size?" she asked me. "It must be old goods—doesn't what I say make sense?"

At this point I felt myself getting angry. Why would I lie? "I just know what they've told me," I responded lamely, and to my relief at that moment Big Sister Zhao arrived to rescue me. Zhao patiently explained that we received the goods in small lots and that the shipments included many colors, but the range of sizes was incomplete. This explanation must have satisfied the young woman, because she bought the coat. I nevertheless was amazed at the customer's suggestion that I had been trying to trick her and insulted at the implication that I was lying.

I quickly learned not to take such encounters personally, for this kind of mistrustful interaction occurred all the time at Harbin No. X. The rise of such marketplace distrust was also the key context for the emergence of distinction work at the state-owned department store, as store workers reacted to a reconfigured retail field.

This chapter considers the appearance of distinction practices at Harbin No. X. In Chapter 3, I argued that, because of the store's state socialist organizational legacy and its continued links to the local state, store management did *not* organize service work to produce social distinctions. This provided room for worker autonomy and reciprocity in worker-customer interactions on the sales floor. In this chapter, however, I will demonstrate that Harbin No. X was not locked in stasis but in fact was changing in the face of an altered environment and new market conditions. While managers continued to take their cues from the local party-state and the city's municipal commerce committee, salesclerks at Harbin No. X had begun to innovate practices of distinction-making on the sales floor.

The impetus for workers to innovate distinction practices was found in the crisis of trust that Harbin No. X experienced as a retail setting patronized by working-class consumers. Confronted with competitive pressures from *geti* markets like The Underground, salesclerks developed an elaborate repertoire of trust-producing practices meant to set Harbin No. X, both its workers and its wares, apart from the risky *geti* marketplace. But in stark contrast to the Sunshine Department Store, where distinction work was carefully engineered and enforced by store management, at Harbin No. X distinction work was the creation of salesclerks themselves. In many ways, the high levels of workplace autonomy described in Chapter 3 provided Harbin No. X's clerks with the freedom to innovate their own form of organizational distinction.

Workers did so by drawing upon ideological and cultural resources acquired under state socialism. By calling forth both the store's waning symbolic capital as a state-owned entity as well as their cultural resources as part of Harbin's stolid working class, salesclerks at Harbin No. X produced a particular configuration of distinction practices that traced a trajectory from socialism to a new market society. In what amounted to a working-class strategy of cultural representation, workers attempted to deploy the reconstructed symbolic capitals of a state-owned enterprise and traditional working-class social relations. In the process, they staked out a "distinctive" location in the city's retail field.

CULTURAL INNOVATION AND
POST-SOCIALIST TRAJECTORIES

The innovation of distinction practices by salesclerks at Harbin No. X raises questions about both social change and cultural continuity. Chapter 3 considered the role of workplace culture in "sustaining existing strategies of action" (Swidler 1986: 278). This chapter takes a different tack, examining instead how people draw upon culture to construct new practices and strategies. To do so, I turn to Bourdieu's concept of "trajectory."

When do the unspoken values that make up cultural dispositions gain a voice? Swidler (1986) suggests that during "unsettled times," cultural values become more explicit. Pierre Bourdieu similarly argues that social change can create dissonance between unconscious dispositions and social circumstances. For sociologists, such tensions can demystify the more common and "seemingly miraculous adjustment" of individual dispositions to the social positions that people occupy (Bourdieu 1984: 110). Contexts of rapid social change also enable us to recognize that cultural practices and dispositions are not frozen in time but are also reproduced and altered as people move through social space and historical time.

In other words, the social conditions under which an individual's or group's *habitus* developed may not be the same as those under which that *habitus* comes to be exercised. This can result from individual class mobility, as when people move upward or downward in status or class position, something Bourdieu dubs "the trajectory effect" (1984: 111). This trajectory effect may also be the result of the collective upward or downward movement of a class or class fraction within the broader social structure, resulting in discord between group practices and expectations, on the one hand, and the objective possibilities open to that group under changed social circumstances, on the other. For individual or group, the relationship between *habitus* and class position is not frozen in time but reflects a historical trajectory, either an individual one through layers of social space or a collective one through transformations of social structure. In other words, the strategies people use to adapt to social change are shaped by historically constituted dispositions. In China, the urban proletariat is a prime example of a group that is experiencing downward mobility and loss of status in a society that increasingly disavows its state-socialist past.

The reform years have brought a host of troubles for China's state sector workers, especially in China's northeastern "rust belt" (Lee 2007). Numerous scholars have documented this "fall of the worker," the rise of unemployment among state sector workers, and other problems faced by China's urban working class (Blecher 2002; Hurst 2004; Hurst and O'Brien 2002; Hung and Chiu 2003; Lee 1999, 2000, 2002, 2007; Solinger 2002, 2004; Won 2004). The loss of what was expected to be lifetime employment within the secure and defined boundaries of a work unit can produce personal, family, and community crises as well as a profound sense of social loss. As one unemployed worker in Beijing told Sian Liu, "Workers have no social position" (Liu 2007: 42). The overall result has been a loss of symbolic capital for China's urban working class and the social spaces with which they are associated.

Within China's retail field, class trajectories take on concrete forms of strategy and practice. By locating the workers, managers, and customers at Harbin No. X within the city's retail field and, beyond that, within China's contemporary consumer environment and the country's evolving class structure, we can see how social actors attempt to adapt their resources to changing circumstances. On the sales floors at Harbin No. X, we also come to see the overlap between two distinct trajectories: The downward trajectory of a state-owned retailer within the retail field, paralleled by the broader decline of China's urban working class.

This chapter explores the questions of social innovation and social trajectory by focusing on salesclerks' reactions to new customer behaviors and orientations. Unlike Harbin No. X's managers, who were aware of changes to Harbin's retail field but felt largely insulated from them (a consequence of close relations with the local party-state), store workers faced daily the consequences of the state-owned department store's descending position among the city's retailers. It was on the sales floor—that largely autonomous space populated by salesclerks and their customers—where changing consumer practices interacted with salesclerks' work culture and their broader class *habitus*. As clerks regularly encountered customers who failed to recognize the boundaries between Harbin No. X and the *geti* free market with which it increasingly competed for business, these clerks felt compelled to reassert the once obvious and unchallenged distinction between the state-run retail sector and the untrustworthy realm of the *geti* merchant. As with Sunshine and The Underground, this distinction work was relational, and it engaged Harbin No. X salesclerks symbolically with other settings in the city's retail field.

These salesclerks' trajectory through historical and social circumstances becomes clear, however, from the particular cultural resources store workers drew on to create distinctions. Specifically, workers defended against the store's downward trajectory in the new, market economy context by attempting to translate the store's, and their own, *socialist* era symbolic and cultural capital into forms their customers could recognize. As a means to re-establish customer trust, workers evoked Harbin No. X's status as a reliable state enterprise. Through their interactions with shoppers, salesclerks also produced a setting characterized by many of the hallmarks of traditional working-class culture. Frank, sociable service interactions conveyed the underlying message that Harbin No. X was the appropriate place for working-class consumers seeking to avoid the new perils of the reform-era marketplace. These new, reform-era practices were the fruits of a working-class *habitus* encountering changed social circumstances. In a reconstituted retail field, salesclerks at the Harbin No. X Department Store staked out their position by practicing a form of distinction work with distinctively (post)socialist characteristics.

It is important to clarify the connections between the arguments laid out in this chapter and those presented in Chapter 3, as they are not contradictory. The mutual disrespect described earlier and the friendly or *reqing* interactions outlined below have common roots in a particular organization of service work that entailed high levels of clerk autonomy, parity between customer and clerk, and no managerially organized extraction of deference from salesclerks. However, whereas "mutual disrespect" was enabled by a state socialist managerial orientation and revealed clerks' ability, at one level, to opt out of distasteful or degrading social interactions, the practices and interactions that are the focus of this chapter should be viewed as *strategy*—both sales strategy and a counter strategy of distinction—squarely situated in a market context.

THE SKEPTICAL SHOPPER AND A
MARKETPLACE OF DISTRUST

Customers at Harbin No. X were nothing if not careful shoppers. As my weeks at the Ice Day down coat counter slipped by, I repeatedly marveled at the time and attention our customers devoted to the purchase of a single item: a down coat. Customer distrust—and an accompanying, deep-seated fear of being tricked or taken advantage of—manifested itself in a variety of forms. These skeptical shoppers would interrogate salesclerks about price, brand name, quality of the merchandise, and store return policies. They feared that if an item was priced high, they were being ripped off, yet they also feared that an inexpensive item was of poor quality. These skeptical shoppers seemed to feel that the slightest detectable flaw was evidence that an item would fall apart soon after purchase. They would examine important purchases like a down coat with the greatest concentration.

Later, when I salesclerked at the Sunshine Department Store, I infrequently encountered such skeptical shoppers. When I asked my fellow Sunshine salesclerks why only a handful of our cashmere sweater customers insisted on careful inspection of merchandise, Zhang Xin shrugged her shoulders and replied, "Some people are just so . . . earnest [*renzhen*] when it comes to life, I guess." At Sunshine, skeptical shoppers could be viewed as individuals of great intensity and thoroughness.

Skeptical shopping was, however, a class-coded practice, and at Harbin No. X these customers were far too prevalent to be attributed to mere personal quirks. Rather, such patterns of shopper behavior were a clear reaction to the perceived risks of the marketplace, especially at its lower tiers. Many of Harbin No. X's customers honed these practices in inexpensive *geti* markets like The Underground, where they also shopped and to which their limited incomes frequently restricted them. Often, customer fears and skepticism grew out of bad experiences, as was the case with one woman who grilled me about the quality of our coats. "I bought a coat last year, paid over 400 yuan for it, and the feathers came out. . . . One bad experience and now I'm afraid!"

Granted, a down coat was an expensive purchase for most Harbin residents, consuming more than half a month's wages for many individuals. Yet the care and attention customers devoted to their purchases represented a more complex phenomenon than hesitation over spending a fair sum of money. For while most shoppers at the Sunshine Department Store could buy their way out of China's risky urban marketplaces by shopping in exclusive settings, shoppers with more modest incomes had to strategize against the hazards of a risk-filled marketplace on a daily basis. At Harbin No. X, this meant that the sharp lines that once had defined the store's reputation as a reliable state-owned retailer and that set it apart from the risky *geti* marketplace were now no longer distinct.

Risk in the Marketplace

The skeptical shoppers appearing on Harbin No. X's sales floors were very much a product of China's broader consumer environment. But as I have suggested above, both perceptions of and exposure to marketplace risks were not distributed equally, and for ordinary Chinese the consumer marketplace was a realm fraught with dangers. In Chapter 5, I discussed negative popular perceptions of The Underground and other *geti* markets, where Harbin shoppers regarded sellers with distrust and moral distaste and viewed the goods as cheap and of dubious quality. In contrast to the country's planned economy days, when (as one informant described) "quality might be poor, but at least everything was cheap," China's consumers today face a marketplace where quality, price, and the authenticity of merchandise are all subject to question and generate anxiety for shoppers.

To some degree, these consumer attitudes reflect China's historical experiences with a planned economy and state socialism, and parallels exist between marketplace anxieties in China and other post-socialist contexts. In Russia, for example, markets are frequently associated with disorder, and for older Russians, years of state-mandated pricing made the relation between price and value a source of suspicion and anxiety (Humphrey 2002; see also Kaneff 2002). In China, traditional mistrust of merchants (Mann 1987) interweaves with a recent history of planned economics, state-mandated prices, and inexperience with the market (Stockman 1992). A generation gap exists between young and old Chinese, similar to that in Russia, and in Harbin, older people were most likely to convey unease with the new ambiguities of price, style, and the dangers of fake merchandise. During a formal group interview I conducted among retired state sector workers, participants expressed their discomfort with the need to haggle over purchases made in new market settings. "The country's economy has developed and changed so fast," said one retired cadre, "but older people are slow to accept these changes." Harbin No. X was one of the few clothing retailers in the city where elderly shoppers could be found in substantial numbers. But with the retail sector increasingly dominated by non-state businesses and merchants, even elderly consumers were more and more apt to shop in less expensive *geti* settings.

The threat of purchasing fake or poor quality goods created even more anxiety than haggling over prices, however. Like many developing economies, China's marketplaces are rife with shoddy merchandise, copycat and fake brands, and numerous schemes to cheat or deceive consumers. Many people have personal experiences of being "cheated" (*shangdang*) in some way, though usually on the relatively small scale of being overcharged for something or being sold a defective item. Ann Veeck's (2000) description of Nanjing residents toting their own scales to outdoor food markets captures a pervasive consumer sentiment in China. Beverly Hooper (2000) notes the growth of consumer complaints related to quality, safety and product deception through the 1980s and '90s and the publicizing of these issues through newspaper reports, television programs, and even the Internet. The sense of danger and distrust associated with shopping is heightened by regular media reports on consumer marketplace deceptions and scams. For example, in 2001, Harbin local and Chinese national media reported on numerous incidents relating to the quality of consumer goods, including a faulty medicine, *Meihua K*, that poisoned more than 70 people in southwestern Hunan province, and the discovery of a reputable manufacturer in the city of Nanjing using year-old, moldy filling to produce moon cakes for the Mid-Autumn festival.[1]

At the local level, the most popular city newspapers offered daily "consumption" pages largely devoted to reporting on consumer complaints and official efforts to redress these issues. Brief articles would frequently appear reporting such distressing trends as "60% of wood

---

[1] For one report on *Meihua K*, see "How did the fake medicine 'Meihua K' enter the marketplace?" (*Jia yao 'meihua K' shi ruhe liuru shichang de?*), Xinhua Net, Changsha, April 2, 2002, http://202.84.17.73.7777, accessed 5/13/2003; on the Nanjing moon cakes, "Nanjing Guanshengyuan will be broken up: 'Old filling mooncakes' incident threatens company leadership" (*Nanjing Guanshengyuan yao bei jiesan: jiu xian yuebing shijian weixie gongsi lingdao anquan*), *Harbin Life Daily* (*Shenghuo Bao*), hereafter *Life Daily*, Oct. 20, 2001, p. 11.

flooring materials [are] substandard" and "Four companies' down coats do not meet standards."[2] Problems with food and food markets were extensively publicized,[3] and regular columns detailed consumer complaints about local businesses ("The voice of the consumer") and exposés of devious practices at Harbin restaurants ("Eat in the know").[4] Pricing and discounting schemes received heavy reporting throughout 2001–2 (for example, not listing prices on official tags is considered price deception [*jiage qipian*] and is a finable offense),[5] as did problems with fake and poor quality merchandise across Harbin's retail sector, though clothing, shoes, cellular phones and medicine complaints took top billing.[6] A habitual reader of the local news would quickly get the

---

[2] "Sixty percent of wood flooring materials substandard" (*liu cheng diban kuai bu hege*), *Life Daily*, May 22, 2002, p. 5; "Four companies' down coats do not meet standards" (*sijia yurongfu bu hege*), *Life Daily*, Dec. 7, 2001, p. 33.

[3] A small selection of headlines from articles reporting on defective or dangerous food products or food-related scams include: "The food products at Hakelong [a Harbin supermarket] have quite a few problems: milk candy is soured, dried sausage is stinky" (*Hakelong shipin wenti bu shao: naitang hala le, kuchang chou le*), *Harbin New Evening News* (*Xinwanbao*), hereafter *New Evening News*, April 10, 2002, p. 17; "On demand, 30% of food import certificates are substandard" (*shipin jinhuo suozheng sancheng bu hege*), *Life Daily*, June 5, 2002, p. 6; "An endless stream of poison meat, poison rice, poison rice noodles—consumer, what can you still eat?" (*Du rou, du mi, du fensi ceng chu bu qiong—xiaofeizhe, hai neng chi shenme?*), *Life Daily*, Nov. 22, 2001, p. 8; "Last year's mooncake filling, used this year to make tangyuan" (*Qunian yuebingxian, jinnian zuo tangyuan*), *Life Daily*, Jan. 29, 2002, p. 26; "One chicken injected with 200 ml water" (*yi zhi ji zhuru 200 haosheng shui*), *Life Daily*, June 21, 2002, p. 6; "Morning markets: Encounters with shorted *jin* [approx. half a kilo] and skimped *liang* [1/10 of a *jin*]" (*zaoshi: zaoyu duanjin shaoliang*), *Life Daily*, June 25, 2002, p. 6.

[4] Harbin's *New Evening News*' "Voice of the consumer" (*Xiaofei zhi sheng*) column printed consumer complaints ranging from refusals to grant refunds and overcharging to defective or pirated merchandise (see, e.g., *New Evening News*, Oct. 11, 12, and 13, p. 18). The same newspaper's "Eat in the Know" (*Chi ge mingbai*) series reported refusals to issue official receipts (a form of tax evasion), charging of illegal fees, and charging more for dishes than the prices listed in the menu (see, e.g., *New Evening News*, April 6–13, 2002, pp. 1 and 18).

[5] Again, the number of reports appearing just in Harbin's *Life Daily* and *New Evening News* are too extensive to list here. For some representative reports from *Life Daily*, see Dec. 23, 2001, p. 6, "Making 'price deception' go away" (*Rang "jiage qipian" zoukai*); March 21, 2002, p. 5, "When product prices are not posted, you rely entirely on feeling" (*Shangpin bu biaojia quan ping ganjue lai*); and May 13, 2002, p. 4, "Nine major cases of price law violations" (*Jiage weifa jiu da anli*).

[6] On fake goods, see, e.g. "6280 yuan Western suit—fake" (*6280 yuan xizhuang, jia de*), *New Evening News*, Oct. 20, 2001, p. 18. On general areas of consumer com-

sense that in modern-day China, scams to cheat you out of your money lurked everywhere and just about anything could be fake—including police officers or marriage introduction services.[7] In a context where a market economy is still relatively new and of questionable legitimacy, these reports of fraud and deception have contributed to what sociologist Sun Liping (2003) has termed a general "crisis of trust" (*xinren weiji*) in Chinese society.

So despite the development of consumer protection laws and growing publicity of consumer's rights (Hooper 2000), the average Chinese shopper continued to perceive the marketplace as fraught with risk. Friends and acquaintances in Harbin regularly informed me of examples of market dangers, some personally experienced and others garnered from acquaintances or newspaper reports. Customers I encountered at Harbin No. X were also careful readers of reports on consumer issues, and on one occasion a customer and I discovered we had read the same article on down coats. The most astonishing story—and quite possibly apocryphal—was of a small *geti* store in one of the city's more fashionable shopping districts that had been discovered to be selling secondhand clothing collected from people who had died of infectious diseases! The young woman who related this story to me explained that this was one of the reasons that she only shopped for clothing at "big stores" (*da shangdian*), department stores.

Indeed, most department stores would try to distance themselves from untrustworthy market settings by offering customers explicit guarantees for merchandise quality and customer satisfaction. As one Beijing-based retail industry specialist explained to me, "When customers buy something, spend money, they are taking a risk." She added that at one high-end shopping complex in Beijing, the store explicitly promised customers that their "shopping risk" (*gouwu fengxian*) would be "zero." At Sunshine, the existence of such consumer protections was

---

plaints, see "Five hotspots appear for consumer complaints" (*Xiaofeizhe tousu chuxian wu da redian*), *Life Daily*, Dec. 28, 2001, p. 6.

[7] For several separate incidents of "fake police" accused of falsely fining taxi drivers and others, see "Fake traffic police appear in front of train station" (*Jia jiaojing zhan qian xianxing*), *New Evening News*, Oct. 31, 2001, p. 3; "Fake civil police deceive twice" (*Jia minjing liangci xingpian*), *Life Daily*, April 11, 2002, p. 27; and "Law enforcers turn out to be fake traffic police" (*Zhifa de yuan shi jia jiaojing*), *New Evening News*, April 22, 2002, p. 3. On a marriage introduction service that cheated customers out of money, see *Life Daily*, Nov. 14, 2001, p. 6 and Nov. 19, 2001, p. 6.

generally taken for granted by shoppers, who tended to ask only about the specific terms of return policies and quality guarantees. Returns and exchanges were commonplace, and customers were quick to appeal to management, who overwhelmingly sided with these authoritative customers.

But for many customers, risk-free shopping came at too high a monetary price. Given the rock-bottom prices offered by *geti* merchants, who often have few overhead costs, low taxes, and can survive on very slim profit margins, many Harbin residents were willing or felt compelled to give up the more expensive security of respectable stores for lower-priced but risky market venues. And, as I explore below, shopping in the *geti* marketplace called forth a whole set of defensive practices—ranging from intensive haggling over prices to microscopic inspections of merchandise—that had become a deeply ingrained orientation toward shopping in general. So even though cash-strapped consumers might still shop in a department store for relatively large purchases, like winter coats, shopping in a formal department store setting had become a luxury. Even a department store like Harbin No. X, which targeted working-class shoppers, had substantial overhead costs and stocked "branded" merchandise, and so charged significantly more than *geti* merchants. As one man remarked of the woman for whom he was purchasing a down coat, "So extravagant, having to buy the coat at Harbin No. X!" He then asked me, "How is the price on this coat, is it inexpensive?" His comments were echoed by a retired man who remarked, "The common people [*laobaixing*] rarely buy fancy things . . . buying from a *geti* merchant is good enough."

The Crisis of Trust at Harbin No. X

At the end of my time salesclerking at Harbin No. X, one of the store's assistant general managers asked me to present my thoughts about store operations. Wanting to avoid discussing my co-workers, I settled on a topic that focused instead on customers: namely, their expressions of distrust. I began my presentation by asking the audience, made up of both managers and workers, what they felt was Harbin No. X's major strength. "What is it about the store that attracts customers?" I asked.

Members of the audience were quick to reply. The head of the propaganda department was the first to answer. "The quality [*suzhi*] of the sales staff, and the reputation [*xinyu*] the store has with customers," she said confidently. Another woman, a department manager, also commented, listing basically the same things: quality of service, Harbin No. X's long history, and the trustworthiness of the store—especially the fact that the store did not carry fake goods (*jiamao*).

These were the kinds of responses I had anticipated. I then explained to my assembled listeners that I believed a consumer environment fraught with risk had combined with a changing retail sector to produce a crisis of trust within Harbin No. X's walls. I argued that despite the fact that Harbin No. X offered return policies and product guarantees, consumer fears had nevertheless made their way into the store. This was evidenced by the elaborate shopping strategies employed by the store's customers and indicated a precipitous decline of Harbin No. X's trustworthiness.

On the one hand, customers could no longer clearly distinguish between many *geti* settings and a store run by a centralized management and offering uniform quality, return and exchange policies. Indeed, some old state-owned stores in the city now rented all their counter space to independent *geti* merchants, and some new shopping centers that looked like department stores were also entirely rented out. In such cases, quality and service might not be guaranteed by the store, only by the individual seller. Just by looking, there was no way for a customer to know that Harbin No. X had remained largely impermeable to these *geti* influences.

At the same time, customers had imported their shopping anxieties into the state-owned department store. Because the shoppers who patronized Harbin No. X also tended to shop in low-priced *geti* markets like The Underground, they had grown accustomed to confronting marketplace risks. In many ways, the sales floors of Harbin No. X had been invaded by *geti* market practices through the vehicle of wary, skeptical customers and their shopping strategies. The result, for salesclerks, were daily encounters with distrustful customers and the repeated need to establish trust in order to sell enough merchandise to earn a decent monthly wage. The store, I told my audience, needed to aid clerks in this endeavor by making store guarantees clear to customers at the more formal, organization level.[8]

[8] In retrospect, I now realize that I was probably making a prescription for distinction work organized by managers.

By the end of the discussion that followed my presentation, it became clear that store managers recognized the change in consumer practices but were unwilling to acknowledge a crisis of trust in the store. Instead, the assistant general manager who had organized the meeting declared that just by entering the store, customers were expressing their trust in Harbin No. X. This dubious logic was taken up by another assistant manager, who closed the session by re-listing the store's "five strengths" in didactic fashion: its long history, worker "quality," product selection, large size, and, not surprisingly, its universally recognized trustworthiness. The irony, of course, was that a trustworthiness that had once been state-mandated—and made evident through Harbin No. X's lofty position within the formerly state-dominated retail sector—now had to be produced, on a daily basis, in the course of service interactions and by means of clerks' sales counter strategies of distinction-making.

A Question of Distinctions

Once installed at the Ice Day counter, I quickly encountered the blurred boundaries that had produced this crisis of trust in the store. One of my first surprises at Harbin No. X was the frequency with which customers hoped, even expected, to negotiate prices with salesclerks. "*Dazhe ma?*" "Is there a discount?" customer after customer would ask.

Prices at Harbin No. X were, however, *not* negotiable, and the store continued to sell goods only at the prices marked on official price tags. But given the prevalence of bargaining in other retail settings—including Sunshine and, especially, The Underground—shoppers were loathe to relinquish price haggling. They often refused to believe salesclerks' insistence on printed prices. In one case, when I explained to a woman customer that there were no discounts, she replied in surprise, "You [really] can't?" On another occasion, a pair of customers simply asked me a second time, as if I had not already responded to their question, "Is there a discount?" One man was so astonished that there was no price haggling at Harbin No. X that he exclaimed, "But that now we have a market economy [*shichang jingji*], things have changed. What do you mean I can't bargain [*jiangjia*]?"

Indeed, the skeptical shopper never took a price at face value, fearing he would miss out on a discount by not pushing hard enough. For example, when Big Sister Lin quoted a 300 yuan price to a customer, he responded, "How about 280?" "I'm telling you the truth," Lin replied plaintively. "I can't bargain, not even one penny [*fen*]. This is the lowest price, any lower and we don't earn anything!" The man did not make the purchase. In another instance, after I refused to offer a discount, a woman customer leaned over and asked in an undertone if it was possible to "speak to the manager" about a discount. Many customers seemed convinced that, if they just asked in the right way, a discount would be forthcoming.

Over time, I came to realize that the problem was one of distinguishing among retail settings. Given all the changes to department store organization in China, it is understandable that customers would be unclear about where the rules for shopping had changed and where they had stayed the same. As detailed in Chapter 4, stores like Sunshine offered some opportunities for discounting, especially to the most privileged, "gold card" customers. (Indeed, at Sunshine bargaining seemed less about thrift and more about shopping connoisseurship and a sense of privilege and entitlement, including the recognition of "face," as Ellen Hertz [2001] argues about prices and discounts.) Other new retail venues were increasingly the purview of *geti* merchants, but they often *looked* the same as a traditional department store, complete with uniformed salespeople. Even at Harbin No. X the occasional corner of unused space might be turned over to a private merchant selling discounted goods. In the single instance I witnessed of this, the salesperson was not only *not* a Harbin No. X salesclerk, but she also collected cash payments directly from customers and made change herself, completely separate from the store's cashier system. Most important, the prices she charged were open to negotiation. So when customers entered Harbin No. X, they often did not know just what kind of retail system they were dealing with. As a local shopkeeper explained when I discussed with her the constant discount requests at No. X, "People don't understand, they don't know how things work."

At Harbin No. X, the problem was one of distinctions. This was revealed to me one day when, after I declined to offer a discount, a woman customer asked me, "Is this counter Harbin No. X's?"

"What?" I replied, confused.

"Are you an individually operated [*geren*] counter, or . . ."

I understood. "We are factory-direct sales [*changjia zhixiao*]," I chirped, indicating that the counter was not a *geti* operation. "We can't bargain."[9]

Such confusion meant that, in the eyes of most shoppers, Harbin No. X was not significantly different from a *geti* merchant, and this drastically eroded much of the symbolic capital Harbin No. X might have claimed in pre-reform days and through the early years of economic reforms. Despite the fact that store managers insisted that simply by entering the store, "customers express their trust in Harbin No. X," in fact most shoppers had little confidence that Harbin No. X or its sales-clerks operated according to anything but the short-term, profit-driven motives that now seemed to define all Harbin retail settings.

It is perhaps unsurprising, then, that it was an elderly couple (the elderly being a group rarely found in newer retail settings), stopping at the Ice Day counter for a brief look, who continued to recognize Harbin No. X as a traditional, fixed-price retailer. The old man made a comment to his wife about bargaining, to which she exclaimed, "This is a state store [*gong jia*]! You can't bargain here!" Our assistant floor manager, Manager Zhou, had been standing at the counter, and on hearing this she smiled at me and then said to them, "That's right, but *we* guarantee the quality of our goods."

Strategies of the Skeptical Shopper

Harbin No. X's promise of quality goods (or your money back!) was not one that customers regarded with confidence, however. The store's customers were skeptical shoppers, and their purchasing strategies clearly revealed this. By importing their broader shopping strategies into the state-owned department store, customers also demonstrated the blurring, in their minds, between retail settings like Harbin No. X and other settings, such as The Underground.

Two of the most common practices were the close inspection of merchandise and a practice called *tiao* in Chinese, a term that literally means "to choose" and in practice refers to selecting the best from a number of

---

[9] My answer to the customer's query was borrowed from my co-workers, who used this appellation—"factory-direct sales"—as a way to allay customer concerns about merchandise quality. But the term was also technically correct, since Harbin No. X had shifted to a modified version of the factory-in-the-store model, discussed in Chapter 2, which involved the manufacturer supplying merchandise directly to the sales area. Pricing and discounting remained under store control.

ostensibly identical items. Both close inspections and *tiao* were practices I would later see regularly exercised in The Underground but rarely at Sunshine, unsurprising given that these strategies reduced the risk of buying shoddy merchandise in a setting without guarantees. In fact, I found that shoppers at Harbin No. X were often more insistent on these two strategies than were Underground shoppers—a situation which partly reflects the greater expense of the down coats I sold at Harbin No. X (about 300 yuan) relative to the jeans, shirts, and blouses sold in Room 28 of The Underground (40 to 100 yuan). Equally important, however, were the class-specific expressions of distrust and perceptions of risk, amplified during costly purchases, that these shopping strategies conveyed. For while bargaining may have become a common practice in most Chinese retail settings, Harbin No. X's working-class customers had introduced other, more class-bounded shopping strategies to the store (such as *tiao*). In doing so, customers enacted the crisis of trust that Harbin No. X, as a once-reputable state-owned department store, faced.

These shopping strategies indicated what life was like at the lower levels of China's retail field. Careful inspection of merchandise was the first line of defense against being tricked into buying the low-quality goods that filled *geti* markets. Shoppers at Harbin No. X would regularly examine every seam, carefully experiment with each zipper, and closely scrutinize collars and cuffs. One woman customer rejected a coat because, after carefully going over every square inch, she discovered the slightest of defects in the stitching on the shoulder. (I could not imagine myself, or most North American shoppers, taking the slightest notice of the irregular stitching.) Other customers would carefully pick over coats after trying them on, examining seams for escaping feathers and looking, as one woman put it, "to see if there are any defects" (*you mei you maobing*). Even a little dust on a coat, a common occurrence given the dry winter air, could bring cries of discovery or distress from a shopper. "Look! Feathers!" exclaimed one woman on seeing a slightly dusty coat. She seemed proud of her discovery, but I quickly responded, "It's not feathers, it's just dust. Feathers aren't so small." This explanation seemed to suffice, and her husband bought the coat.

In fact, on occasion I encountered customers who seemed to view shopping as primarily an exercise in detecting shoddy wares and an opportunity to confront devious salespeople. On one occasion, a woman customer who had been examining a coat suddenly said to me, sharply,

"Miss, feel this, what is it?" There was something hard in the coat, and the customer acted as though she had caught me in an underhanded act of trickery—that is, selling substandard merchandise. (A down coat filled with pebbles, perhaps?) Anxiously, I felt the coat for a moment and then replied triumphantly, "It's a button."

The corollary to close inspection of merchandise was the practice of *tiao*. The basic principle behind *tiao* is that you never buy an item without choosing the best from at least two options. For example, one morning I helped a woman select a winter coat. After she had found a style and color that satisfied her, she asked me to dig out yet another coat of the same size and color so that she could choose "the best" one. This process usually involved identifying a miniscule flaw on one of the coats—rejecting a coat with a wrinkle in the shoulder area or a slightly imperfect stitch, or choosing a coat that seemed to have slightly more down in it (when in fact it was just filled with more air). As the anecdote that opens this chapter illustrates, the logic behind *tiao* was simple: an item of which there was one, and just one, was suspected of being defective in some way. A remnant or leftover, and quite possibly the reject from someone else's inspection.

For this reason, customers were rarely willing to buy "the last one." When we claimed to be selling customers the "last" or "only one" of a particular item, they would express suspicions that we did indeed have others and were lying in order to sell off a defective coat. Sometimes we would have to go through the motions of looking for a coat that we knew did not exist just to allay customer suspicions. After paying for an item at the cashier, customers would return to collect their package, often opening it up to inspect the item yet again. There were even customers who, after trying on a coat pulled from a just-opened box, would say, "Now find me a new one," meaning a coat that no one— even themselves—had ever tried on. "This one is new," I said in bafflement to one father-daughter pair. Miffed and suspicious, they refused to buy the coat.

These shopping practices would appear from time to time in more elite retail settings, like Sunshine, where customers could also be suspicious of salesclerk motives. But at Harbin No. X, inspections of merchandise and *tiao* were not only frequent, they were also just the most prominent of a whole collection of practices calculated to compensate for the lack trust in market settings. Customers would engage in extensive comparison shopping, referred to euphemistically as *zhuan* or "taking a turn" (i.e. browsing through the store or market). Custom-ers would try on items before and *again* after purchase. Some would question us carefully about the down coats we were selling: Where were they made? What material were they filled with? What were the properties of the fabric? Of the filling? Other customers were content to simply rely upon brand recognition for quality guarantees, saying things like, "What's this brand? I've never heard of it before. It's noth-ing special . . . and look, there's not even a pocket inside the coat!" One customer astonished me when, after closely examining the tags on a coat, he indicated to me that the coat did not have an ISO number.[10] "I like to buy products with ISO numbers," he explained, because only then he could be sure that the quality would be reliable.

THE PRODUCTION OF TRUST AND COUNTER
STRATEGIES OF DISTINCTION

Given that customers no longer took for granted Harbin No. X's rep-utation for honesty and quality, the store's salesclerks were faced with the task of producing trust at the individual level, through sales interac-tions. Unlike their managers, store workers encountered daily remind-ers of customer distrust, and their interactions with customers (coupled with their own status as working-class consumers) made salesclerks acutely aware of Harbin No. X's repositioning within the city's retail field.[11] At the same time, clerks' sales commissions made them anxious to assuage customer fears in order to sell merchandise. Given the high

[10] The ISO, or International Organization for Standardization, issues standards— usually technical or technological—to ensure compatibility and quality levels for technology, products, and services across countries. China is a member nation of the ISO, and Chinese companies with products or services meeting ISO standards like to advertise this fact, especially given widespread quality problems. There were even department stores in Harbin that had received an ISO 9000, a standard for quality business management, especially with regards to customer satisfaction. The application of ISO standards to Chinese managerial and service performance seems to support Ann Anagnost's (1997: 77) claim that "the speculative gaze of foreign capital" gets translated into modern notions of "civility" and culture in China.

[11] Salesclerks themselves frequented many other types of retail settings—includ-ing markets like The Underground—in order to economize. They encouraged me to shop at Harbin No. X, however, explaining that since I was a foreigner it was "safer" to shop at a large, reliable department store.

levels of worker autonomy found on the sales floor (discussed in Chapter 3), the department store's salesclerks developed their own set of counter strategies for dealing with customer suspicion and distrust.

Thus we find the rise of distinction work at Harbin No. X, for worker counter strategies centered on the production of social distinctions and the drawing of symbolic boundaries. Recognizing themselves as occupying a kind of middle position among Harbin retailers, salesclerks sought to establish in the minds of shoppers that Harbin No. X was a retail setting both trustworthy and economical, a space appropriate for working-class consumers with modest incomes. This distinction was primarily between a trustworthy state-owned store and the untrustworthy and disreputable private marketplace (such as The Underground), though at times workers also sought to set the store apart from high-priced private retailers like Sunshine. In other words, the production of trust involved the production of distinction.

The resources workers relied on to draw these symbolic boundaries were laden with class meanings and reflected their collective trajectory through China's recent era of economic reforms and rapid social change. That is to say, in constructing strategies to cope with the penetration of new market forces and market mindsets into the store, Harbin No. X's workers relied on their own cultural resources, both workplace-based as well as broader working-class ones. While worker counter strategies were conscious in the sense that they involved the explicit goal of getting customers to make purchases, these practices also drew upon worker dispositions and cultural orientations—the realm of *habitus*—that were steeped in a kind of implicit state-socialist cultural knowledge. Salesclerks' counter strategies found traction with customers precisely because many shoppers at Harbin No. X shared these class- and generationally inflected cultural orientations. Changes to Harbin's retail field had brought forth a set of working-class practices that traced a trajectory across social time and space. By relying on an increasingly devalued cultural knowledge, salesclerk strategies reflected their own (and many of their customers') descending social position.

Here, I identify two specific strategies store workers directed at their distrustful clientele. The first was an explicit evocation of Harbin No. X's status as a state-owned entity and represented a stubborn effort to shore up the long-standing division between state and private businesses and to revive the positive status China's state sector enjoyed until recently. At the same time, workers recognized that Harbin No. X's state enterprise status, once the store's greatest symbolic and material resource, could also be a liability in the new marketized environment, and they drew attention to their state-ownership in a selective manner.

The second trust-producing strategy involved the far more subtle creation of a distinctive shopping culture and set of service interactions at Harbin No. X. This shopping culture revolved around the notion of *reqing* ("warm feeling") and relied on elements of urban working-class culture that resonated both with the work culture at Harbin No. X and the *habitus* of many of the store's customers. Indeed, as I will argue below, expressions of *reqing* by salesclerks took on an almost nostalgic aura in a context of downward mobility for large portions of the city's aging, industrial working class. Both these strategies—explicit claims and implied cultural understandings—produced trust and distinction by means of cultural expressions that were highly intelligible to the more traditional and often older segments of Harbin's working class.

State-Owned Symbolic Capital

If managers at Harbin No. X felt confident that customers continued to recognize the store's reputation as one of its "five strengths," workers on the sales floor had cause, as I have shown, to be less sanguine. At the same time, store workers lacked one of the easiest methods used in other market settings to diminish customer fears and reluctance to buy—the granting of discounts. As a result, salesclerks instead sought to gain customers' trust in order to make sales. Though aware of the declining status of state-owned enterprises (especially retailers) in the city, Harbin No. X salesclerks nevertheless sought to mobilize what remained of the store's diminishing symbolic capital by emphasizing the positive associations with its state-owned status and in particular its reputation for fair prices and trustworthiness in an increasingly chaotic and profit-driven marketplace.

Workers reminded customers of the store's history of trustworthiness by highlighting the distinction between China's honest and reliable state-owned sector and the greedy proprietors of privately owned businesses. An interaction between Big Sister Lin and a male customer was exemplary. The man selected a navy blue coat and asked, "Any cheaper?" Big Sister Lin replied, "We can't bargain here, we can't have one price for you and sell it to him [here Lin indicated the man's friend]

174   *Post-Socialist Distinction Work*

for another. It's not like with private merchants [*siren*]." The man was persistent. "Cheaper?" Lin was steadfast. "We can't bargain, we're a state-owned [store] [*gongjia*]!"

Here, Lin suggested that Harbin No. X operated on principles of fairness, treating all customers equally. Separately, Little Xiao suggested to me that vulnerable customers who were likely to be overcharged—foreigners, like me, but also the elderly and out-of-towners—shopped in places like Harbin No. X because all customers paid the same price, and they would not feel ripped off.[12] At Harbin No. X, workers were at pains to demonstrate, customers would *not* be cheated. Little Xiao followed this logic when dealing with an elderly couple. The man asked Xiao if he might switch the coat he was looking over for another one. "The zipper doesn't work quite right," he worried. Little Xiao gathered up the coat, forcefully zipped it up (thereby demonstrating that the zipper worked fine), and said, "We can't sell you something for more than 200 yuan that doesn't work. Harbin No. X isn't like those private merchants [*getihu*] who are just interested in making money."

Salesclerks frequently sought to tap into Harbin No. X's state-socialist symbolic capital to reinforce the store's integrity with shoppers, believing that the label "state-owned" still denoted honesty, reliability, and fairness. The connection between the two was so strong that Big Sister Zhao mistakenly characterized Bingya, Ice Day's parent company, as "state-run" (*guoying*) even though this well-known company was in fact a private enterprise. On another occasion, Zhao told a customer concerned about our prices, "We are state-run [*guoying*], we don't have any inflated prices [*huang jia*] here, it's not like with privately run places."[13]

---

[12] Ellen Hertz (2001: 279) gives a contrasting example of a man who claimed he never paid "market price" for anything, instead relying on personal connections to secure discounts and lower prices. Hertz argues that this represents the assertion of face—of individual identity—in a seemingly anonymous market context. It could be argued, then, that salesclerks at Harbin No. X were indeed asserting a kind of equality of "the masses" that was an ideal (even if often unrealized) of China's socialist economy.

[13] I do not want to oversimplify: At times, coping with customer distrust involved concealing Harbin No. X's differences from other retailers. This was often the case with customer expectations for discounts. Here, salesclerks might try to face down customer demands by insisting that the merchandise was "already discounted." For example, when a girl asked Big Sister Zhao if there was a discount on a coat she had selected, Zhao launched into a detailed explanation about how Ice Day was "a new brand this year" (*jinnian chuang pai*) and so the price was already set at 15% off.

These distinctions targeted both suspect *geti* merchants and lofty retailers like Sunshine, and Harbin No. X salesclerks frequently reminded customers that only at Harbin No. X could they find good quality *and* good value. As Little Xiao and Big Sister Zhao told one group of customers, "Even with discounts, Sunshine's down coats won't be any cheaper than ours." Little Xiao then related a story to us all, clerks and customers alike, about a man who had come the other day to Harbin No. X to purchase a child's coat. Originally this man had been prepared to buy a coat at Sunshine, where he was friendly with a manager and so could expect a generous discount. Little Xiao explained that this man had even decided on a coat already and was prepared to pay more than 300 yuan for it. But when he saw our coats—the prices and the quality—he immediately bought one. Xiao's story seemed to have the desired effect, and one of the young women purchased a coat from our counter.[14]

These counter strategies were all explicit attempts to differentiate Harbin No. X from the other retailers whom the store's customers also patronized. They reflected salesclerks' attempts to mobilize Harbin No. X's symbolic capital in order to garner customer trust. But this capital was in decline—the store's history as a state-owned enterprise was, for some shoppers, an indication of its out-datedness and inefficiency—and these selling practices were thus more effective with some customers (like the elderly) than others. As noted in Chapter 4, the state-owned Harbin No. X served as an important contrast against which elite retailers like Sunshine defined themselves as modern. Within the confines of Harbin No. X itself, however, salesclerks frequently sought to portray the state-owned store as insulated from unfair market forces.

At other times, the distinction was not so much between state and private retailers as between large, reputable stores and unreliable *geti* merchants operating from rented counter spaces. For example, when a pair of women customers balked at the prospect of buying a display coat, Big Sister Zhao replied, "I just put that coat there this morning.

Zhao added that if she lowered the price, "Auntie will have to take 10 yuan out of my own pocket, and I only earn 400 yuan a month."

[14] During the winter of 2001–2, Sunshine made an initial attempt to cash in on the lucrative mass down coat market in Harbin by setting up a "Down Coat City." Sunshine hoped to rely on its reputation for high quality goods—a reputation linked to the high prices of Sunshine's merchandise—to attract shoppers with modest incomes to the new down coat "city."

This isn't The Underground, we wouldn't sell dirty items, it's not like with *geti*, this is a big store." The customers persisted to be anxious and picky, prompting Zhao to continue in this vein. "This isn't The Underground, we sell real brands [*zhenggui paizi*] here." She added that our merchandise was absolutely of good quality. "You don't have to worry about the [down in the] coat smelling bad after wearing it a couple of weeks," Zhao assured them. This point seemed to hit a cord. "Yes, that's true about the smell, I've had that happen to me," one of the women mused. Given that many older shoppers thought of a "big store" as the equivalent of a "state-run" store, on another occasion, Zhao scolded a skeptical woman shopper, saying "This is a big store, we don't have bad things here."

Given the social proximity of Harbin No. X and The Underground, the clothing bazaar was the primary target of salesclerks' distinction practices. For instance, when a woman shopper commented to her friend that down coats were much cheaper in The Underground, Little Xiao interjected: "But then you run into all sorts of quality problems . . . and lots of those coats are fake [*jia huo*] anyway." The woman agreed, saying that she did not dare buy a down coat in The Underground, given that even there such coats cost a fair amount of money, and the possibility of buying a bad one was so high.

These sales pitches tapped into a broader discourse that portrayed department stores as "risk-free" shopping environments where customers were protected by formal policies guaranteeing customer satisfaction. Whether salesclerks drew attention to the store's state-sector status or to its large size (which once had correlated quite perfectly with state ownership), they attempted to bring a diminishing symbolic capital to bear in a new market context. In this way, workers deployed a set of increasingly history-bound resources as counter strategies of both trust and distinction.

Reqing *and Working Class Nostalgia on the Sales Floor*

In seeking to distinguish Harbin No. X from other retail settings—at the one end, markets like the chaotic, precarious Underground, at the other, formal, highly regulated settings like Sunshine—salesclerks at the department store also created a space that *felt* distinct to shoppers. Salesclerks modeled their interactions with customers on a notion of straightforwardness and warmth—*reqing*—that both clerks and customers identified as characteristic of traditional working-class culture and, even, expressive of a kind of genuine feeling that had been greatly dampened by economic reforms, market relations, and the downward mobility of China's urban industrial proletariat. *Reqing* expressed a sense of mutuality between workers and customers that was, in many ways, the flipside of the mutual disrespect described in Chapter 3. In both cases, the resulting interactions were marked by straightforwardness and blunt candor, though as noted above *reqing* represented a sales strategy whereas mutual disrespect reflected the ability of clerks to *not* engage in a sale that would cost them too much personal dignity.

In service settings, the term *reqing* has been broadly adopted by promoters of new, modern standards of service (e.g. Zhu and Wang 2000), and salesclerk training classes at Sunshine and elsewhere exhorted salesclerks to engage in "warm service" (*reqing fuwu*). Managers at Harbin No. X also spoke of these new notions of service, describing a progression from the "two dragons" (*liang tiao long*) of service in the 1980s (good service and convenience to the customer) to the "service with a smile" (*weixiao fuwu*) of the 1990s to the latest "exceeding customers' expectations" service (*chaoyue guke de qidai de fuwu*). One former Sunshine salesclerk I interviewed described "service with a smile" as a kind of *reqing*, "greeting customers with a smile and giving them a good feeling." But as I have tried to demonstrate in Chapter 4, in elite settings like Sunshine this notion of *reqing* was often translated into enforced deference toward the customer.

At Harbin No. X, however, the notion of *reqing* took on a distinct significance, caught up as it was in a politics of nostalgia and what might be labeled, to borrow a term from Lisa Rofel (1999: 135), a working-class "strategy of representation." At a time when many in Harbin faced layoffs and unemployment, salesclerk performances of *reqing* service created a social space evocative of the positive qualities associated with the urban working class. Performances of *reqing* by salesclerks simultaneously asserted both Harbin No. X's difference and the value of working-class social relations.

Literally, the Chinese term *reqing* means "warm feeling" and refers to genuine expressions of warmth and enthusiasm. In everyday life, the word is used to describe people of honest friendliness and warm hospitality, and the people of China's Northeast understand themselves to be especially endowed with these qualities of welcoming and generosity. For the working class, expressions of *reqing* are also linked to perceptions of themselves as honest and straightforward (*laoshi* and *zhishuai*). But whereas traits like *laoshi* ("honest," "frank") and *zhishuai* ("straightforward," "candid") can carry the negative connotations, especially in the reform era, of "ingeniousness and naïveté" (Yang 1994: 66; for parallels in post-socialist Poland, see Dunn 1999), *reqing* commands a uniformly positive meaning.

Such character traits and cultural expectations are closely associated with the earthy working-class culture of China's northeastern cities, reflected in the cultural ideals that William Jankowiak (1993) identified in working-class neighborhoods in the northern city of Huhhot (see also Whyte and Parish 1984: 332–56, on personal relations and the "comradely ethic" found in urban China). Similarly, traditional urban work units were social institutions characterized not only by the instrumental and despotic elements of loyalism and clientelism identified by Andrew Walder (1986) but also by a stable community of highly personalized relations and, as Brantly Womack (1991: 328) argues, an "expectation of continuity" resulting in strong, long-term relationships and a sense of collective interests (see also Hertz 2001: 278; Li 1993).

These positive, idealized features associated with working-class settings—the strength of human feeling, and the honesty and straightforwardness of social relationships—parallel the reform-era nostalgic themes described by both Lisa Rofel (1999) and Guobin Yang (2003). In the 1980s, Rofel found that older women factory workers harkened back to a pre–Cultural Revolution China when "an innocent state [was] at one with its citizens" (1999: 131), especially its workers. Yang (2003) catalogs the more recent "*zhiqing* nostalgia" of the 1990s among the urban Cultural Revolution generation.[15] In both cases, socialist nostalgia challenges the marginalization of certain groups (e.g. older women workers and the Cultural Revolution generation) in the reform era by "creating a certain distance" between dominant representations and group identities (Rofel 1999: 137; Yang 2003).[16]

[15] *Zhiqing* or "educated youths" are also known as the "Cultural Revolution generation" and were the cohort who came of age during the Cultural Revolution (1966–76). This group was sent as youths to the countryside for re-education during the latter years of the Cultural Revolution. I should note that the *zhiqing* nostalgia Yang describes locates positive themes such as human connection in rural, not urban, life.

[16] Rofel (1999) argues that the construction of modernity in China is in part dependent on the portrayal of the country's Cultural Revolution generation as "abjected figures": "One proves oneself a modern subject in the post-Mao era by expunging what the Cultural Revolution generation has come to represent" (190). On other examples of nostalgia as a kind of resistance or expression of unease in contemporary

Reqing service at Harbin No. X performed a similar kind of socialist, working-class nostalgia by evoking a space and a set of social relations that harkened back to a time when urban workers enjoyed greater status and security. But as Rofel notes, even if it may recall more innocent times, nostalgia itself "is not an innocent sentiment" (135). Indeed, *reqing* operated as part of a strategy of representation that invoked not an authentic past but an imagined one (Dai 1997) in order to stake a claim on the present. To be sure, people's actual memories of service prior to and in the early years of economic reforms are not ones of *reqing fuwu*. As noted in Chapter 2, stories of bad service experiences and abusive sales clerks abound. Ellen Hertz (2001: 281) points out that the cold and impersonal interactions people had with shop assistants were a central aspect of an uncomfortable urban anonymity found in both Maoist and post-Maoist China, and in the mid-1980s the state targeted "civilization and politeness" (*wenming limao*) campaigns at state service workers. Discussions of civility and courtesy in China today tend to portray state sector service workers as suffering from a "lack" (Anagnost 1997) of these attributes.

On the sales floor at Harbin No. X, however, the concept of *reqing* countered such portrayals. In the hands of working-class salesclerks dealing with their largely working-class customers, *reqing* conveyed levels of care and concern for the customer that workers felt set Harbin No. X apart from newer, more profit-driven retail settings. In this sense, expressions of *reqing* were as much a working-class strategy of cultural representation as they were counter strategies of the distrustful marketplace. They were strategies that appealed to a cultural identity shared by workers and customers; it was in this sense that sales strategies were also cultural representations.

The following scene was exemplary of the sentiment labeled *reqing*: An elderly couple arrived at the counter. The man was energetic and excited, gesturing at the coat he wanted "for an old lady to wear." When Big Sister Zhao walked up, the old man exclaimed, "Ah! There you are!" and it became clear that this was not his first visit to our counter. Zhao attended to the couple, patiently outfitting both the man and woman with down coats. After they left, Big Sister Zhao explained

China, see Barmé 1999; O'Brien and Li 1999; and Dai 1997; on Shanghai nostalgia in support of reforms, see Lu 2002. Lee (2007) notes that nostalgia for and criticisms of the socialist era often co-exist among China's laid-off workers.

to me that the man had come the other day and spent a considerable length of time talking with her. Afterward, someone scolded Zhao for wasting so much time with a customer who did not make a purchase, and Zhao told me that management had explicitly discouraged sales-clerks from "chatting" with customers. "But I know that this is how old people make their purchases, first they come and take a thorough look around before coming out a second or third time to buy." The old man even told Zhao that he had visited Sunshine's new "Down Coat City" and had failed to find anything he liked. "It's still best to shop at Harbin No. X," Zhao agreed.

Certainly, this kind of *reqing* was not a formal store policy—and as this incident illustrates, expressions of *reqing* could be interpreted by management as chattiness or socializing. In addition, not all workers used *reqing* as a strategy to create rapport with customers, believing it a waste of time and energy. But on my sales counter as well as the surrounding ones, I repeatedly saw instances where workers went to considerable lengths to create a feeling of concern and intimacy be-tween themselves and their customers. These *reqing* practices were in part rooted in a work culture that fostered intimacy, sociability, and ul-timately trust among workers and could be extended to include cus-tomers. These practices also stood in stark contrast to *both* my other set-tings, the restrained Sunshine and as well as The Underground, where sellers and buyers tended not to identify with one another. At Harbin No. X, by contrast, *reqing* built upon a sense of shared place in the world and a mutual understanding of needs and desires. The "trueness" of these interactions was reinforced by the fact that workers were not in-variably *reqing*, as Chapter 3 demonstrated. And as the example above suggests, *reqing* also distinguished Harbin No. X as a suitable—and comfortable—space for the city's working-class shoppers.

In practical terms, *reqing* involved hands-on involvement with cus-tomers and close but unaffected personal attention to their needs—like one might expect from a friend or, in some cases, a slightly bossy aunt. Big Sister Zhao was the most forthright about performing—and then declaring—friendly service. On one occasion, as Zhao pulled out coat after coat for a pair of shoppers, she exclaimed, "See how *reqing* we are with you, pulling out all these different coats for you to try on!" When the couple joked with Zhao about her commission, she responded that she had been working as a salesclerk for 20 years and really did enjoy the work. "You don't get to meet so many people if you hang around at home," she said. "It's really interesting [at the store]!" On one occasion Zhao even declared to a set of customers that serving them was a kind of "spiritual enjoyment" (*jingshen xiangshou*). At other times, both Big Sister Lin and Little Xiao also went to great lengths to accommodate customers. In one case, Little Xiao spent a considerable amount of time introducing a coat to a woman customer, but the customer left, somewhat awkwardly, without making a purchase. Lin explained to me that the customer was embarrassed not to buy a coat "after Little Xiao had been so *reqing*."

Indeed, performances of *reqing* often resulted in a sense of mutuality between workers and their customers. Given that *reqing* was most definitely part of a sales strategy, there were times when salesclerk performances of *reqing* were portrayed as a personal connection with customers that verged on an obligation to make a purchase. On one occasion, Big Sister Zhao joked with a customer whom Big Sister Lin had handled with great patience (but who had not made a purchase), saying "We're so *reqing*, and still you don't buy!" To my surprise, even customers could present this point of view. For example, after a man customer failed to find a coat that met all his specifications, he apologized to Big Sister Lin and me for not buying a coat, adding, "And we got along so well!"

On another occasion, Big Sister Lin carefully tended to a pair of women—both wearing heavy work clothing—teasing as she wrote out the sales slip and packaged up the coat, "How good we are to you!" One of the women asked, "Is it at all possible that the coat is a fake?" No, Lin replied, "We are not *chengbao* [rental space]," and she went on to explain that since we were not a *geti* operation we did not have fake goods. Lin then asked, "Where are you from?" The two women explained that they sold vegetables in a local wholesale market, to which Lin jokingly replied, "Well then, you'll have to give me a discount!" In this case, Big Sister Lin's *reqing* interaction included a distinction between "us" and "*geti*" merchants (though ironically the sale was being made to a pair of *geti* merchants!). At the same time she established a sense of empathy and common interest with the pair of women shoppers.

For while clerks engaged in *reqing* treatment of customers in order to sell merchandise, they produced an atmosphere of comradely sociability in which both clerks and customers would participate. *Reqing* interactions sat on a continuum of mutuality, the far end of which was the mutual disrespect detailed in Chapter 3. Indeed, unlike at Sunshine, the behavior of salesclerks was not choreographed by management, and so workers were *reqing* with customers when they felt so disposed—and rude when they did not. This mutuality could be seen in the ways that all sorts of personal information would be solicited or shared between my co-workers and their customers, and salesclerks felt entitled to question customers about their occupations, the relations among people shopping together, and above all customers' appearances. Big Sister Zhao (whose own daughter was considered obese by Chinese standards) offered weight-loss advice to the parents of a fat girl. Big Sister Lin made informed recommendations regarding coat sizes for growing children. At times the sales floor would break out into jovial repartees between clerks and customers, as shoppers participated in the production of *reqing*. Big Sister Lin tended a gaggle of young soldiers, one of whom tried on coat after coat while one of his mates pulled out a camera and began shooting photos. On another occasion, a pair of men looking over a down coat jokingly asked Xu Li-mei, at the neighboring counter, for a knife. "A knife?" she asked, nonplussed. "Why?" "Because," one of the men said, a twinkle in his eye, "We want to cut this open and see the inside!"

Workers would regularly enlist the help of passing shoppers in order to aid customers (and, of course, to make a sale). For example, when a woman from the nearby city of Jiamusi came to buy a coat for her father, Big Sister Zhao recruited an appropriately sized male shopper to serve as a model. "Sir, sir, would you come over here for a minute and help us out?" Zhao called out to the tall man. "We'd like to use you as a model. We spotted you from quite a ways away." He was happy to help, the coat fit, and the woman made the purchase. As our model departed, Zhao thanked him and said brightly, "Sorry for holding you up!"

At other times, customers would freely insert themselves into ongoing interactions between salesclerks and other shoppers. Sometimes this could provide a seemingly objective, third-party opinion that would smooth a purchase. For instance, as an elderly couple considered a men's coat, the woman noticed the slit in the back of the coat and remarked loudly, "Cold! Won't it be cold this way?" To my surprise, a passing customer, an older man, intervened. He stopped and explained earnestly, "It won't be cold, the slit only opens when you sit down, it's there to protect the zipper. These things have their logic." This explanation seemed to satisfy the woman. The passing customer began to admire the coat. "It's really not expensive!" he exclaimed, adding, "And the workmanship is quite good. It's really a nice coat!"

Passing customers would frequently stop to observe happenings on the sales floor, though at times a gregarious shopper could inadvertently sabotage a sale. On one occasion a passing woman customer stopped to look on while I laid out a short pink coat for a young couple to look over. "My daughter bought a coat here this weekend," the new arrival offered helpfully. "But she said she's already cold wearing it, the down is too thin." Great, I thought, this is just what I need. "But this coat is O.K.," the woman continued, turning to the young woman. "This one is thick enough." A look of doubt passed across the young woman's face, and though she tried on the coat it was clear she was not going to buy it. The other woman continued to chat with me cheerfully, oblivious to the fact that she had ruined my sale. In short, Harbin No. X was a public space in which strangers, customers, and workers alike regularly engaged in friendly, if brief, interactions. By contrast, in The Underground strangers only tended to insert themselves into an ongoing interaction to get a word in edgewise—that is, to give someone a scolding (e.g. "If you're not going to buy then shut up!") or to emphasize an insult that had already been dished out. The friendly, open interactions at Harbin No. X were partly what identified the store as "massified" (*dazhonghua*, a term that evokes the socialist, revolutionary "masses"), as one manager had pointed out to me.

Like the examples of mutual disrespect I described in Chapter 3, the sociability that *reqing* represented was meant to be reciprocal between customer and clerk. Failure by a customer to respond to *reqing* was viewed by clerks as a breach of etiquette. For instance, a skeptical customer read the tags on a coat (which listed the filling as 90% down and 10% feathers) and asked, "What if they just write anything they want on these tags [*suibian xie*]?" Big Sister Zhao's reply was in the form of a clever pun: "A young lady might wear a *suibian* [braid], but the information on the coat tags is not *suibian* [casually (written)]!" The customer, however, remained surly and skeptical, and after he left Zhao remarked that he "wasn't a thing [*wanyir*]." I was confused. She smiled slyly and explained, "He wasn't a thing [*dongxi*] [an insult in Chinese], after we treated him so well he didn't buy anything!"

These *reqing* performances at Harbin No. X were not full-fledged, explicit examples of nostalgia or resistance like those described by Yang (2003), Rofel (1999), O'Brien and Li (1999), and others. Workers did not produce the kind of articulated critical consciousness that Ching Kwan Lee (2000, 2002, 2007) identified in restive portions of China's laid-off state industrial workers. Rather, salesclerks at Harbin No. X engaged in a more subtle counter strategy of remembering that traced a trajectory of social change and the rise of new patterns of class stratification in urban China. In fact, it was only within a broader social context of post-socialist socio-economic change and the general disenchantment of the urban working class—phenomena which studies of nostalgia and more overt worker resistance help us understand—that *reqing* could actually take on the significance of a practice of class distinction.

CONCLUSION

In a context where shoppers in China's retail marketplaces have become stratified by exposure to and perceptions of risk, Harbin No. X perched precariously at the cusp of two eras of retailing. Changes to the business of buying and selling consumer goods in urban China resulted in the rapid expansion of choice for consumers, in terms of both the kinds of goods available and the places in which to purchase them. This was accompanied, at the retail sector's lower echelons, by uncertainties about price, quality, and the authenticity of goods. At Harbin No. X, the consequence was a crisis of trust, as shoppers carried their anxieties and deep distrust of the marketplace into the state-owned store. An institution that had once commanded customer patronage by virtue of scarce competition and enjoyed high status as one of the premier state-run retail outlets in the city, the Harbin No. X Department Store could no longer elicit trust by virtue of its place in the Chinese state-socialist universe.

As Harbin No. X tracked a descending trajectory in the city's retail field, the dynamics of buying and selling had begun to change dramatically for store workers. The counter strategies workers developed in order to cope with this crisis of trust can be seen, I have suggested above, as a form of distinction work. Conscious of the competitive environment they now inhabited and sensitive to the increasingly murky boundaries between reputable and disreputable marketplaces, salesclerks at this state-owned store sought to re-establish the sharp moral boundaries that once set Harbin No. X apart, and above, the expanding private retail sector.

But the strategies salesclerks relied on to counter customer suspicion and distrust simultaneously traced the downward trajectory of China's urban working class. Indeed, their counter strategies only make sense within this context. In the course of distinguishing Harbin No. X from its new competitors, salesclerks also engaged in a nostalgic strategy of representation that portrayed Harbin No. X as still endowed with the symbolic capital of state socialism. Salesclerks endeavored to create a space, on the sales floor, characterized by a set of earthy, sociable interactions that recollected an imagined, pre-marketized golden era of genuine warmth and feeling among strangers—among, really, the urban working class. Here we find, much as Michele Lamont's work (1992; 2000; see also Lamont and Molnár 2002) would lead us to expect, that moral boundaries are laden with class-coded meanings and cultural practices. We also find, however, that moral boundaries are shaped by the social trajectories of the groups they define. At Harbin No. X, the production of trust and distinction mapped a social trajectory in which the past became a resource in the present. In reaction to a downward slide, the store's salesclerks staked a claim about value and moral worth in the here and now by reaching back into a reconstructed working-class past.

CHAPTER SEVEN

Conclusion

Whether she staffs a high-end boutique or labors at a cramped market stall, the daily work of an ordinary Harbin salesclerk involves many of the same tasks. She organizes stock, assists her customers with merchandise, and, of course, tries to sell them that merchandise. Yet at the same time that the women selling goods in various settings engage in separate, if parallel, work activities, their labors are also crucially interconnected. A fundamental aspect of their work is to distinguish themselves, their workplace, and their customers from the people doing the buying and selling elsewhere in the city.

Indeed, as I have demonstrated in the preceding chapters, service work in China today can be centrally organized around the construction and communication of symbolic boundaries, in particular those demarcating class differences. I call this distinction work. Distinction work was clearest at the Sunshine Department Store, where management was deeply committed to the creation of a distinctive sales force who could not only communicate the elite position of the store within Harbin's retail field but could also ably recognize customers' claims to high social position and class entitlements in the course of service interactions. That elite position was most easily conveyed when Sunshine situated itself in contrast to other key retail settings in the city, such as Harbin No. X and The Underground. Both were easily intelligible to local shoppers, the former as a "proletarian" and "socialist" space, the latter as an unruly and disreputable lower-class one. As I noted in Chapter 4, recognition of the kind of social space Sunshine *was* required recognizing what it *was not*. In this way, distinction work and the construction of class boundaries are deeply relational in nature.

However, the distinctions carefully built up at Sunshine were frequently chipped away in The Underground, as the saleswomen there challenged the boundaries that marked their marketplace, their wares, and even their persons as lowly and untrustworthy. I have suggested that by destabilizing the distinctions separating *geti* bazaars from exclusive retail outlets like Sunshine, the women working in The Underground engaged in counter strategies of distinction. And yet their sales work drew them into a larger symbolic economy in which they remained unable to escape the highly gendered class boundaries that marked them. More often than not, the same resources they brought to bear in this symbolic economy also reinscribed their low social position.

The Harbin No. X Department Store, by contrast, revealed conditions under which distinction work does—and does not—appear. Because store management focused more on their relations with the local party-state than with either their customers or their retailing competitors, they did not engineer the sales floor as a space of distinction. Instead, that sales floor was a place where a work culture with socialist characteristics could flourish. But as Chapter 6 demonstrated, the sales floor at Harbin No. X was also a place where workers had begun to innovate a relational labor process and create their own form of distinction work. Confronted daily with the pressures of market competition and the encroachment of *geti* marketplace practices and mindsets, Harbin No. X salesclerks attempted to distinguish the store by reminding shoppers of the store's state-socialist pedigree. Distinction work in this setting aimed to translate state-socialist symbolic capital into a currency recognized in a new, market era.

In all three cases, the organization of service work suggests that the production of class distinctions can be a key aspect of what service work is organized to produce. The production of class meanings also puts different service settings in conversation with one another. As I have argued in the preceding chapters, we can only recognize the role of distinction work in one service setting if we take into account how it is shaped by its relations with other positions within the field. This approach to service work, and to the symbolic construction of class boundaries, provides insight into the practical and relational aspects of class—class as, in the words of E. P. Thompson, "not . . . 'structure,' nor even . . . 'category,' but as something which in fact happens . . . in human relationships" (1966: 9), or what Pierre Bourdieu has described as "not as something given but as *something to be done*" (1998: 12).

The symbolic boundaries that stake out the cultural borders of social classes are critical aspects of both everyday social interactions and the construction of enduring hierarchies of domination and power. These boundaries are also contested and changing. Salesclerks at Harbin No. X sought to bank on a kind of socialist-era symbolic capital that was, ultimately, in decline. Indeed, the downward trajectory of Harbin No. X, and its workers, says much about the gendered implications of distinction work for service workers and the implications of a new structure of entitlement in urban China. This is also a good point to take us back, briefly, into this tale of three marketplaces.

HARBIN REVISITED

In March 2005, some two-and-a-half years after completing my field research, I returned to Harbin to revisit all three market sites. The city, still in the grip of a lingering winter, bore stretch marks from economic growth: main boulevards choked on a swollen fleet of personal cars, and residential and business districts were dotted with construction sites. Shopping areas glistened with new shop façades. Hong Kong–based retailer Lane Crawford had opened a store in downtown Harbin where, one friend informed me, a man's shirt sold for 4,000 yuan (roughly US$500). "There must be a lot of rich people in Harbin now," he said to me, a bit ruefully.

The Sunshine Department Store was largely unchanged, except for an impressive set of new chrome doors at the store entrance. I rode the escalators up to the fourth floor cashmere department, where Goat King and its competitors still operated sweater boutiques. The salesclerks, however, were all new. I passed through the store anonymously, spotting only a single clerk whom I recognized. My experience in The Underground was similar. Room 28 continued to house ten counter spaces, but only three of the original merchants (all experienced and middle-aged) were still there, seeming to confirm Mr. Zhou's estimate three years prior that only 30% of Underground merchants actually made a profit. But Mr. Zhou was at his counter, and I stopped to chat with him. "What happened to everyone else?" I asked. Some had gone out of business, others had sought new avenues of making a living, and some had moved to other locations. And while a few of the merchants had remained in the room, all the sales help had experienced turnover, moving to other counters in the market or seeking work elsewhere in the city's service sector.

Then I headed over to the Harbin No. X Department Store. Having heard rumors that the store had been sold, I did not know what to expect as I rode the escalator up to women's department. But as soon as I stepped out onto the second floor, someone recognized me. "Ai-mei, you're back!" exclaimed a clerk whom *I* did not recognize. At my request, she quickly directed me to Big Sister Zhao's sales area. After a happy greeting (and a scolding for not staying in touch), Zhao took me to see Big Sister Lin, and the three of us went up to the fifth floor—the new location for down coats—to visit Little Xiao and take photographs together. In typical Harbin No. X fashion, my old co-workers knew where everyone in the store was working, what shift they were on, and recent events in their personal lives.

But in truth, Harbin No. X was in the throes of change. The city had not yet sold its stake in the store, but a sale was slated to go through in less than a month's time. The deal had been arranged by the municipal commerce office in Harbin, and a large, state-controlled business conglomerate ("group," or *jituan* in Chinese) would soon acquire a majority interest in the store. A store manager gave me a rough outline of the changes, explaining that the new owners were planning to expand the store to include a movie theater and other entertainment venues. As for workers, they would be "rehired" (*yingpin*) under a new, fully marketized employment system. Current store employees would have the option of signing one of two types of labor contracts. The first option was a short-term, three-year contract at the end of which the worker would be "bought out" (*maiduan*) by the store. Employment would terminate, and the worker would be paid a yet-to-be-determined severance package, largely based on the number of years the worker had been with the store. The second type of contract would last until the worker decided to retire. "All the details haven't been worked out yet," the manager told me, but he and the other managers I spoke with all assured me that I certainly would be able to find them at Harbin No. X the next time I visited the city.

That night, I met up with several of my old Harbin No. X co-workers for a reunion dinner. Big Sister Zhao, Big Sister Lin, and Xu Li-mei brought me up-to-date on their lives as the four of us ate, and our meal was punctuated by laughter and periodic toasts with the local beer. When Big Sister Zhao discovered I was not going to finish my last glass of beer, she insisted that I allow her to drink it for me. "This beer is made from Chinese grain," she told me sagely. "We shouldn't waste a drop!"

As we ate, I probed my three friends about the looming changes at Harbin No. X. What did they think of them? What were their plans? It turned out that the upcoming sale of the store was the culmination of a series of changes that had made my former co-workers rather unhappy. Xu Li-mei explained that over the past two years or so management had gotten much stricter at the store. "Now they've drawn a line in each sales area where you have to stand when there are no customers to assist. If you don't and get caught, you lose a point—and one point is 30 yuan!" A similar fine could be applied for talking with another salesclerk.[1]

We then discussed the contract options that Zhao, Lin, and Xu faced. Big Sister Zhao said she might expect about 20,000 yuan for her 20 years of work at the store if she signed a terminal, "buy-out" contract. She was still undecided as to which contract she would choose, but she was mulling over the possibility of starting up her own small clothing business with the buy-out money. Big Sister Lin, at the store for over 10 years, was reticent about her options. "I'm sure there will be something at the store I can do . . . they'll need people to staff the movie theater," she suggested hopefully.

Workers with less than 10 years of tenure at the store were to be bought out at a lower rate, so Xu, who at 29 years of age had only worked at Harbin No. X for nine years, believed she would receive a mere 7,000 yuan or so if she signed a "buy-out" contract. "Wouldn't it make sense for you to sign the long-term contract, then?" I asked Xu Li-mei. She was uncertain. "They can still fire you, it doesn't actually guarantee employment," she explained. "They could fire you if they want, for some little thing, like standing in the wrong spot!" Besides, she added, there were plans to institute an age limit for salesclerks, but what the actual limit would be was still unclear. "By the time the store re-opens under the new ownership, I could be 30 and over their age limit!"

[1] It is impossible for me to know how strictly these new fines were enforced. Both Big Sister Zhao and Big Sister Lin left their work posts to go take photos with me, and when the three of us visited Little Xiao up on the fifth floor, he told Zhao and Lin that it "wasn't strict" there. Nevertheless, the requirement about where a worker must stand, and fines of 30 yuan (previously only 5 yuan), were new.

Big Sister Zhao was optimistic. She suggested the store would never behave in such a way, pointing out that age discrimination had been explicitly discouraged by the most recent session of the National People's Congress. Zhao added that the government was committed to protecting "vulnerable groups" (*ruoshi qunti*). Xu Li-mei was utterly unconvinced. "It won't be a state enterprise anymore, how can the government object? It will be all about profits."

GENDER, GENERATION, AND THE FACE
OF POST-SOCIALISM

Service organizations like the department stores I studied are invested in a structure of differentiated entitlement that sets them—and their customers—apart from others. When I worked at Harbin No. X, it was the workers who sensed their interest in distinguishing themselves from the lower position of *geti* merchants. But as the local government's desire to cut itself loose from the store's financial woes became clear, managers had also adopted a new stance toward store business. Ironically, it seemed that Harbin No. X was now to be distinguished from . . . itself.

As Harbin No. X's managers adopted what are perceived to be the trappings of capitalist labor discipline in China—including strict control over workers' physical movements (cf. Rofel 1999; Lee 1998)—they were simultaneously distancing the store from its socialist legacy. The requirement that salesclerks stand in a single, pre-designated location seemed a mindless attempt to copy the successful service model offered up by top department stores like Sunshine. In the hopes of attracting a wealthier clientele who desired the trappings of elite service, decision-makers at Harbin No. X sought to cast off the store's associations with the socialist era by acquiring a new, modern face and the veneer of capitalist workplace discipline.

That face was not just symbolic but also physical, and the large, state-owned retailer would likely shed its aging female workforce as well. In an expanding service sector where young women workers serve as representatives of a new market society, the politics of post-socialist transformation have combined with class and gender inequalities to weigh especially heavily on middle-aged, working-class women. These urban women were among the first to experience state sector lay-offs in the

1980s and '90s (Wang Zheng 2000). Ironically, the gendered distribution of jobs during the more egalitarian Mao era placed many of these women in the low-skill jobs that have been targeted by reforms and privatization efforts (ibid.).

But the fact that middle-aged, state sector workers are not considered suitable for modern interactive service sector jobs—even if they have twenty years' experience on the sales floor—has just as much to do with the imageries of change and progress in China today. Many scholars have explored the fate of laid-off state and collective sector workers in China, detailing the troubles they face in the labor market and the numerous reasons behind this—such as competition from rural migrants, inexperience in the job market, and the lingering effects of the Cultural Revolution on education and skill levels (e.g. Solinger 2002; Hung and Chiu 2003; Won 2004). I want to suggest, however, that the value of labor in China has been "temporalized" such that workers associated with socialism are viewed as incapable of producing value in a market economy (Junghans 2001). Much like workers in Eastern Europe (Kideckel 2002), or China's own "lost" Cultural Revolution generation (Hung and Chiu 2003), China's urban working class and the social spaces with which they are associated have lost symbolic capital in the course of the reform era as a result of their associations with a broken and seemingly unreformable state sector. The result has been, in the words of Dorothy Solinger, a "crumpling of [socialist] status hierarchies" (2004: 52).

But Harbin No. X salesclerks were not simply associated with socialism by virtue of their gender and their age. Their vibrant work culture and their egalitarian stance with customers also identified them as unruly, undisciplined, and disrespectful—unproductive as service workers and unwilling to conform to the strictures of discipline in a capitalist marketplace. Much like the department stores where one might find these women selling merchandise, they were viewed by many industry specialists as anachronisms destined to fade away and rejoin the past to which they purportedly belong. As one of my informants said of retailers like Harbin No. X, "Those state-owned stores will have to change . . . or they will disappear." Department stores, of course, can disappear, their old buildings occupied by new businesses. Thirty- and forty-something women salesclerks, however, are doomed to living out their obscurity.

Once state employers shed their middle-aged women workers, these women face almost certain downward mobility in a job market that deems them suited for largely invisible, backroom service jobs offering low wages and no benefits: laundry, food service, or domestic work such as housecleaning or elderly care (Wang Zheng 2000). Two different job advertisements I encountered during my March 2005 trip to China encapsulated the gender- and age-segregated labor market that urban, working-class women encounter. In Harbin, a new Parkson Department Store posted a large employment notice in the window of the soon-to-open department store. The notice declared that the store intended to hire "2,000 salesclerks meeting the following specifications," the most prominent of which was being "under 30 years of age." Later, in the small city of Chengde near Beijing, a sign posted in a small fried cruller shop advertised for kitchen workers. "Laid-off women workers given priority."

The threat is that not just a single generation, but rather that generations, of working-class women will be successively purged from well-paying service sector jobs because age is viewed as an indicator of productivity—and a condition of employability. What does it mean when there is simply no ladder for advancement beyond age 30? Where do no-longer-youthful salesclerks go when they exceed store age limits? Going into "small business" (*xiao shengyi*) for oneself carries a very high risk of failure—as my return visit to The Underground suggests—and could easily consume a family's already-precious resources (see Solinger 2004; Liu 2007). Many of these questions are empirical in nature, and while the fate of aging service workers is an issue beyond the scope of my study, these questions point to important directions for future research.

MORE COUNTER STRATEGIES?

Another question raised by this research is one of worker resistance. As service work regimes become more despotic and more temporary, and as employers shed their responsibilities for workers (but not their control over them) in increasingly fragmented service work settings like Sunshine, what are the possibilities for workers' resistance? And for salesclerks like those at Harbin No. X, where I have argued a socialist work culture once flourished, what is the likelihood that their critical consciousness might be redeployed against the erosion of worker privileges?

Ching Kwan Lee (2000, 2002, 2007) has argued, for example, that a critical class consciousness is, in fact, forged in the ashes of socialism as workers use the tenets of socialist ideology to challenge class relations in a market society, a phenomenon that she describes as "postsocialist labor insurgency." Direct confrontation with market reforms and market inequalities can awaken a "positive" class consciousness and provide the memories of socialism with a new target. At the same time, Lee finds that the persistence and effectiveness of collective industrial labor struggles are often severely constrained by a work unit's political and economic situation and by workers' ties to their unit. The feeblest work units leave workers most emboldened, but this has also meant workers are least likely to achieve their aims. In such cases, Lee writes, "successful action usually led to a formal dissolution of employment relations with the state, and the loss of their status as state workers with all its moral, economic and political rights" (Lee 2000: 232).

As Harbin No. X's socialist work culture was threatened by changing managerial practices (like restriction of movement), the individualized nature of employment packages precluded mass resistance. The option of getting seed money for a future small business could easily deter workers like Big Sister Zhao from joining together with co-workers like Big Sister Lin, who hoped to retain her position at the store. Indeed, as the dinner conversation I described above reveals, workers were hard put to make greater demands of their employer when what was happening fit neatly into the legal framework of enterprise reforms and followed the logic of a market economy. This is not to say that workers felt recent developments to be fair, as Marc Blecher's (2002) argument about the hegemony of market values might suggest. In fact, many workers believed these changes to be very *un*fair, but they also saw little opening for protest. In the end, workers would have to "choose," on an individual basis, their own fate with the store.

At Sunshine and in The Underground, worker strategies were even more fragmented and individualized. Given that salesclerks were not technically store employees, Sunshine clerks did not belong to a branch of the state-run trade union, as was true at Harbin No. X. Indeed, the labor arrangements at Sunshine were deeply antithetical to collective action, and sales floor dynamics created fractured, competitive, and even distrustful relations among salesclerks. And in contrast to salesclerks at Sunshine, the young women hired to sell merchandise in The Underground had even fewer resources: They could not even turn to a personnel department for recourse when disputes with employers arose. In both settings, workers would largely resist with their feet, leaving to seek employment elsewhere. But, as Ching Kwan Lee points out, when "some 30 percent of both urban and rural labor is considered 'surplus'" (2002: 198), it is managers who have considerable leverage over their workers. At the very least, it is clear that changes to the organization of service work like those found in department stores have been, in many ways, a recipe for worker disempowerment (Hanser 2007).

Changes to the Field

The day after my reunion dinner, and my last day in Harbin, I visited Sunshine's new store, and its third outlet in the city. It was, in many ways, a reproduction of the original one where I had worked: chrome-plated doors, marble floors, and highly polished mirrored pillars. Sales areas displayed carefully arrayed racks of expensive, brand name fashions. The only obvious difference from the other Sunshine outlet was that the color of salesclerks' uniforms had migrated from burgundy to hot pink.

To my surprise, the parallels with Sunshine's flagship store did not end there. Just outside the new Sunshine outlet I found an entrance leading down below the street to another underground market. This market catered to a retail clientele, but the merchandise was the same mix of goods found in The Underground (and may well have been purchased wholesale from that larger, more centrally located *geti* market). The two types of markets—one high-end and exclusive, the other inexpensive and common—seemed locked in a symbiotic, and symbolic, relationship.

But when I gazed across the busy intersection to the large store situated there, instead of a drab state-owned retailer there sat a massive superstore operated by the French company Carrefour. This reconfiguration of retail stores not only marks the arrival of transnational retailers in Harbin and other large Chinese cities but also suggests the erasure of the past as well.

Distinction Work and Subordination

Aside from issues of job security, job opportunity, and possibilities for collective action, service workers' interests clearly center on the service interactions that comprise the bulk of their workdays. Service work that is organized as distinction work—which creates distinctions among organizations and enacts distinctions among people—has involved some fundamental shifts in the nature of service work for Chinese retail workers. In particular, relations between workers and customers in luxury retail settings are stripped of much of the reciprocity and mutuality that was once a broader feature of such social interactions. As the previous chapters have attempted to show, personal dignity in the workplace is of great importance to the workers and merchants I studied (cf. Hodson 2001), and yet increasingly this is also what "good" service can preclude. A profound subordination of the worker is built into models of service work that are organized around the recognition of class entitlements (Sherman 2006). And as developments at Harbin No. X show, such service settings may increasingly serve as a model and standard for service more generally in China.

Why should a service worker have to be cheerful and pleasant all the time? Why must a salesclerk be forced to deal with an unreasonable customer, and with a pleasant demeanor to boot? In the West, the performance of deference by service workers is often so extensive and routine that we are not even aware of it: Grocery store cashiers perform bodily deference by standing at their registers, and a surly store clerk draws disparaging comments. The expectations we have about good service are not simply based on standards of courteous interaction but, in fact, often require performances of social inequality. One need not adhere to the culture-bound concepts of self and authenticity at the core of Arlie Hochschild's work on emotional labor to recognize, as she does, that "good" service frequently involves expressions of symbolic violence against the worker and enactments of social hierarchy between customer and salesclerk.

I am not, of course, suggesting that China prior to market reforms was a workers' paradise. As Andrew Walder's (1986) study of the Chinese workplace testifies, the intense competition for scarce rewards and resources that occurred under that system created coercive, divided workplaces. Indeed, it could be argued that deference was actually structured into the pre-reform workplace in the form of *biaoxian*, displays of political and personal cooperativeness with work unit leadership and the party-state more broadly. Such displays were often enactments of dependency and social hierarchy. Yet the fact remains that when I carried out this study, service workers in state-owned department stores like Harbin No. X conducted their work with levels of dignity and respect that find no equivalents in more "modern" models of service work in urban China.

The rise of distinction work is not simply a question of the enactment of subordination in social interactions, for it is a pattern of interaction in which for-profit organizations become deeply invested and compel their employees to engage. This can be viewed as one of the institutionalized forms that inequality takes in China today, much like organized dependence (Walder 1986) of past workplaces. But in the modern context, domination by the state and its agents has been replaced by the seemingly impartial forces of markets and capitalism. Increasingly in China today, a belief in the power of markets to regulate service interactions—that customers will simply take their business elsewhere if they are not adequately catered to—suggests that a customer's money buys not only merchandise but also polite and attentive service. That money is also seen as rightfully buying a worker's deference and submission.

At the same time that distinction work involves acts of interpersonal domination and subordination on the sales floor, it is also pitched to create institutional distinctions. Indeed, employers' efforts to "distinguish" themselves in a competitive market setting revolve around sets of inclusions and exclusions that limit job opportunity and social mobility, and these exclusions structure inequalities based on class, gender, and age. These boundaries are fundamental to the production of inequality, and for its justification, in urban China today.

Difference and the Structure of Entitlement

It is the link between difference, class entitlements, and service work that gives us a sense of how a story of three marketplaces fits into the bigger picture of social transformation and inequality in modern China. Indeed, the social organization of department stores and markets provides a window onto how "the market" more broadly writ serves as a central context in which inequality is enacted, understood, and justified. Worker disempowerment is closely tied to a broad acceptance in China of new levels and forms of inequality that are often seen as unavoidable accompaniments to economic reforms (Wang Xiaoming 2003; Wang Jing 2001). To be sure, the model of service work pursued by China's most elite retailers—and now mimicked, to some degree, by failing state-owned ones—invests in a new structure of entitlement that not only dictates who is deserving of a job on the sales floor but also who is entitled to the levels of deference and respect distributed there. Acts of deference on the sales floor, I have tried to show, recognize class difference and do not simply express respect for the sensibilities of individuals. Service interactions that involve such expressions of deference must, I contend, be located in a context much broader than the worker-customer dyad or even the manager-worker-customer triad. These social interactions are situated in a wider social context in which wealthy elites are increasingly viewed as rightfully entitled to esteem, respect, and deference. Rituals of class recognition embedded in service interactions are indicative as well as constitutive of these new class hierarchies and help create a culture of differentiated privileges and a new structure of entitlement in urban China. They are, in effect, enactments of social hierarchy and as such make up the very substance of inequality (Sherman 2006: 259).

A structure of entitlement that enables the few to extract deference from, and enforce a symbolic violence upon, other groups of people is also integral to the legitimization of inequality (Sherman 2006: 262). No doubt, the categories that mark symbolic boundaries and construct a field of differences among retail settings, among workers, and between workers and customers are a central strut of this structure of entitlement. As Pun Ngai has noted, "The play of difference is highly political" (1999: 11). Symbolic boundaries are important in large part because they can translate into social boundaries (Lamont and Molnár 2002: 168–69). Powerful groups rely on "their legitimate culture" not only to mark difference but also to maintain and reproduce group membership and its privileges as they convert "symbolic distinction into [social] closure" (ibid.: 172). As Charles Tilly has argued (1998), the social and cultural categories that create concrete social groupings become embedded in both formal and informal institutional settings. As highly intelligible, and often commonsensical, ways of understanding the world, such categories of difference form the basis for what Tilly calls "durable inequality."

There are other reasons to believe that this new structure of entitlement, institutionalized in service work settings, is of great social significance. For example, recent research on consumption and consumerism in China has begun to explore the emergence of consumer rights and entitlements (Hooper 2000), especially those related to home ownership, as a sphere for collective action and the assertion of entitlements and rights (Tomba 2004, 2005; Read 2003; Davis 2005, 2006). In a context

The last hurrah. Photo by the author.

in which consumers are increasingly viewed as a key engine of China's economic growth (Dirlik 2001; Croll 2006), the "consumer" may become a vehicle for claims made against the state, legal institutions, and powerful economic agents such as real estate development companies. But, as this book has detailed, consumer entitlements and the kinds of social and political demands they engender are structured by inequalities. As Luigi Tomba (2004) has ably demonstrated, work unit affiliation and a state-engineered effort to "create" a middle class in China's large cities have strongly mediated the ability to purchase housing in high-price real estate markets. The form of collective action that results from home ownership, as Luigi Tomba (2005) and Deborah Davis (2006) separately argue, is narrow and exclusive. Given the extremely limited development of political rights in China, whatever empowerment experienced by consumers in China is apt to be shaped not only by broader economic inequalities but also by the cultural contours of a structure of entitlement.

Indeed, as the previous chapters have detailed, a structure of entitlement and new class inequalities in urban China are institutionalized in service settings that draw upon legitimating discourses of gender and of economic transition. When middle-aged, working-class women are associated with the inefficiencies and absurdities of the Mao era, their downward mobility and shrinking employment opportunities in the reform era seem self-evident. When young women working in free markets and clothing bazaars are associated with moral deviance and unrefined culture, their lack of upward mobility seems justified and self-imposed. At the top of the retail hierarchy, the organization of work produces class meanings that serve as a powerful public buttress to these broader social inequalities, helping to create, as Barbara Ehrenreich has said of service work in the U.S. context, "not just an economy but a culture of . . . inequality" (2001: 212).

THE LAST HURRAH

After Big Sister Zhao downed that last, precious glass of Chinese beer, my three dinner companions and I strolled out into the frigid Harbin night. Before going our separate ways, Zhao had us form a huddle, into the center of which we each stuck our right hand. Over this collective, four-way handshake we made promises to stay in touch, and I assured my friends that I would return again soon. Would I still be able to find them at Harbin No. X? We all hoped so.

Works Cited

Works Cited

Acker, Joan. 1990. "Hierarchies, Jobs, Bodies: A Theory of Gendered Organizations." *Gender & Society* 4: 139–58.

Adkins, Lisa. 2002. *Revisions: Gender and Sexuality in Late Modernity*. Buckingham: Open University Press.

Anagnost, Ann. 1989. "Prosperity and Counterprosperity: The Moral Discourse on Wealth in Post-Mao China." Pp. 210–34 in *Marxism and the Chinese Experience*, edited by A. Dirlik and M. Meisner. Armonk, NY: M. E. Sharpe.

———. 1997. *National Past-Times: Narrative, Representation, and Power in Modern China*. Durham: Duke University Press.

———. 2004. "The Corporeal Politics of Quality (suzhi)." *Public Culture* 16: 189–208.

Asia Pulse. Apr. 12, 2005. "China Enters New Stage in Opening of Commercial Sector." Beijing.

———. Apr. 15, 2005. "Market Share of State-Owned Retailers Drops in China." Beijing.

———. Feb. 27, 2007. "Wal-Mart Further Consolidates in China." Beijing.

Bakken, Borge. 2000. *The Exemplary Society: Human Improvement, Social Control, and the Dangers of Modernity in China*. Oxford: Oxford University Press.

Baldoz, Rick, Charles Koeber, and Philip Kraft. 2001. *The Critical Study of Work: Labor, Technology, and Global Production*. Philadelphia: Temple University Press.

Barboza, David. 2005. "China, New Land of Shoppers, Builds Malls on Gigantic Scale." *New York Times*, May 25, p. 1.

Barmé, Geremie. 1999. *In the Red: On Contemporary Chinese Culture*. New York: Columbia University Press.

Bendix, Reinhard. 1956. *Work and Authority in Industry: Ideologies of Management in the Course of Industrialization*. Berkeley: University of California Press.

Benson, Susan Porter. 1986. *Counter Cultures: Saleswomen, Managers, and Customers in American Department Stores, 1890–1940*. Urbana: University of Illinois Press.

Bergère, Marie-Claire. 1989. *The Golden Age of the Chinese Bourgeoisie, 1911–1937*. Translated by Janet Lloyd. Cambridge: Cambridge University Press.

Bettie, Julie. 2003. *Women Without Class: Girls, Race, and Identity*. Berkeley: University of California Press.

Bian, Yanjie. 2002. "Chinese Social Stratification and Social Mobility." *Annual Review of Sociology* 28: 91–116.

———. 1994. *Work and Inequality in Urban China*. Albany: State University of New York Press.

Blecher, Marc J. 2002. "Hegemony and Workers' Politics in China." *The China Quarterly* 170: 283–303.

Bourdieu, Pierre. 1977. *Outline of a Theory of Practice*. Cambridge: Cambridge University Press.

———. 1981. "Men and Machines." Pp. 304–17 in *Advances in Social Theory and Methodology: Toward an Integration of Micro- and Macro-Sociologies*, edited by K. Knorr-Cetina and A. V. Cicourel. Boston: Routledge and Kegan Paul.

———. 1984. *Distinction: A Social Critique of the Judgment of Taste*. Cambridge: Harvard University Press.

———. 1990. *In Other Words: Essays Towards a Reflexive Sociology*. Stanford: Stanford University Press.

———. 1993. *The Field of Cultural Production: Essays on Art and Literature*. New York: Columbia University Press.

———. 1996. *The Rules of Art: Genesis and Structure of the Literary Field*. Translated by S. Emanuel. Stanford: Stanford University Press.

———. 1998. *Practical Reason: On the Theory of Action*. Stanford: Stanford University Press.

———. 2001. *Masculine Domination*. Stanford: Stanford University Press.

Bourdieu, Pierre, and Loïc J. D. Wacquant. 1992. *An Invitation to Reflexive Sociology*. Chicago: University of Chicago Press.

Braverman, Harry. 1974. *Labor and Monopoly Capital: The Degradation of Work in the Twentieth Century*. New York: Monthly Review Press.

Brownell, Susan. 1995. *Training the Body for China: Sports and the Moral Order of the People's Republic*. Berkeley: University of California Press.

———. 2001. "Making Dream Bodies in Beijing: Athletes, Fashion Models, and Urban Mystique in China." In *China Urban: Ethnographies of Contemporary Culture*, edited by N. Chen, C. Clark, S. Gottschang, and L. Jeffery. Durham: Duke University Press.

Bruun, Ole. 1993. *Business and Bureaucracy in a Chinese City: An Ethnography of Private Business Households in Contemporary China*. Berkeley: Institute for East Asian Studies, University of California.

Buckley, Christopher. 1999. "How a Revolution Becomes a Dinner Party: Stratification, Mobility and the New Rich in Urban China." Pp. 208–29 in *Culture and Privilege in Capitalist Asia*, edited by M. Pinches. London: Routledge.

Burawoy, Michael. 1991. "The Extended Case Method." Pp. 271–87 in *Ethnography Unbound: Power and Resistance in the Modern Metropolis*, edited by M. Burawoy et al. Berkeley: University of California Press.

———. 1985. *The Politics of Production: Factory Regimes under Capitalism and Socialism*. London: Verso.

————. 1979. *Manufacturing Consent: Changes in the Labor Process under Monopoly Capitalism*. Chicago: University of Chicago Press.

Burawoy, Michael, and Janos Lukács. 1992. *The Radiant Past: Ideology and Reality in Hungary's Road to Capitalism*. Chicago: University of Chicago Press.

Campbell, Colin. 1987. *The Romantic Ethic and the Spirit of Modern Consumerism*. London: Basil Blackwell.

Cao, Yang, and Victor Nee. 2000. "Comment: Controversies and Evidence in the Market Transition Debate." *American Journal of Sociology* 105: 1175–89.

Carter, James H. 2002. *Creating a Chinese Harbin: Nationalism in an International City, 1916–1932*. Ithaca: Cornell University Press.

Chai, Joseph C. H. 1992. "Consumption and Living Standards in China." *The China Quarterly* 131: 721–49.

Chan, Wellington K. K. 1998. "Personal Styles, Cultural Values and Management: The Sincere and Wing on Companies in Shanghai and Hong Kong, 1900–1941." Pp. 66–89 in *Asian Department Stores*, edited by K. MacPherson. Honolulu: University of Hawai'i Press.

Chen, Bingyan. 1984. "Research into the Problems of the Socialist Market in Heilongjiang Province" (*Heilongjiang sheng shehui zhuyi shichang wenti yanjiu*), part 2. *Shangye jingji* (Nov.): 1–10.

Chen, Tina Mai. 2003a. "Female Icons, Feminist Iconography? Socialist Rhetoric and Women's Agency in 1950s China." *Gender & History* 15: 268–95.

————. 2003b. "Proletarian White and Working Bodies in Mao's China." *positions: East Asia cultures critique* 11: 361–93.

Cheng, Tiejun, and Mark Selden. 1994. "The Origins and Social Consequences of China's Hukou System." *The China Quarterly* 139: 644–68.

China Economic Review. Mar. 1999. "Shopping in the Dark."

————. May 1999. "Paradise Lost."

Clunas, Craig. 1991. *Superfluous Things: Material Culture and Social Status in Early Modern China*. Cambridge: Polity Press.

Cohen, Lizabeth. 2003. *A Consumers' Republic: The Politics of Mass Consumption in Postwar America*. New York: Vintage Books.

Cochran, Sherman. 2006. *Chinese Medicine Men: Consumer Culture in China and Southeast Asia*. Cambridge: Harvard University Press.

Collins, Randall. 1992. "Women and the Production of Status Cultures." Pp. 213–31 in *Cultivating Differences: Symbolic Boundaries and the Making of Inequality*, edited by M. Lamont and M. Fournier. Chicago: University of Chicago Press.

Cook, Daniel T. 2004. *The Commodification of Childhood: Personhood, the Children's Wear Industry and the Rise of the Child-Consumer, 1917–1962*. Durham: Duke University Press.

Croll, Elisabeth J. 1991. "Imagining Heaven: Collective and Gendered Dreams in China." *Anthropology Today* 7: 7–12.

————. 1995. *Changing Identities of Chinese Women: Rhetoric, Experience and Self-Perception in Twentieth-Century China*. London: Zed Books.

————. 2006. *China's New Consumers: Social Development and Domestic Demand*. London: Routledge.

Dai, Jinhua. 1997. "Imagined Nostalgia." *boundary* 2(24): 143–61.

Dalton, Melville. 1974. "The Ratebuster: The Case of the Saleswoman." Pp. 206–14 in *Varieties of Work Experience: The Social Control of Occupational Groups and Roles*, edited by P. Stewart and M. Cantor. New York: Halsted Press.

Datamonitor. 2006. Apparel Retail in China: Industry Profile. Aug.

Davis, Deborah S. 2006. "Urban Chinese Homeowners as Citizen-Consumers." Pp. 281–99 in *The Ambivalent Consumer: Questioning Consumption in East Asia and the West*, edited by S. Garon and P. Maclachlan. Ithaca: Cornell University Press.

———. 2005. "Urban Consumer Culture." *The China Quarterly* 183: 692–709.

———. 2000a. "Social Class Transformation in Urban China: Training, Hiring, and Promoting Urban Professionals and Managers after 1949." *Modern China* 26: 251–75.

———, ed. 2000b. *The Consumer Revolution in Urban China*. Berkeley: University of California Press.

———. 1999. "Self-Employment in Shanghai: A Research Note." *The China Quarterly* 157: 22–43.

———. 1993. "Urban Households: Supplicants to a Socialist State." Pp. 50–76 in *Chinese Families in the Post-Mao Era*, edited by D. Davis and S. Harrell. Berkeley: University of California Press.

de Certeau, Michel. 1984. *The Practice of Everyday Life*. Berkeley: University of California Press.

Deng, Suiyu. 1984. "A Consideration of Management System Reforms in Small-Scale State-Run Retail Enterprises" (*Guoying xiaoxing lingshou qiye guanli tizhi gaige de tantao*). *Caimao jingji* 11: 33–36.

Department of Commerce. 1989. *Chinese Dry Goods Business* (*Zhongguo baihuo shangye*). Beijing: Beijing University Press.

Diao, Zengtang, Zicun Yang, and Yuexia Zhang. 1988. "A New Form for Reforming Retail Businesses—A Survey of the Renting of Counter Space at Yetai City's Shengxing Department Store" (*Lingshou shangye gaige de yi zhong xin xingshi—Yetai shi shengxing baihuo shangchang tanwei chuzu de diaocha*). *Caimao jingji* 12: 51–53.

DiMaggio, Paul J., and Walter W. Powell. 1991 [1983]. "The Iron Cage Revisited: Institutional Isomorphism and Collective Rationality." Pp. 63–82 in *The New Institutionalisim in Organizational Analysis*, edited by W. Powell and P. DiMaggio. Chicago: University of Chicago Press.

Dirlik, Arif. 2001. "Markets, Culture, Power: The Making of a 'Second Cultural Revolution' in China." *Asian Studies Review* 25: 1–33.

Dong, Shuangyin. 1987. "A Discussion of Some Difficulties with the Chengbao System" (*Dui chengbao zhi ji nan wenti de tantao*). *Caimao jingji* 12: 55–57.

Donnithorne, Audrey. 1967. *China's Economic System*. New York: Frederick A. Praeger Publishers.

Donovan, Frances. 1930. *The Saleslady*. Chicago: University of Chicago Press.

Douglas, Mary, and Baron Isherwood. 1979. *The World of Goods*. London: Basic Books.

Drakulic, Slavenka. 1991. *How We Survived Communism and Even Laughed*. New York: W. W. Norton & Co.

Dudley, Kathryn Marie. 1994. *The End of the Line: Lost Jobs, New Lives in Postindustrial America*. Chicago: University of Chicago Press.

du Gay, Paul. 1996. *Consumption and Identity at Work*. Thousand Oaks: Sage Publications.

Duneier, Mitchell. 1999. *Sidewalk*. New York: Farrar, Straus and Giroux.

Dunn, Elizabeth. 1999. "Slick Salesmen and Simple People: Negotiated Capitalism in a Privatized Polish Firm." Pp. 125–50 in *Uncertain Transition: Ethnographies of Change in the Postsocialist World*, edited by M. Burawoy and K. Verdery. Lanham, MD: Rowman & Littlefield.

———. 2004. *Privatizing Poland: Baby Food, Big Business, and the Remaking of Labor*. Ithaca: Cornell University Press.

Dutton, Michael. 1998. *Streetlife China*. Cambridge: Cambridge University Press.

Ehrenreich, Barbara. 2001. *Nickel and Dimed: On (Not) Getting By in America*. New York: Owl Books.

Erickson, Rebecca, and Amy Wharton. 1997. "Inauthenticity and Depression: Assessing the Consequences of Interactive Service Work." *Work and Occupations* 24: 188–213.

Fang, Cheng, Xiaobo Zhang, and Shenggan Fan. 2002. "Emergence of Urban Poverty and Inequality in China: Evidence from Household Survey." *China Economic Review* 13: 430–43.

Fantasia, Rick. 1995. "Fast Food in France." *Theory and Society* 24: 201–43.

Fernandez-Kelly, Maria Patricia. 1983. *For We Are Sold, I and My People: Women and Industry in Mexico's Frontier*. Albany: State University of New York Press.

Fligstein, Neil. 2001a. "Social Skill and the Theory of Fields." *Sociological Theory* 19: 105–25.

———. 2001b. *The Architecture of Markets: An Economic Sociology of Twenty-First-Century Capitalist Societies*. Princeton: Princeton University Press.

Foley, Douglas E. 1990. *Learning Capitalist Culture: Deep in the Heart of Tejas*. Philadelphia: University of Pennsylvania Press.

Foucault, Michel. 1988. "Technologies of the Self." In *Technologies of the Self: A Seminar with Michel Foucault*, edited by L. Martin, H. Gutman, and P. Hutton. Amherst: University of Massachusetts Press.

———. 1990 [1978]. *The History of Sexuality*, volume 1: *An Introduction*. New York: Vintage Books.

———. 1990 [1985]. *The History of Sexuality*, volume 2: *The Use of Pleasure*. New York: Vintage Books.

———. 1995 [1977]. *Discipline and Punish: The Birth of the Prison*. New York: Vintage.

Fraser, David. 2000. "Inventing Oasis: Luxury Housing Advertisements and Reconfiguring Domestic Space in Shanghai." Pp. 25–53 in *The Consumer Revolution in Urban China*, edited by D. Davis. Berkeley: University of California Press.

Freeman, Carla. 2000. *High Tech and High Heels in the Global Economy: Women, Work and Pink-Collar Identities in the Caribbean*. Durham: Duke University Press.

Fuller, Linda, and Vicki Smith. 1996. "Consumers' Reports: Management by Customers in a Changing Economy." Pp. 79–90 in *Working in the Service Society*, edited by C. Macdonald and C. Sirianni. Philadelphia: Temple University Press.

Furth, Charlotte. 2002. "Blood, Body, and Gender: Medical Images of the Female Condition in China, 1600–1850." in *Chinese Femininities/Chinese Masculinities: A Reader*, edited by S. Brownell and J. Wasserstrom. Berkeley: University of California Press.

Gerth, Karl. 2003. *China Made: Consumer Culture and the Creation of the Nation.* Cambridge: Harvard University Asia Center.

Giddens, Anthony. 1984. *The Constitution of Society: Outline of the Theory of Structuration.* Berkeley: University of California Press.

Gieryn, Thomas F. 1983. "Boundary-Work and the Demarcation of Science from Non-Science: Strains and Interests in Professional Ideologies of Scientists." *American Sociological Review* 48: 781–95.

Gillette, Maris Boyd. 2000. *From Mecca to Beijing: Modernization and Consumption Among Urban Chinese Muslims.* Stanford: Stanford University Press.

Glenn, Evelyn Nakano. 1992. "From Servitude to Service Work: Historical Continuities in the Racial Division of Paid Reproductive Labor." *Signs: Journal of Women in Culture and Society* 18: 1–43.

———. 1985. "Racial Ethnic Women's Labor: The Intersection of Race, Gender and Class Oppression." *Review of Radical Political Economics* 17: 86–108.

Goffman, Erving. 1967. *Interaction Ritual: Essays on Face-to-Face Behavior.* New York: Pantheon Books.

———. 1983. "The Interaction Order: American Sociological Association, 1982 Presidential Address." *American Sociological Review* 48: 1–17.

Gold, Ray. 1952. "Janitors versus Tenants: A Status-Income Dilemma." *American Journal of Sociology* 57: 486–93.

Gold, Thomas B. 1989. "Guerrilla Interviewing Among the *Getihu*." Pp. 175–92 in *Unofficial China: Popular Culture and Thought in the People's Republic*, edited by P. Link, R. Madsen, and P. Pickowicz. Boulder: Westview Press.

Goodman, David S. 1995. "New Economic Elites." Pp. 132–44 in *China in the 1990s*, edited by R. Benewick and P. Wingrove. Vancouver: UBC Press.

Gu, Chaolin, Hu Xiuhong, Liu Haiyong, and Song Guochen. 2004. "Situation of the Urban Rich" (*Chengshi fuyu jiceng zhuangkuang*). Pp. 264–82 in *Social Stratification in China Today (Zhongguo shehui fenceng)*, edited by P. Li, Q. Li, and L. Sun. Beijing: Zhongguo shehui fenceng.

Guan, Xinlin. 1998. "An Exploration of Certain Problems Associated with Sales Commissions" (*Guanyu xiaoshou huikou ruogan wenti tanjiu*). *Finance and Trade Economics (Caimao jingji)* (Sept.): 54–57.

Guo, Hongchi, and Liu Fei. 1998. "New China's Flagship Emporium: The Beijing Wangfujing Department Store." Pp. 114–38 in *Asian Department Stores*, edited by K. MacPherson. Honolulu: University of Hawai'i Press.

Guo, Kesha, and Wang Yanzhong. 1999. *Zhongguo chanye jiegou biandong qushi ji zhengce yanjiu [Changes to China's Industrial Structure and Policy Research].* Beijing: Jingji Guanli Press.

Guo, Zhijun, Wang Xilai, Cui Xun, and Wu Xiaohui. 1992. "The Current Situation of State-Run Commercial Wholesale Enterprises and Relevant Policies" (*Guoying shangye pifa qiye de xianzhuang ji duice*). *Finance and Trade Economics (Caimao jingji)* (Apr.): 46–51.

Gutek, Barbara A. 1995. *The Dynamics of Service: Reflections on the Changing Nature of Customer/Provider Interactions.* San Francisco: Jossey-Bass.

Guthrie, Douglas. 1998. "Organizational Uncertainty and Labor Contracts in China's Economic Transition." *Sociological Forum* 13: 457–94.

———. 1997. "Between Markets and Politics: Organizational Responses to Reform in China." *American Journal of Sociology* 102: 1258–1304.

Hall, Elaine J. 1993. "Smiling, Deferring, and Flirting: Doing Gender by Giving 'Good Service.'" *Work and Occupations* 20: 452–71.

Hall, John R. 1992. "The Capital(s) of Cultures: A Nonholistic Approach to Status Situations, Class, Gender, and Ethnicity." Pp. 257–85 in *Cultivating Differences: Symbolic Boundaries and the Making of Inequality*, edited by M. Lamont and M. Fournier. Chicago: University of Chicago Press.

Hamilton, Gary G., and Chi-kong Lai. 1989. "Consumerism Without Capitalism: Consumption and Brand Names in Late Imperial China." Pp. 253–79 in *The Social Economy of Consumption*, edited by H. Rutz and B. Orlove. Lanham, MD: University Press of America.

Hanser, Amy. 2002. "The Chinese Enterprising Self: Young, Educated Urbanites and the Search for Work." Pp. 189–206 in *Popular China: Unofficial Culture in a Globalizing Society*, edited by P. Link, R. Madsen, and P. Pickowicz. Lanham, MD: Rowman & Littlefield.

———. 2005. "The Gendered Rice Bowl: The Sexual Politics of Service Work in Urban China." *Gender & Society* 19(4): 581–600.

———. 2007. "A Tale of Two Sales Floors: Changing Service-Work Regimes in China." Pp. 77–97 in *Working in China: Ethnographies of Labor and Workplace Transformation*, edited by C. K. Lee. London: Routledge.

Harbin City Almanac (Ha'erbin shi zhi). 1996. Harbin: Heilongjiang People's Press (*Heilongjiang renmin chubanshe*), vol. 15.

Hartmann, Heidi. 1976. "Capitalism, Patriarchy and Job Segregation by Sex." Pp. 137–69 in *Women and the Workplace: The Implications of Occupational Segregation*, edited by M. Blaxall and B. Reagan. Chicago: University of Chicago Press.

Henson, Kevin, and Jackie Krasas Rogers. 2001. "'Why Marcia You've Changed!' Male Clerical Temporary Workers Doing Masculinity in a Feminized Occupation." *Gender & Society* 15: 218–38.

Hershkovitz, Linda. 1985. "The Fruits of Ambivalence: China's Urban Individual Economy." *Pacific Affairs* 58: 427–50.

Hertz, Ellen. 2001. "Faces in the Crowd: The Cultural Construction of Anonymity in Urban China." Pp. 274–93 in *China Urban: Ethnographies of Contemporary Culture*, edited by N. Chen, C. Clark, S. Gottschang, and L. Jeffery. Durham: Duke University Press.

Heyat, Farideh. 2002. "Women and the Culture of Entrepreneurship in Soviet and Post-Soviet Azerbaijan." Pp. 19–31 in *Markets and Moralities: Ethnographies of Postsocialism*, edited by R. Mandel and C. Humphrey. Oxford: Berg.

Hochschild, Arlie Russell. 1997. *The Time Bind: When Work Becomes Home and Home Becomes Work*. New York: Metropolitan Books.

―――. 1983. *The Managed Heart: Commercialization of Human Feeling*. Berkeley: University of California Press.

Hodson, Randy. 2001. *Dignity at Work*. Cambridge: Cambridge University Press.

Hoffman, Lisa. 2001. "Guiding College Graduates to Work: Social Constructions of Labor Markets in Dalian." Pp. 43–66 in *China Urban: Ethnographies of Contemporary Culture*, edited by N. Chen, C. Clark, S. Gottschang, and L. Jeffery. Durham: Duke University Press.

Holt, Douglas B. 1997. "Poststructuralist Lifestyle Analysis: Conceptualizing the Social Patterning of Consumption in Postmodernity." *Journal of Consumer Research* 23: 326–50.

Honig, Emily, and Gail Hershatter. 1988. *Personal Voices: Chinese Women in the 1980s*. Stanford: Stanford University Press.

Hooper, Beverly. 2000. "Consumer Voices: Asserting Rights in Post-Mao China." *China Information* 16: 92–128.

Hossfield, Karen. 1990. "Their Logic Against Them: Contradictions in Sex, Race and Class in Silicon Valley." In *Women Workers and Global Restructuring*, edited by K. Ward. Ithaca: ILR Press.

Hsing, You-tien. 1998. *Making Capitalism in China: The Taiwan Connection*. Oxford: Oxford University Press.

Humphrey, Caroline. 2002. *The Unmaking of Soviet Life: Everyday Economies After Socialism*. Ithaca: Cornell University Press.

Hung, Eva P. W., and Stephen W. K. Chiu. 2003. "The Lost Generation: Life Course Dynamics and *Xiagang* in China." *Modern China* 29: 204–36.

Hurst, William. 2004. "Understanding Contentious Collective Action by Chinese Laid-off Workers: The Importance of Regional Political Economy." *Studies in Comparative International Development* 39: 94–120.

Hurst, William, and Kevin J. O'Brien. 2002. "China's Contentious Pensioners." *The China Quarterly* 170: 345–60.

Hyde, Sandra Teresa. 2007. *Eating Spring Rice: The Cultural Politics of AIDS in Southwest China*. Berkeley: University of California Press.

IGD. 2003. "Asia Pacific Will Be Instrumental to Carrefour's Future Growth, Says IGD." *International Journal of Retail & Distribution Management* 31: 478.

Jankowiak, William R. 1993. *Sex, Death, and Hierarchy in a Chinese City: An Anthropological Account*. New York: Columbia University Press.

Ji, Yongkai. 2002. "Entry into the WTO: The Opportunities and Challenges Faced by Large-Scale Retail Businesses and Countermeasures." Unpublished manuscript.

Junghans, Lida. 2001. "Railway Workers Between Plan and Market." Pp. 183–200 in *China Urban: Ethnographies of Contemporary Culture*, edited by N. Chen, C. Clark, S. Gottschang, and L. Jeffery. Durham: Duke University Press.

Kaneff, Deema. 2002. "The Shame and Pride of Market Activity: Morality, Identity and Trading in Postsocialist Rural Bulgaria." Pp. 33–51 in *Markets and Moralities: Ethnographies of Postsocialism*, edited by R. Mandel and C. Humphrey. Oxford: Berg.

Katz-Gerro, Tally. 2002. "Highbrow Cultural Consumption and Class Distinction in Italy, Israel, West Germany, Sweden and the United States." *Social Forces* 81: 207–29.

Kelley, Robin D. G. 1994. *Race Rebels: Culture, Politics, and the Black Working Class*. New York: The Free Press.

Khan, Azizur Rahman, and Carl Riskin. 2005. "China's Household Income and Its Distribution, 1995 and 2002." *The China Quarterly* 182: 356–84.

———. 2001. *Inequality and Poverty in China in the Age of Globalization*. Oxford: Oxford University Press.

———. 1998. "Income and Inequality in China: Composition, Distribution and Growth of Household Income, 1988 to 1995." *The China Quarterly* 154: 221–53.

Kideckel, David A. 2002. "The Unmaking of an East-Central European Working Class." Pp. 114–32 in *Postsocialism: Ideals, Ideologies and Practices in Eurasia*, edited by C. Hann. London: Routledge.

Konrad, George, and Ivan Szelenyi. 1979. *The Intellectuals on the Road to Class Power*. Translated by A. Arato and R. Allen. New York: Harcourt Brace Jovanovich.

Kornai, Janos. 1980. *Economics of Shortage*. Amsterdam: North Holland.

Kou, Senlin. 1991. "Facing Market Choices" (*Miandui shichang de xuanze*). *Caimao jingji* 2: 49–51.

Kraus, Willy. 1991. *Private Business in China: Revival between Ideology and Pragmatism*. Translated by E. Holz. Honolulu: University of Hawaii Press.

Kunda, Gideon. 1992. *Engineering Culture: Control and Commitment in a High-Tech Corporation*. Philadelphia: Temple University Press.

LaBarbera, Priscilla A. 1988. "The Nouveaux Riches: Conspicuous Consumption and the Issue of Self-Fulfillment." *Research in Consumer Behavior* 3: 179–210.

Lahusen, Thomas. 2001. "Harbin and Manchuria: Place, Space, and Identity." Durham: Duke University Press.

Lamont, Michele. 1987. "Review: *The Practice of Everyday Life*." *American Journal of Sociology* 93: 720–21.

———. 1992. *Money, Morals, and Manners: The Culture of the French and American Upper-Middle Class*. Chicago: University of Chicago Press.

———. 2000. *The Dignity of Working Men: Morality and the Boundaries of Race, Class, and Immigration*. New York: Russell Sage Foundation.

Lamont, Michele, and Marcel Fournier. 1992a. *Cultivating Differences: Symbolic Boundaries and the Making of Inequality*. Chicago: University of Chicago Press.

———. 1992b. "Introduction." Pp. 1–17 in *Cultivating Differences: Symbolic Boundaries and the Making of Inequality*, edited by M. Lamont and M. Fournier. Chicago: University of Chicago Press.

Lamont, Michele, and Virág Molnár. 2002. "The Study of Boundaries in the Social Sciences." *Annual Review of Sociology* 28: 167–95.

Lan, Pei-Chia. 2001. "The Body as a Contested Terrain for Labor Control: Cosmetics Retailers in Department Stores and Direct Selling." Pp. 83–105 in *The Critical Study of Work: Labor, Technology and Global Production*, edited by R. Baldoz, C. Koeber, and P. Kraft. Philadelphia: Temple University Press.

———. 2003. "Working in a Neon Cage: Bodily Labor of Cosmetics Saleswomen in Taiwan." *Feminist Studies* 29: 21–45.

Langer, Beryl. 1988. "Review: *The Practice of Everyday Life.*" *Contemporary Sociology* 17: 122–24.

Larenaudie, Sarah Roper. 2005. "Luxury for The People!" *Time* 165: 48–52.

Ledevena, Alena V. 1998. *Russia's Economy of Favours: Blat, Networking, and Informal Exchange.* Cambridge: Cambridge University Press.

Leach, William R. "Transformations in a Culture of Consumption: Women and Department Stores, 1890–1925," *Journal of American History* 71 (2) (Sept.): 319–42.

Lee, Ching Kwan. 1998. *Gender and the South China Miracle: Two Worlds of Factory Women.* Berkeley: University of California Press.

———. 1999. "From Organized Dependence to Disorganized Despotism: Changing Labour Regimes in Chinese Factories." *The China Quarterly* 157: 44–71.

———. 2000. "The 'Revenge of History': Collective Memories and Labor Protests in North-Eastern China." *Ethnography* 1: 217–37.

———. 2002. "From the Specter of Mao to the Spirit of the Law: Labor Insurgency in China." *Theory and Society* 31: 189–228.

———. 2007. *Against the Law: Labor Protests in China's Rustbelt and Sunbelt.* Berkeley: University of California Press.

Lei, Guang. 2003. "Rural Taste, Urban Fashions: The Cultural Politics of Rural/Urban Difference in Contemporary China." *positions: East Asia cultures critique* 11: 613–46.

Leidner, Robin. 1993. *Fast Food, Fast Talk: Service Work and the Routinization of Everyday Life.* Berkeley: University of California Press.

———. 1996. "Rethinking Questions of Control: Lessons from McDonald's." Pp. 29–49 in *Working in the Service Society,* edited by C. Macdonald and C. Sirianni. Philadelphia: Temple University Press.

Li, Bin. 1993. "*Danwei* Culture as Urban Culture in Modern China: The Case of Beijing from 1949 to 1979." Pp. 345–52 in *Urban Anthropology in China,* edited by G. Guldin and A. Southall. Leiden: E. J. Brill.

Li, Conghua. 1998. *China: The Consumer Revolution.* Singapore: John Wiley & Sons (Asia).

Li, Dianjia. 1987. "Promoting Commercial Rental Operations a Step Further" (*Jin yi bu tuijin shangye zuzhai jingying*). *Juece tansuo* 5: 19–21.

Li, Peilin, and Zhang Yi. 2004. "Stratification of Consumption in China: An Important Perspective on Jump-Starting the Economy" (*Zhongguo de xiaofei fenceng: qidong jingji de yi ge zhongyao shidian*). Pp. 225–44 in *Social Stratification in China Today (Zhongguo shehui fenceng),* edited by P. Li, Q. Li, and L. Sun. Beijing: Social Sciences Academic Press (*Shehui kexue wenxian chubanshe*).

Li, Qiang. 2000. *Shehui fencen yu pinfu chabie (Social stratification and the gap between rich and poor).* Macao: Lujiang Press.

Li, Shaomin, He Xiaofeng, and You Youming. 2001. *China's Industrial and Commercial Operations (zhongguo gongshang jingying).* Beijing: Beijing University Press.

Li, Xianghua. 1987. "Making Use of the Full Set of Modern Management Techniques to Advance Management Improvements: A Survey of the Implementation of Modern Management at Shenyang City's Tiexi Department Store" (*Peitao yingyong xiandai guanli fangfa tuijin guanli jinbu: shenyang shi tiexi baihuo shangdian tuixing xiandaihua guanli de diaocha*). *Shangye yanjiu* 58(2): 20–21.

Liechty, Mark. 2003. *Suitably Modern: Making Middle-Class Culture in a New Consumer Society*. Princeton: Princeton University Press.

Liu, Guanglu. 1989. "A Survey of the Situation of State- and Collective Commerce Renting Out Counter Space" (*Guoying, jiti shangye chuzu guitai qingkuang de diaocha*). *Liaoning shangye jingji* (Apr.): 20–21.

Liu, Sian Victoria. 2007. "'Social Positions': Neighborhood Transitions After *Danwei*." Pp. 38–55 in *Working in China: Ethnographies of Labor and Workplace Transformation*, edited by C. K. Lee. London: Routledge.

Lo, T. Wing-Chun, Ho-Fuk Lao, and Gong-Shi Lin. 2001. "Problems and Prospects of Supermarket Development in China." *International Journal of Retail & Distribution Management* 29: 66.

Lockwood, David. 1989. *The Blackcoated Worker: A Study in Class Consciousness*. New York: Oxford University Press.Barlow, Tani E. 1994. "Politics and Protocols of Funü: (Un)making National Woman." In *Engendering China: Women, Culture and the State*, edited by C. Gilmartin, G. Hershatter, L. Rofel, and T. White. Cambridge: Harvard University Press.

Loe, Mieka. 1996. "Working for Men—At the Intersection of Power, Gender, and Sexuality." *Sociological Inquiry* 66: 399–421.

Lombard, George. 1955. *Behavior in a Selling Group: A Case Study of Interpersonal Relations in a Department Store*. Cambridge: Harvard University Graduate School of Business Administration.

Lu, Hanchao. 2002. "Nostalgia for the Future: The Resurgence of an Alienated Culture in China." *Pacific Affairs* 75: 169–89.

Lu, Hanlong. 2000. "To Be Relatively Comfortable in an Egalitarian Society." Pp. 124–41 in *The Consumer Revolution in Urban China*, edited by D. Davis. Berkeley: University of California Press.

MacPherson, Kerrie L. 1998. "Introduction: Asia's Universal Providers." Pp. 1–30 in *Asian Department Stores*, edited by K. MacPherson. Honolulu: University of Hawai'i Press.

Mann, Susan. 1987. *Local Merchants and the Chinese Bureaucracy, 1750–1950*. Stanford: Stanford University Press.

Martin, John Levi. 2003. "What Is Field Theory?" *American Journal of Sociology* 109: 1–49.

Melosh, Barbara. 1982. *"The Physician's Hand": Work Culture and Conflict in American Nursing*. Philadelphia: Temple University Press.

Milkman, Ruth. 1987. *Gender at Work: The Dynamics of Job Segregation by Sex During World War II*. Urbana: University of Illinois Press.

Miller, Daniel. 1987. *Material Culture and Mass Consumption*. Oxford: Blackwell.

Miller, Michael B. 1981. *The Bon March: Bourgeois Culture and the Department Store, 1869–1920*. Princeton: Princeton University Press.

Murphy, Rachel. 2004. "Turning Peasants into Modern Chinese Citizens: 'Population Quality' Discourse, Demographic Transition and Primary Education." *The China Quarterly* 177(1): 1–20.

Naughton, Barry. 1995. *Growing Out of the Plan: Chinese Economic Reform, 1978–1993*. Cambridge: Cambridge University Press.

Nee, Victor. 1989. "A Theory of Market Transition: From Redistribution to Markets in State Socialism." *American Sociological Review* 54: 663–81.

———. 1996. "The Emergence of a Market Society: Changing Mechanisms of Stratification in China." *American Journal of Sociology* 101: 908–49.

Newby, Howard. 1979. *The Deferential Worker: A Study of Farm Workers in East Anglia*. Madison: University of Wisconsin Press.

Newman, Katherine. 1999. *No Shame in My Game: The Working Poor in the Inner City*. New York: Knopf and the Russell Sage Foundation.

Nickum, James E. 2003. "Review Essay: Broken Eggs in the Market: The Rise of Inequality in China." *The China Journal* 49: 119–26.

O'Brien, Kevin J., and Lianjiang Li. 1999. "Campaign Nostalgia in the Chinese Countryside." *Asian Survey* 39: 375–93.

Ong, Aihwa. 1987. *Spirits of Resistance and Capitalist Discipline: Factory Women in Malaysia*. Albany: State University of New York Press.

———. 1997. "The Gender and Labor Politics of Postmodernity." Pp. 61–97 in *The Politics of Culture in the Shadow of Capital*, edited by L. Lowe. Durham: Duke University Press.

Ortner, Sherry B. 1991. "Reading America: Preliminary Notes on Class and Culture." Pp. 163–89 in *Recapturing Anthropology: Working in the Present*, edited by R. Fox. Santa Fe: School of American Research Press.

Otis, Eileen M. 2007. "Virtual Personalism in Beijing: Learning Deference and Femininity at a Global Luxury Hotel." Pp. 101–23 in *Working in China: Ethnographies of Labor and Workplace Transformation*, edited by C. K. Lee. London: Routledge.

———. 2003. "Serve the People: Gender, Class and Ethnicity in China's Emergent Service Sector." Ph.D. dissertation, Sociology, University of California, Davis.

Pan, Yao. 1988. "Improving and Developing the Contract Management System in Commercial Enterprises" (*Wanshan yu fazhan shangye qiye chengbao jingying zerenzhi*). *Shangye jingji yu guanli* 4: 135–40.

Paules, Greta Foff. 1991. *Dishing It Out: Power and Resistance Among Waitresses in a New Jersey Restaurant*. Philadelphia: Temple University Press.

Perry, Elizabeth J. 1993. *Shanghai on Strike: The Politics of Chinese Labor*. Stanford: Stanford University Press.

Pierce, Jennifer L. 1995. *Gender Trials: Emotional Lives in Contemporary Law Firms*. Berkeley: University of California Press.

Pringle, Rosemary. 1988. *Secretaries Talk: Sexuality, Power and Work*. London: Verso.

———. 1992. "What Is a Secretary?" In *Defining Women: Social Institutions and Gender Divisions*, edited by L. McDowell and R. Pringle. Cambridge: Polity Press.

Pun, Ngai. 1999. "Becoming Dagongmei (Working Girls): The Politics of Identity and Difference in Reform China." *The China Journal* 42: 1–18.

———. 2000. "Opening a Minor Genre of Resistance in Reform China: Scream, Dream, and Transgression in a Workplace." *positions: East Asia cultures critique* 8: 531–55.

———. 2003. "Subsumption or Consumption? The Phantom of Consumer Revolution in 'Globalizing' China." *Cultural Anthropology* 18: 469–92.

———. 2005. *Made in China: Women Factory Workers in a Global Workplace*. Durham, NC, and Hong Kong: Duke University Press and Hong Kong University Press.

Qiao, Run. 1989. "It Is Not Appropriate for Large and Mid-Sized State-Run Retail Enterprises to Rent Counters to *Getihu*" (*Guoying da zhong xing shangye lingshou qiye buyi dui getihu chuzu guitai*). *Caimao jingji* (May): 61.

Ray, Raka. 1999. *Fields of Protest: Women's Movements in India*. Minneapolis: University of Minnesota Press.

Read, Benjamin L. 2003. "Democratizing the Neighborhood? New Private Housing and Home-Owner Self-Organization in Urban China." *The China Journal* 49: 31–59.

Riskin, Carl, Zhao Renwei, and Li Shi. 2001. *China's Retreat from Equality: Income Distribution and Economic Transition*. Armonk, NY: M. E. Sharpe.

Rivas, Lynn. 2003. "Invisible Labors: Caring for the Independent Person." Pp. 70–84 in *Global Woman: Nannies, Maids, and Sex Workers in the New Economy*, edited by B. Ehrenreich and A. Hochschild. New York: Metropolitan Books.

Rofel, Lisa. 1999. *Other Modernities: Gendered Yearnings in China After Socialism*. Berkeley: University of California Press.

———. 1992. "Rethinking Modernity: Space and Factory Discipline in China." *Cultural Anthropology* 7: 93–114.

Rollins, Judith. 1996. "Invisibility, Consciousness of the Other, and Resentment Among Black Domestic Workers." Pp. 223–43 in *Working in the Service Society*, edited by C. Macdonald and C. Sirianni. Philadelphia: Temple University Press.

———. 1985. *Between Women: Domestics and Their Employers*. Philadelphia: Temple University Press.

Rose, Nikolas. 1998. *Inventing Our Selves: Psychology, Power, and Personhood*. Cambridge: Cambridge University Press.

Rosen, Stanley. 2004. "The State of Youth/Youth and the State in Early 21st-Century China." Pp. 159–79 in *State and Society in 21st-Century China: Crisis, Contention, and Legitmation*, edited by P. Gries and S. Rosen. New York: Routledge Curzon.

Sallaz, Jeffery J. 2002. "The House Rules: Autonomy and Interests Among Service Workers in the Contemporary Casino Industry." *Work and Occupations* 29: 394–427.

Salzinger, Leslie. 2003. *Genders in Production: Making Workers in Mexico's Global Factories*. Berkeley: University of California Press.

Saporito, Bill. 2003. "Can Wal-Mart Get Any Bigger?" *Time*, Jan. 13, pp. 38–42.

Schein, Louisa. 2000. *Minority Rules: The Miao and the Feminine in China's Cultural Politics*. Durham: Duke University Press.

Schell, Orville. 1984. *To Get Rich Is Glorious: China in the Eighties*. New York: Pantheon Books.

Schoenberger, Erica. 1997. *The Cultural Crisis of the Firm.* Cambridge, MA: Blackwell Publishers.

Schurmann, Franz. 1968. *Ideology and Organization in Communist China.* Berkeley: University of California Press.

Scott, James C. 1985. *Weapons of the Weak: Everyday Forms of Peasant Resistance.* New Haven: Yale University Press.

Segura, Denise. 1997. "Chicanas in White Collar Jobs: 'You Have to Prove Yourself More.'" Pp. 292–310 in *Situated Lives: Gender and Culture in Everyday Life,* edited by L. Lamphere, H. Ragone, and P. Zavella. New York: Routledge.

Sennett, Richard, and Jonathan Cobb. 1972. *The Hidden Injuries of Class.* New York: Vintage Books.

Sewell, Jr., William H. 1992. "A Theory of Structure: Duality, Agency, and Transformation." *American Journal of Sociology* 98: 1–29.

Shamir, Boas. 1980. "Between Service and Servility: Role Conflict in Subordinate Service Roles." *Human Relations* 33: 741–56.

Sherman, Rachel E. 2003. "Class Acts: Producing and Consuming Luxury Service in Hotels." Ph.D. dissertation, Sociology, University of California, Berkeley.

———. 2005. "Producing the Superior Self: Strategic Comparison and Symbolic Boundaries Among Luxury Hotel Workers." *Ethnography* 6: 131–58.

———. 2006. *Class Acts: Service and Inequality in Luxury Hotels.* Berkeley: University of California Press.

Shirk, Susan L. 1982. *Competitive Comrades: Career Incentives and Student Strategies in China.* Berkeley: University of California Press.

Simmel, Georg. 1957. "Fashion." *American Journal of Sociology* 62: 541–58.

Siu, Helen F. 1993. "Reconstituting Dowry and Brideprice in South China." Pp. 165–88 in *Chinese Families in the Post-Mao Era,* edited by D. Davis and S. Harrell. Berkeley: University of California Press.

Smith, Dorothy. 1987. *The Everyday World as Problematic: A Feminist Sociology.* Boston: Northeastern University Press.

Smith, Vicki. 1994. "Braverman's Legacy: The Labor Process Tradition at 20." *Work and Occupations* 21: 403–22.

Solinger, Dorothy J. 2004. "The New Crowd of the Dispossessed: The Shift of the Urban Proletariat from Master to Mendicant." Pp. 50–66 in *State and Society in 21st-Century China: Crisis, Contention, and Legitimation,* edited by P. Gries and S. Rosen. New York: Routledge Curzon.

———. 2002. "Labour Market Reform and the Plight of the Laid-off Proletariat." *The China Quarterly* 170: 304–26.

———. 1999. *Contesting Citizenship in Urban China: Peasant Migrants, the State, and the Logic of the Market.* Berkeley: University of California Press.

———. 1993. *China's Transition from Socialism: Statist Legacies and Market Reforms, 1980–1990.* Armonk, NY: M. E. Sharpe.

———. 1984. *Chinese Business Under Socialism: The Politics of Domestic Commerce in Contemporary China.* Berkeley: University of California Press.

Statistical Yearbook of Harbin. Various years. Beijing: China Statistics Press.

Steedman, Carolyn Kay. 1987. *Landscape for a Good Woman.* New Brunswick: Rutgers University Press.

Stinchcombe, Arthur L. 1965. "Social Structure and Organizations." Pp. 142–93 in *Handbook of Organizational Behavior Management*, edited by J. March. New York: Rand McNally and Co.

Stockman, Norman. 1992. "Market, Plan and Structured Inequality in China." Pp. 260–76 in *Contesting Markets: Analyses of Ideology, Discourse and Practice*, edited by R. Dilley. Edinburgh: Edinburgh University Press.

Sun, Liping. 2003. *Cleavage: Chinese Society Since the 1990s (Duanli: 20 shiji 90 niandai yilai de zhongguo shehui)*. Beijing: Social Sciences Documentation Publishing House.

Swidler, Ann. 1986. "Culture in Action: Symbols and Strategies." *American Sociological Review* 51: 273–86.

Tannock, Stuart. 2001. *Youth at Work: The Unionized Fast-Food and Grocery Workplace*. Philadelphia: Temple University Press.

Thompson, E. P. 1966. *The Making of the English Working Class*. New York: Vintage Books.

Tilly, Charles. 1998. *Durable Inequality*. Berkeley: University of California Press.

Tolich, Martin. 1993. "Alienating and Liberating Emotions at Work: Supermarket Clerk's Performance of Customer Service." *Journal of Contemporary Ethnography* 22: 361–81.

Tomba, Luigi. 2004. "Creating an Urban Middle Class: Social Engineering in Beijing." *The China Journal* 51: 1–26.

———. 2005. "Residential Space and Collective Interest Formation in Beijing's Housing Disputes." *The China Quarterly* 184: 934–51.

Veblen, Thorstein. 1899 [1934]. *Theory of the Leisure Class: An Economic Study of Institutions*. New York: Modern Library.

Veeck, Ann. 2000. "The Revitalization of the Marketplace: Food Markets of Nanjing." Pp. 107–23 in *The Consumer Revolution in Urban China*, edited by D. Davis. Berkeley: University of California Press.

Verdery, Katherine. 1998. *What Was Socialism, and What Comes Next?* Princeton: Princeton University Press.

Walder, Andrew G. 1986. *Communist Neo-Traditionalism*. Berkeley: University of California Press.

———. 1996. "Workers, Managers, and the State: The Reform Era and the Political Crisis of 1989." Pp. 43–69 in *The Individual and the State in China*, edited by B. Hook. Oxford: Clarendon Press.

———. 2002. "Markets and Income Inequality in Rural China: Political Advantage in an Expanding Economy." *American Sociological Review* 67: 231–53.

Wang, Fei-Ling. 2005. *Organizing Through Division and Exclusion: China's Hukou System*. Stanford: Stanford University Press.

Wang, Guisen. 1988. "Courage to Reform, Opening and Moving Forward: A Survey of Huaibei City's Department Store" (*Yong yu gaige kaikuo qianjin: huaibei shi baihuo dalou de diaocha*). *Caimao jingji* (Mar.): 60–62.

———. 1987. "Spare No Effort at Enterprising Competition, Enliven Enterprise Operations: A Survey of Huaibei City's Huaihai Market in Anhui Province" (*Fenli jingzheng kaituo, gaohuo qiye jingying: anhui sheng huaibei shi huaihai shangchang de diaocha*). *Caimao jingji* (June): 56–57.

———. 1986. "Perfecting the Operation Responsibility System, Raising Economic Efficiency: A Survey of Huaibei City Huaihai Market" (*Wanshan jingying zerenzhi, tigao jingji xiaoyi: huaibei shi huaihai shangchang de diaocha*). *Caimao jingji* 2: 66–68.

———. 1984. "Enlivening Business, Increasing Economic Efficiency: A Survey of Huaibei City's Xiangshan Department Store" (*Zuohuo shengyi, tigao jingji xiaoyi: huaibei shi xiangshan baihuo shangdian de diaocha*). *Caimao jingji* (Jan.): 50–52.

Wang, Jing. 2001. "Culture as Leisure and Culture as Capital." *positions* 9: 69–104.

Wang, Shaoguang. 1995. "The Politicis of Private Time: Changing Leisure Patterns in Urban China." Pp. 149–72 in *Urban Spaces in Contemporary China: The Potential for Autonomy and Community in Post-Mao China*, edited by D. Davis, R. Kraus, B. Naughton, and E. Perry. Cambridge: Cambridge University Press.

Wang, Shaoguang, and An-kang Hu. 1999. *The Political Economy of Uneven Development: The Case of China*. Armonk, NY: M. E. Sharpe.

Wang, Shiquan. 1982. "Converting Urban Cooperative Stores into Real Collective Enterprises" (*Ba chengshi hezuo shangdian bancheng zhenzheng de jiti qiye*). *Caimao jingji* 5: 48–51.

Wang, Shuguang, and Ken Jones. 2001. "China's Retail Sector in Transition." *Asian Geographer* 20: 25–51.

———. 2002. "Retail structure of Beijing." *Environment and Planning A* 34: 1785–1808.

Wang, Xiaoming. 2003. "China on the Brink of a 'Momentous Era.'" *positions* 11: 585–611.

Wang, Yanhong. 2001. "Sectoral Position Analysis." Unpublished manuscript.

Wang, Zheng. 2000. "Gender, Employment and Women's Resistance." Pp. 62–82 in *Chinese Society: Change, Conflict and Resistance*, edited by E. Perry and M. Selden. London: Routledge.

Wank, David L. 1999. *Commodifying Communism: Business, Trust, and Politics in a Chinese City*. Cambridge: Cambridge University Press.

Warhurst, Christopher. 1998. "Recognizing the Possible: The Organization and Control of a Socialist Labor Process." *Administrative Science Quarterly* 43: 470–97.

Wharton, Amy. 1993. "The Affective Consequences of Service Work: Managing Emotions on the Job." *Work and Occupations* 20: 205–32.

Whyte, Martin King. 1974. *Small Groups and Political Rituals in China*. Berkeley: University of California Press.

Whyte, Martin King, and William L. Parish. 1984. *Urban Life in Contemporary China*. Chicago: University of Chicago Press.

Whyte, William Foote. 1946. "When Workers and Customers Meet." Pp. 123–47 in *Industry and Society*, edited by W. F. Whyte. New York: McGraw-Hill Book Co.

———. 1948. *Human Relations in the Restaurant Industry*. New York: McGraw-Hill Book Co.

Wilkes, Chris. 1990. "Bourdieu's Class." Pp. 109–31 in *An Introduction to the Work of Pierre Bourdieu: The Practice of Theory*, edited by R. Harker, C. Mahar, and C. Wilkes. Houndmills: Macmillan.

Williams, Christine. 2004. "Inequality in the Toy Store." *Qualitative Sociology* 27: 461–86.

———. 2006. *Inside Toy Stores: Shopping, Retail Work, and Social Inequality*. Berkeley: University of California Press.

———. 1989. *Gender Differences at Work: Women and Men in Nontraditional Occupations*. Berkeley: University of California Press.

———. 1995. *Still a Man's World: Men Who Do Women's Work*. Berkeley: University of California Press.

Williams, Raymond. 1977. *Marxism and Literature*. Oxford: Oxford University Press.

Willis, Paul. 1977. *Learning to Labor: How Working Class Kids Get Working Class Jobs*. New York: Columbia University Press.

Winship, Janice. 2000. "New Disciplines for Women and the Rise of the Chain Store in the 1930s." Pp. 23–45 in *All the World and Her Husband: Women in Twentieth-Century Consumer Culture*, edited by M. Andrews and M. Talbot. London: Cassell.

Woetzel, Jonathan R. 2003. *Capitalist China: Strategies of a Revolutionized Economy*. Singapore: John Wilely & Sons (Asia).

Wolff, David. 1999. *To the Harbin Station: The Liberal Alternative in Russian Manchuria, 1898–1914*. Stanford, CA: Stanford University Press.

Womack, Brantly. 1991. "Transfigured Community: Neo-Traditionalism and Work Unit Socialism in China." *The China Quarterly* 125: 313–32.

Won, Jaeyoun. 2004. "Withering Away of the Iron Rice Bowl: The Reemployment Project of Post-socialist China." *Studies in Comparative International Development* 39(2): 71–93.

Woo, Margaret Y. K. 1994. "Chinese Women Workers: The Delicate Balance Between Protection and Equality." In *Engendering China: Women, Culture and the State*, edited by C. Gilmartin, G. Hershatter, L. Rofel, and T. White. Cambridge: Harvard University Press.

Woronov, T. E. 2004. "In the Eye of the Chicken: Hierarchy and Marginality Among Beijing's Migrant Schoolchildren." *Ethnography* 5(3): 289–313.

Wu, Huiqiang. 1984. "The Three Reform Projects at Southern Mansion" (*Nanfang dasha de san xiang gaige*). *Shangye yanjiu* 28(2): 24–27.

Wu, Jane Peihsun. 1997. "The Development of China's Retail Industry Since the Economic Reform in 1978." Ph.D. dissertation Thesis, Department of Agricultural Economics, Cornell University.

Wu, Xiaogang. 2002. "Work Units and Income Inequality: The Effect of Market Transition in Urban China." *Social Forces* 80: 1069–99.

Wu, Xiaogang, and Donald J. Treiman. 2004. "The Household Registration System and Social Stratification in China: 1955–1996." *Demography* 41: 363–84

Xu, Liren. 1985. "Contracting Is Necessary to Raise the Economic Efficiency of Retail Businesses: Recording the Before and After of Pulandian Department

Store's Contract [System]" (*Chengbao shi lingshou shangye tigao jingji xiaoyi de xuyao: ji pulandian baihuo shangdian chengbao qianhou*). *Shangye yanjiu* (May): 21–22.

Xu, Xinxin. 2004. "The Evolution of Wealth Disparities Between Rich and Poor in China's Cities" (*Zhongguo chengzhen zhumin pinfu chaju yanbian qushi*). Pp. 76–92 in *Social Stratification in China Today (Zhongguo shehui fenceng)*, edited by P. Li, Q. Li, and L. Sun. Beijing: *Zhongguo shehui fenceng*.

Xue, Jinjun, and Wei Zhong. 2003. "Unemployment, Poverty and Income Disparity in Urban China." *Asian Economic Journal* 17: 383–405.

Yan, Hairong. 2003. "Neoliberal Governmentality and Neohumanism: Organizing Suzhi/Value Flow Through Labor Recruitment Networks." *Cultural Anthropology* 18: 493–523.

Yanagisako, Sylvia Junko. 2002. *Producing Culture and Capital: Family Firms in Italy*. Princeton: Princeton University Press.

Yang, Chunxiang, and Wang Guangrun. 1985. "Getting Reforms Right, Increasing Enterprise Vigor: A Survey of Large and Medium Sized State-Run Retailing and Commerce-Operated Industrial Enterprises" (*Gaohao tizhi gaige zengqiang qiye huoli: dui da zhong xing guoying lingshou he shangban gongye qiye de diaocha*). *Shangye yanjiu* 36(1): 7–9.

Yang, Guobin. 2003. "China's *Zhiqing* Generation: Nostalgia, Identity, and Cultural Resistance in the 1990s." *Modern China* 29: 267–96.

Yang, Lian. 2005. "Dark Side of the Chinese Moon." *New Left Review* 32: 132–40.

Yang, Mayfair Mei-hui. 1999. *Spaces of Their Own: Women's Public Sphere in Transnational China*. Minneapolis: University of Minnesota Press.

———. 1994. *Gifts, Favors and Banquets: The Art of Social Relationships in China*. Ithaca: Cornell University Press.

Yang, Weiwen. 1983. "A Successful Example of Reform to Large-Scale Retail Enterprise System" (*Daxing lingshou shangye tizhi gaige chenggong yi li*). *Caimao jingji* (Apr.): 39–41.

Yang, Wenjie, and Yuhong Zhu. 1998. "The Path Out of Difficulty for State-Owned Commercial Wholesale Enterprises" (*Guoyou pifa shangye zou chu kunjing zhi lu*). *Caimao jingji* 5: 51–52.

Yang, Yiyong. 1997. *Shiye chongjibo—zhongguo jiuye fazhan baogao (Unemployment Wave—A Report on the Development of Employment in China)*. Beijing: Jinri Press.

Yen, Ching-hwang. 1998. "Wing On and the Kwok Brothers: A Case Study of Pre-War Overseas Chinese Entrepreneurs." Pp. 47–65 in *Asian Department Stores*, edited by K. MacPherson. Honolulu: University of Hawai'i Press.

Young, Louise. 1999. "Marketing the Modern: Department Stores, Consumer Culture, and the New Middle Class in Interwar Japan." *International Labor and Working-Class History* 55: 52–70.

Young, Susan. 1995. *Private Business and Economic Reform in China*. Armonk, NY: M. E. Sharpe.

Zelizer, Viviana A. 1994. *The Social Meaning of Money*. New York: Basic Books.

Zang, Xiaowei. 2002. "Labor Market Segmentation and Income Inequality in Urban China." *The Sociological Quarterly* 43: 27–44.

———. 2000. *Children of the Cultural Revolution: Family Life and Political Behavior in Mao's China*. Boulder: Westview Press.

Zavisca, Jane. 2004. "Consumer Inequalities and Regime Legitimacy in Late Soviet and Post-Soviet Russia." Ph.D. dissertation, Sociology, University of California, Berkeley.

Zhang, Li. 2001. *Strangers in the City: Reconfigurations of Space, Power, and Social Networks Within China's Floating Population*. Berkeley: University of California Press.

Zhang, Zhen. 2000. "Mediating Time: The 'Rice Bowl of Youth' in Fin de Siecle Urban China." *Public Culture* 12: 93–113.

Zhang, Xiaojun. 2004. "Land Reform in Yang Village: Symbolic Capital and the Determination of Class Status." *Modern China* 30: 3–45.

Zhao, Yuezhi. 2002. "The Rich, the Laid-off, and the Criminal in Tabloid Tales: Read All About It!" Pp. 111–35 in *Popular China: Unofficial Culture in a Globalizing Society*, edited by P. Link, R. Madsen, and P. Pickowicz. Lanham, MD: Rowman & Littlefield.

Zhou, Xuegang. 2000. "Economic Transformation and Income Inequality in Urban China: Evidence from Panel Data." *American Journal of Sociology* 105: 1135–74.

Zhu, Ping, and Wang Chunjian. 2000. *Sales Assistant Training and Administration: Necessary Professional Reading for Store Sales People (Yingyeyuan peixun yu guanli: shangdian xiaoshou renyuan jiuzhi bidu)*. Beijing: Zhonghua gongshang lianhe chubanshe.

Zhu, Xinhua. 1990. "Store Managers Need to Get a Good Grasp of Store Operation Management" (*Shangchang jingli yao zhuahao jingying xianchang guanli*). *Caimao jingji* 5: 59.

Zukin, Sharon. 2004. *Point of Purchase: How Shopping Changed American Culture*. New York: Routledge.

Zukin, Sharon, and Ervin Kosta. 2004. "Bourdieu Off-Broadway: Managing Distinction on a Shopping Block in the East Village." *City & Community* 3: 101–14.

Zukin, Sharon, and Jennifer Smith Maguire. 2004. "Consumers and Consumption." *Annual Review of Sociology* 30: 173–97.

Index

Age: as distinction marker, 100, 101; generational differences, 16, 17, 18; as indicator of productivity, 17, 100, 101–5, 193. *See also* Middle-aged women; Young women
Age discrimination, 18, 191–92, 193
Agriculture, 31, 35

Beauty: natural, 100; of private department store salesclerks, 100; relationship to productivity, 100, 101–5; rice bowl of youth, 17–18, 97, 98–99, 118
Beijing: luxury hotels, 10, 50; Number One Department Store, 34; wealthy residents, 49–50n23
Benson, Susan Porter, 52, 63
Bettie, Julie, 7, 132–33
Blecher, Marc J., 194
Bodies: employer control, 97; hypersexualized, 18, 133, 136; of private department store salesclerks, 87, 97, 99–100, 102, 108; sexualized female, 17, 99–100; symbolic messages, 97
Bodily labor, 97
Boundaries: moral, 185; social, 6. *See also* Symbolic boundaries
Bourdieu, Pierre, 5, 6, 7, 9, 57, 105–6, 123, 124, 156, 187
Brands: counterfeit goods, 142–43, 161–64, 176; development, 46; at

private department store, 89–90, 111; recognition of, 171; Western, 89n1, 142
Burawoy, Michael, 56, 58, 64, 68, 70, 73
Bureau of Industry and Commerce (*gongshang ju*), 22, 126

Capitalism: in China, 3; class differences and deferential service interactions, 106, 196; commodity fetishism, 122–23; low levels, 15, 136. *See also* Economic reforms; Markets
Carrefour, 41, 42n17, 195
Cashmere sweaters: knowledge about, 111; as luxury product, 92, 111; private department store selling area, 92–94, 93 (photo), 96, 188
Chain stores, 40
Chinese Communist Party, 12, 14, 28
Class consciousness, 194
Class mobility: downward, 157, 172, 177, 192–93, 200; lack of upward, 135; trajectory effects, 156–57
Classes: cultural construction of, 4–5, 6–7; customer status claims, 9, 88, 105–7, 111; deference acts related to, 106, 117, 197, 198; definitions, 4–5; gender and, 16–18, 96, 106, 136; impact of economic reforms, 3, 198; in imperial China, 27; marginalized groups, 15, 83–84, 136;

luxury hotels, 9–10, 106; service work, 7, 9–10; Wal-Mart, 41–42, 42n17, 71

Urban areas: incomes, 12, 13; life in Mao-era China, 25, 32. *See also* Harbin; Rural migrants

Urban working class: behaviors, 99; blurring of distinctions from rural people, 135; culture, 177–78; customers of private marketplace, 121, 129, 153; customers of state-run department store, 79, 81, 153, 176–77, 180; distinction from rural residents, 83–84; downward mobility, 157, 172, 177, 192–93, 200; effects of economic reforms, 15–16, 157, 191–93; femininity, 17–18; lack of upward mobility, 135; in socialist China, 32; Underground customers, 121, 129; women, 16, 17–18, 135; work units, 12, 17, 32, 130, 178. *See also* Working class

Veeck, Ann, 161
Virtuocracy, 72

Wacquant, Loic, 5
Wages: paid by manufacturers, 45, 47–48, 67, 75, 91, 93–94; of rural migrants, 13; of salesclerks, 44, 93–94, 104, 109, 131–32. *See also* Incomes
Walder, Andrew G., 32, 64, 178, 196
Wal-Mart, 41–42, 42n17, 71
Wanamaker, John, 52
Wang, Jing, 51
Wang, Shaoguang, 49
Wang, Shuguang, 39
Warhurst, Christopher, 68
Warm feeling, *see Reqing*
Wealth, 49–50n23, 51. *See also* Elites
Weber, Max, 4, 5
Weddings, 50, 51
Wholesalers: customers of Underground marketplace, 128,

140n13; in Guangzhou, 128; in socialist China, 29; state-run, 29, 35, 43n18

Whyte, William F., 106, 117
Williams, Christine, 10
Williams, Raymond, 8
Willis, Paul, 7
Womack, Brantly, 178
Women: beauty standards, 100, 133; class differences, 16; effects of economic reforms, 191–93, 200; employment, 28; factory workers, 13, 98, 104, 118, 178; generational differences, 17–18; maiden workers, 118; private department store managers, 98n6; rice bowl of youth, 17–18, 97, 98–99, 118; rural, 16, 135; service work, 192–93; sexualized bodies, 17; unemployment, 191–92; working wives and mothers, 118; working-class, 16, 17–18, 132–33, 191–93. *See also* Femininity; Gender; Middle-aged women; Young women

Work cultures: in service settings, 63; socialist, 54, 57–58, 63–64, 85; in state-run store, 57–58, 63–68, 73–78, 85, 158, 180

Work units, 12, 17, 32, 130, 178
Workers: disempowerment, 194–95, 197; in Eastern Europe, 64, 73, 192; manufacturing, 13, 68n8, 98, 104, 118, 178; in pre-reform China, 64, 196; resistance, 193–95; self-organization of work, 68; temporalized value of labor, 192; trade unions, 194. *See also* Salesclerks; Service workers; State sector workers; Unemployment

Working class: femininity, 18, 132–33, 135–36; strategies of representation, 177, 179. *See also* Urban working class

World Trade Organization (WTO), Chinese membership, 41, 71